Table of Contents

Renaissance

Revolution & Independence

Wars

Scientific & Industrial Revolutions

ANCIENT WORLD

THE BEGINNING OF CIVILISATION

Thousands of years ago, human beings lived in caves and forests. They wandered from one place to another in search of food and water. They hunted animals and gathered fruit, nut, and grain. Soon, they began domesticating animals like goats, dogs, and hens. Not only did the animals offer safety, they provided a regular supply of meat, milk, and eggs. However, human life was still predominantly nomadic.

All this improved a great deal when human beings began farming around 12,000 years ago, starting with peas, lentils and barley. As they learned more from nature, their life grew more stable. They saw how grains grew well near river banks and how crops grew better during certain months. Staying near water meant they no longer had to wander long distances searching for it. This settled way of life marks the start of civilisation! One of the oldest known settlements is a 9,500-year-old site in Turkey.

▲ Ancient Egyptians began farming c. 6500 BCE. It was so important to their success, they recorded it in paintings and murals

Cultivating crops

Storing food

What Makes a Civilisation?

As more and more settlements appeared, the earliest civilisations began to emerge between 4000 and 3000 BCE. These were located in the Fertile Crescent, a sickle-shaped land stretching from the upper Nile River in Egypt to the Tigris and Euphrates Rivers in western Asia. People discovered better ways of farming, invented tools to help them and soon had a **surplus** of crop! More food meant fewer people died of hunger. Villages grew larger and larger.

▲ *Pottery from the late **Neolithic** Period*

 ## Emergence of Cities

The oldest cities came up roughly between the 5th and 2nd millennium BCE in Mesopotamia, Iran, and Egypt. With more people to support, cities began to divide labour. New jobs like that of a carpenter, plumber, scribe, trader, and administrator came into being. The first cities that flourished in Mesopotamia had names like Eridu, Uruk, and Ur.

In Asia, one of the oldest cities came up around 2600 BCE, called Mohenjo-Daro. It was located in the Indus Valley and was home to about 50,000 people. The earliest American cities were built in the Andes and Mesoamerica (the strip of land that connects North and South America). These flourished over the 30th–18th century BCE.

▼ *Skara Brae is a Neolithic settlement built of stones. It consisted of eight houses and might have been built between 3180–2500 BCE. Today, it is found in modern-day Scotland*

▲ *These paintings depict life in ancient Egypt*

🏠 Early Diversity

Ancient cities varied a good deal in form and function. Keeping a surplus meant that people could store a lot of grains and not worry about their next meal. For example, while people near fields practised agriculture, people near water bodies practised fishing. Some cities were centres of trade while others were considered holy. None of the cities were densely populated. The most important ones grew into centres of political might and became the nuclei of future empires!

▲ *Tools such as this basic mortar and pestle, were invented to process grains that were grown in the field*

🏠 Division of Labour

As there was a surplus of food, everyone did not have to participate in farming. Human beings started dividing work among themselves depending on the needs of the city, and for some lucky few, their own interests. So, each person was involved in an occupation. Some brought water from the river to the fields, some made pots for cooking and storage, some gathered fruit and seeds, some practised farming, and others learned fishing. People also cross-bred and cultivated new, more productive varieties of plants and animals for various purposes such as eating, milking, labour, etc.

◀ *A number of female figurines, in the form of clay mother goddesses and soapstone dancers, have been found at Harappa*

▲ *Mayan hieroglyphs carved on a stone*

🏠 Religion and Society

Ancient people worshipped nature, the earth and sky because their livelihood depended on these powerful forces. They developed rituals, in the hope of pleasing higher powers and steady rain, sunshine, and fertile land in return. Rituals gradually became more complex. They turned into important traditions and cherished beliefs. Religious leaders thus, became powerful. People looked to them for guidance in moral matters and to protect their homes and families from wrathful gods. In Mohenjo-Daro, there is a seal from c. 2000 BCE showing a seated yogi-like man, surrounded by animals. Experts call him *Pasupati* or 'lord of animals'.

🏠 Language and Writing Systems

As human interactions in cities grew more complex, people started keeping records of transactions. They also needed ways to send messages from one place to another. Thus, they invented writing. The oldest scripts are mostly **pictographic** in nature, which means they are made of fixed symbols to denote sounds. Ancient human beings wrote on leaves and barks of trees, soft clays or stones, papyrus, hides of animals, clothes, and finally, on paper when it was invented.

Xia/Shang

Mesopotamia

Indus
Valley

Nile Valley

Mesoamerica

◄ The map identifies locations
of the ancient civilisations

Peru

■ NEW WORLD

■ OLD WORLD

River:
The Cradle of Civilisation

Civilisations grew when human beings first settled near fertile river valleys. Almost all the oldest and major civilisations developed near these cradles of the river valleys; hence, they are called River Valley Civilisations.

🏠 Classifying Civilisations

There are six ancient civilisations in total, of which four are called old world civilisations and the other two are new world civilisations. The former are the largest civilisations that developed primarily around rivers. Some of them continue to exist in developed forms till today.

👤 In Real Life

Chocolate came from Mesoamerica and was introduced to the rest of the world through the Mexican Conquistadors (Mexican conquerors). The word 'chocolate' is derived from the Aztec word 'Xocoatl', which was considered to be a gift from the God Quetzalcoatl. It was drunk only by the kings and Aztec elites during rituals and festivals.

▶ A sculpture of an Aztec
man holding a cocoa pod

⭐ Incredible Individuals

Queen Hatshepsut was one of the first female rulers of the world. She ruled for almost 20 years. She was one of the most able rulers of Egypt. She developed trade relations and built many monuments. There is a temple in Dayr al-Bahri (ancient archaeological site) dedicated to her.

◄ Queen Hatshepsut depicted at her
tomb as Osiris, Goddess of fertility
and resurrection

🏠 Old World Civilisations

This group comprises the Mesopotamian Civilisation that developed around the River Euphrates; the Ancient Egyptian Civilisation around the River Nile; the Indus Valley Civilisation along the River Indus (in India and Pakistan) and the Chinese Civilisation along the Yangtze and Yellow Rivers.

🏠 New World Civilisations

The new world civilisations are also called the Pre-Columbian Civilisations. They developed in and around present-day Mexico and Central America as well as in South America. The first of these two is the **Mesoamerican** Civilisation. It consisted of various groups, including the Mayans, Zapotecs, Totonacs and Teotihuacans, which are together called the Olmecs. The Andean Civilisation is the second one. It developed around the western region of South America. It is home to the Peruvian and Incan Civilisations, among others.

Mesopotamia: The Land Between Two Rivers

▲ *Lamassu is an ancient Assyrian deity with the head of a human and the body of a lion or bull. It also has wings*

Mesopotamia is derived from the Greek words 'Meso' which means middle, and 'potamos', which means river. Thus, the land between the two rivers Euphrates and Tigris was known as Mesopotamia. Today, Mesopotamia is identified with the land spread over Iraq, Turkey, Syria, and the Gulf.

🏛 Contribution to Culture

The Mesopotamian civilisation lasted from c. 5000 BCE to 1100 BCE. It was the birthplace of the Sumerian, Akkadian, Babylonian and Assyrian cultures. Archaeological evidence shows that Mesopotamians advanced science, technology, astronomy, literature, law, philosophy, and religion.

▲ *The bust of an unknown Akkadian ruler made during the **Bronze Age***

🏛 A Dynastic Civilisation

The Akkadian Civilisation was part of Northern Mesopotamia. Akkadians ruled over the Sumerian regions of Mesopotamia, or modern Syria, and Lebanon. Hebrew and Arabic languages developed from the Akkadians. In c. 2334 BCE, Sargon of Akkad came to power and established the first **dynastic** rule in the world. This empire collapsed around 2154 BCE, within 180 years of its founding.

🏛 The Great Warriors

The Assyrians first rose to power when the Akkadians fell. Though they were considered some of the best warriors, their empire fell quite a number of times. They made deadly weapons using iron and bronze technology. Akkadians excelled **siege warfare**. They used physical force such as battering rams to break walls and gates. They also used other tactics such as cutting off water and food supply to bring their enemies out of hiding. The strongest rule the Assyrians was during the time of Tiglath Pileser III, Sargon II, and Ashurbanipal. Tiglath Pileser III built good roads so that his army and messengers could travel efficiently.

▶ **Relief** *showing the Assyrian King Ashurbanipal hunting a lion*

Sumerians:
The Inventors

For ancient cities, the day began at sunrise and ended at sunset. There was no 24-hour system. It were the Sumerians who first divided the day into 24 hours, with 60 minutes in an hour, and 60 seconds in every minute. This is just one of their gifts to the world.

▲ *Sumerians in a battle or hunting scene carved on a stone slab*

Rise of the Sumerians

The Sumerian Civilisation developed in southern Mesopotamia (modern Iraq and Kuwait) in around 4000 BCE. It is often considered to be the first urban civilisation. The most astounding fact about the Sumerian Civilisation is that many did not know about its existence before the 19th century. Sumer was discovered by accident when archaeologists were searching for proof of a flood mentioned in the *Bible*.

Gifts from the Sumerians

Sumerians were among the first people to invent writing, and build ships. They also invented the wheel. They were experts at record-keeping and mathematics. The abacus that children use to learn counting may also have been invented by these talented people.

Sir Leonard Woolley, an archaeologist, found remains of two four-wheeled wagons at the site of an ancient city called Ur, which flourished in the 3rd millennium BCE. These are the oldest wheeled vehicles ever discovered in history.

The Sumerians traded with other civilisations, such as the people of the Indus Valley, using the ships they built. They traded textile, jewellery, pearl, ivory, etc.

🛈 In Real Life

The oldest poem to have survived belonged to the Sumerians. It is called *The Epic of Gilgamesh*. It was written in cuneiform script on nearly 12 clay tablets. It is a poem about a semi-mythical king of an ancient Sumerian city called Uruk.

 Cuneiform

The written language of the Sumerians, cuneiform literally means wedge-shaped. It was adopted by other regions and used for around 2,000 years.

◀ *Sumerians inscribed cuneiform into stone plaques*

▼ *The Sumerians worshipped multiple gods and built temples upon massive structures called ziggurats, located at the heart of their cities*

The Babylonian Empire

Babylon is one of the most famous cities of Ancient Mesopotamia. Its ruins are found in the town of Al-Hillah near Baghdad in Iraq. The Greeks called it Babylon after its Akkadian name 'bav-ilim', meaning 'the gate of gods'.

▲ Aerial view of the ruins of the ancient palace of Nebuchadnezzar, currently in Iraq. Alexander the Great died in this palace

 ## King Hammurabi

Babylon, a minor **city state** in Mesopotamia, emerged as a powerful empire under King Hammurabi (c. 1810–1750 BCE). He was an able ruler who brought stability to the city. His famous code of laws can still be seen on stone steles (large stone slabs) and clay tablets. This code is one of the oldest deciphered writing of the world. It consists of 282 laws outlining punishments such as the famous phrase, 'an eye for an eye, a tooth for a tooth'.

▲ King Hammurabi raises his right arm in worship

Babylon fell from power after King Hammurabi passed on the throne to his heirs. It was brought back to glory by Nebuchadnezzar II (c. 605–c. 562 BCE). He ruled for a long time, around 43 years! The hanging gardens of Babylon, one of the seven wonders of the ancient world, are said to have been built by him. After his death, Babylon was conquered by the Persians, in c. 529 BCE.

Babylon is famous as the place where Alexander the Great, the conqueror, breathed his last. He captured Babylon in c. 331 BCE while returning from Asia. He died here in c. 323 BCE in the palace of Nebuchadnezzar II. In the ensuing struggle for power Babylonia was seized in c. 312 BCE by his general Seleucus, founder of the Seleucid Dynasty.

◀ The Hammurabi stele codified the laws of ancient Mesopotamia

💡 Isn't It Amazing!

The Bible tells us that people once wanted to build a tower that reached the heavens. God cursed them to speak in different languages—in a babel of tongues—so they could not understand each other. Thus, he stopped them from building the tower. The city of Babylon takes its name from the Hebrew word 'bavel', which means confusion.

Egypt:
The Land of Pyramids

▲ *An Egyptians sarcophagus which was used as part of their funeral rites*

Have you ever been fascinated with the pyramids, mummies, and scarabs? Do you know who Hatshepsut, Nefertiti, and Tutankhamen were? They belonged to ancient Egypt, one of the six major river civilisations of the old world. Its cities were situated on the banks of the River Nile, the world's longest river.

The annual flooding of the Nile deposited nutrient-rich soil along its coast. This fertile soil was used for farming, which in turn produced an abundance of crops, making Egypt rich and powerful.

🏠 Advancements of Ancient Egyptians

The Egyptian Civilisation first developed in two parts—Upper Egypt and Lower Egypt. It was united by King Menes (also called Narmer) in the year 3200 BCE, though **nomadic** people had already settled in the Nile valley. They subsisted on farming, hunting, and gathering.

As time passed, Egyptians became more advanced. They became good at mathematics, medicinal science, astronomy and ship building. They were also geniuses of art and architecture, which they showcased by building and painting the temples at Abu Simbel, the Great Sphinx at Giza, and the astounding royal tombs in the Valley of Kings.

Such enduringly magnificent structures created by Egyptians influenced the later Roman emperors to cart away their obelisks (gigantic, tapering stone pillars) to celebrate their victories. Even the 19th century Washington Monument, the world's largest obelisk, is inspired by the architectural marvels of ancient Egypt!

▼ *The Great Pyramid of Giza, the only remaining wonder of the ancient world, was the tallest building in the world for over 3,800 years*

Hieroglyphs

Ancient Egyptian script used lots of pictograms i.e., pictures of birds, animals or objects, to communicate ideas, traditions, stories, practices and even sounds and punctuation. These characters were called hieroglyphs. Egyptians created rudimentary hieroglyphs around 3400–3200 BCE. By c. 2000–1700 BCE, it was a mature writing system with several hundred different signs.

We are able to read Egyptian hieroglyphs today thanks to the discovery of the Rosetta Stone (a temple decree) by one of Napoleon's officers during his Egyptian invasion in 1799.

▲ The ancient hieroglyphs depict a seated pharaoh, animals and other symbols

Divinity in Egypt

The people of Egypt were polytheistic i.e., they worshipped many gods. They had many religious rituals and ceremonies dedicated to these gods. They believed that their king, the Pharaoh, was a living God. The Egyptians also believed in life after death. This is why they **mummified** corpses of people, especially important ones like the king and his family, etc. Egyptians believed that the bodies of these people should be preserved for their next life. They made use of various herbs, embalming products, and medical methods to prevent the bodies from decaying. They further protected the body by binding it in long strips of cloth, making a mummy, and preserved it in a beautiful casket called a **sarcophagus**. These were then placed in tombs filled with fruit, wine, money, gold ornaments, gold vessels, and utensils. Many a times, they also placed the mummies of the dead person's servants, wives, and pets (especially cats) to keep them company on their journey to the next life!

▲ Statue of the Sun God Ra carved in stone

▶ After they were completed, the pyramids of Giza were covered in a layer of white limestone, and the Great Pyramid was topped off with a golden capstone that has gone missing

The Gods of Egypt

There were many gods in Egypt connected to great mythical stories. Many of these stories are about their relationship to nature and ethics. Most of the Egyptian gods were half-animal (like birds) and half-human. Of the many gods, some were considered to be more powerful than others and hence, were worshipped by more people. Ancient Egyptians prayed to these gods with much reverence and worshipped them before special occasions, especially before the annual flooding of the Nile.

Nut, Shu, and Geb

They were the first gods and represented the sky, air, and earth respectively. Shu was Nut and Geb's father. He held up and separated the sky from Earth. Nut swallowed Ra each evening (sunset) and gave birth to him every morning (sunrise). Geb was held in awe, as the father of snakes. His laughter caused earthquakes!

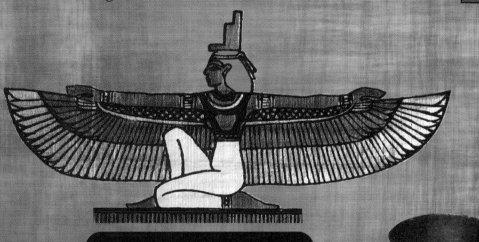

Isis

Isis, the mother of gods, is the Goddess of life, a healer, and the protector of kings. She is shown with wings and a throne on her head. She was the first one to use the mummification process to preserve her husband, Osiris.

Amun

Amun was a later god, the one who held the powers of Ra, the Sun God. Amun, meaning the mysterious one, was the king of gods. He is often shown as a human but can also be a ram or a goose.

Osiris

Osiris, the mythical first king of Egypt, was one of the most important gods. Murdered by his brother Set, he was brought back to life by his wife Isis. He is depicted as a mummy holding a crook and a flail, symbols of kingship. He also wears a white crown.

Bes

Bes is a childbirth deity who guarded people from dangerous animals and demons. He has a grotesque form as a bandy-legged dwarf whose tongue hangs out.

Ma'at

Ma'at was the goddess of truth and justice. She is usually shown as a seated woman with an ostrich feather on her head. She is the ultimate judge in the afterlife where the dead person's heart is weighed against her feather. If the heart is heavier than the feather, it is eaten by Ammut, the crocodile-headed devourer of dead.

Thoth

Thoth is almost always shown with the head of an ibis, holding a pen and a palette but sometimes as a baboon too. He is one of the oldest gods—the god of knowledge and writing, shown as calculating or writing something. He kept records of all deeds done by the dead on their judgement day.

Set

Set is the god of chaos, darkness, and war. He is mostly shown with an unknown animal head but also as a hippopotamus, pig, or donkey. It was believed that when he travelled with Ra, he cast a shadow across the worlds, causing sandstorms.

Anubis

Anubis is the god of death. He is a protector of the dead and the mummified. He takes the dead through the halls of judgement. He is shown as a jackal-faced man or as the jackal himself.

Ra

Ra is the almighty Egyptian Sun god, hawk-headed by day and ram-headed by night. His crown is a solar disk surrounded by a serpent. His **cult** became so powerful that the Pharaoh of Egypt claimed he was a direct descendant and called himself Sa-Ra, the son of Ra.

Egyptian Dynasties

The Great Sphinx of Giza has a human head, a lion's body and is shown sitting down. It was built during the Old Kingdom (2575–2130 BCE) for King Khufu, possibly by his son King Khafre. Between King Khufu and his son, they ruled Egypt for 106 years. Before the Old Kingdom, Egypt had already gone through two dynasties of kings.

▲ *Step Pyramid of Djoser, Saqqara*

Old Kingdom

The first important ruler of the Old Kingdom was Djoser. He was the second king of the 3rd dynasty. The Step Pyramid at Saqqara was built for him by his vizier Imhotep. It was the very first pyramid. Before it, rulers were buried in a *mastaba*, which was a rectangular building. The Old Kingdom lasted until the 6th dynasty of Pharaohs.

Middle Kingdom

The 7th–10th dynasties followed the Old Kingdom and were called the First Intermediate Kingdom (c. 2134–2040 BCE). Then followed the Middle Kingdom, which included the 11th–13th dynasties (c. 2040–1640 BCE). Their Pharaohs were buried in secret tombs, to keep them safe from grave robbers. Sobekneferu, the first female Pharaoh, ruled during this time (1806–1802 BCE).

New Kingdom

The New Kingdom (c. 1550–1070 BCE) was a period when Egyptians defeated foreign armies, especially the Hyksos people who had captured most of Egypt during the Second Intermediate Period (c. 1640–1550 BCE). Hatshepsut, the second and most famous female Pharaoh, ruled during this period.

Egypt's wealth made it a target for invaders. Over time, internal corruption and external aggression caused the empire to fall into foreign hands, most famously to Persia, Rome, and later to Islamic rulers. The ancient Egyptians are still a mystery to us. **Egyptologists** are trying to peel back the layers one by one to understand the people who gave us the amazing sphinx, pyramids, and mummies.

💡 Isn't It Amazing!

The Egyptians admired cats so much that they were mummified and placed in tombs with their dead masters. The cat could then accompany the dead into the afterlife. The Egyptians' love for cats is attested by a discovery made in November 2018 by archaeologists who worked on a 4,500-year-old tomb near Cairo. They were astonished to find more than 100 gilded cat statues planted near dozens of cat mummies.

▶ *Cats were considered to be sacred animals that would protect homes and bring good luck. The penalty for killing a cat, even accidentally, was death*

▼ *The massive size of The Great Sphinx is no match to the wonders of nature. It has fallen victim to stormy winds and sand dunes, which resulted in its complete burial. It was excavated in the 1930s*

Persia:
Expansion & Conquest

It was Cyrus the Great who started the Persian Empire. He captured many empires from c. 550 BCE onwards; most notably, Babylon in c. 529 BCE. Herodotus, a Greek historian, noted that Cyrus developed Babylon to be a great trade centre, bringing prosperity to the land. Those who ruled soon after Cyrus carried his expansion policy forward.

Expansion

Due to its aggressive expansion Persia built one of the largest empires of the ancient world. It stretched from Anatolia (modern Turkey) in the north, Egypt in the south, across western and central Asia, to northern India in the east. This great empire was brought to an end by Alexander the Great in c. 331 BCE.

King Darius I

The Persian Empire is also called the Achaemenid Empire as Shah Darius the Great (c. 522–486 BCE) claimed descent from a mythical figure named Achaemenes. Darius's rule brought stability through a mature administration. He appointed satraps, or governors, to rule over far-flung parts of the empire under his name. There were nearly 20 satraps in his rule. This system was adopted by many other rulers from different parts of the world.

▲ *This bearded profile, carved on the wall of an old palace in Iran, is thought to belong to a Persian king*

Darius I also found a unique way to use the tributes he received. He called it tax and spent it on constructing the navy, public buildings, canals and roads. He also used the money to provide irrigation facilities to farmers.

◀ *Persepolis was the ceremonial capital of the Achaemenid Empire*

Religious Tolerance

One of the most interesting traits of the Persian Empire is said to be their religious tolerance. They allowed everyone to practise their own religion, establishing the laws on secular issues, such as paying taxes. They even allowed the Jews—who were removed from the city of Babylon when the city had been conquered—to travel to Jerusalem and build a temple there.

Persian beliefs were based on the teachings of their prophet Zoroaster. Their religion was hence called Zoroastrianism and their deity, Ahura Mazda, the lord of wisdom.

⊛ Incredible Individuals

Xerxes (486–465 BCE), the son of Darius I and Atossa (daughter of Cyrus the Great), led a vast army to conquer the ancient Greeks. The war came down to a single naval battle, fought at Salamis. The Greeks had a much smaller fleet, but won the day using well thought-out tactics. The battle showed that the mighty Persians could be defeated. Other states, like Egypt, soon rose against Persia. The satraps too became defiant. Eventually, a young Macedonian king, Alexander the Great, conquered the whole empire!

◀ *An Achaemenid king, thought to be Xerxes, killing a Greek soldier*

On the Banks of the Yangtze River

The period from c. 2100–c. 220 CE can be called ancient China, though some experts stretch it all the way to the 17th century CE. Things like gunpowder, paper, printing, the compass, and the abacus are just a handful of its contributions. The Grand Canal, the longest man-made river in the world, was built at this time, as was the first Great Wall of China.

The Yellow River Connection

The Chinese civilisation was born on the banks of the Yangtze River, the longest river in China. By the 5th millennium BCE, people had heavily settled along the lower Yangtze. Soon, rice was being cultivated along its water-rich banks.

But what we today consider Chinese culture more likely started farther north, along the Yellow River—China's second-longest river.

The Chinese dragon is closely connected with power over water, rainfall, typhoons and floods. Thus, it was exclusively used as a symbol by emperors.

The many warring states of this land were first united during c. 221 BCE by Qin Shi Huang, literally meaning the First Emperor of the Qin dynasty. China is the world's oldest lasting continuing civilisation.

▼ *The terracotta army at the tomb of the First Emperor is one of the most impressive discoveries from ancient China*

The Identity of an Empire

The first dynasty lasted a mere 15 years, but it standardised Chinese characters, measurements, road widths and currency. The next major dynasty was the Han (206 BCE–220 CE), during which the Silk Road, the famous trade route, was established.

Lucky Three

The Chinese people believed in 'three ways', which became their way of life, art, and religion. These three ways are the three main religious philosophies—Taoism, Confucianism, and Buddhism. These philosophies were propounded by Tao, Confucius, and Buddha. Three seems to be an important number in Chinese culture as they also believed in three perfections when it came to art. These are painting, poetry, and calligraphy. The art of **Feng Shui** was invented in China. It is a system of laws that decides the arrangement and orientation of things such as furnishings, buildings, and other things, so that the flow of energy is positive.

◄ *This gilded, bronze oil-lamp, shaped like a kneeling servant, was discovered in the tomb of Princess Dou Wan, sister-in-law to Han Emperor Wu (157–87 BCE)*

Paper and Porcelain

If you enjoy writing on paper and admire fine porcelain, then you should thank China for both of them. Paper and porcelain were invented during the Han dynasty. It is believed Cai Lun (c. 50–121 CE), an official who served a number of Han emperors, was responsible for the invention of paper. Although, historians also believe that the Chinese had been trying to improve their papermaking technique even 100 years before that.

Porcelain is made by heating mineral clays to very high temperatures. Han dynasty potters, south of the Yangtze, produced celadon wares (greenish porcelain) of the most incredible hues.

▲ Cai Lun was an inventor and politician from the Han dynasty

▶ Before the invention of paper, the Chinese wrote important text on bamboo strips put together to form a scroll

Chai and China

The Chinese have been drinking tea for thousands of years. Folk tales say it was discovered accidentally when some tea leaves fell into an emperor's hot water cup. The earliest written records of tea also come from China. It was drunk bitter for its supposedly medicinal value. Tea was discovered in the mausoleum of Emperor Jing of Han, suggesting that it was drunk by Han rulers as early as the 2nd century BC.

◀ The Chinese script is read from top to bottom

 Incredible Individuals

Ancient China was a strongly patriarchal society. But from time to time, women broke through its prejudice and made a name for themselves. One such woman was Fu Hao. She was one of the 60 wives of Emperor Wu Ding of the Shang Dynasty (c. 1250–1192 BCE). Yet, she rose to become a military leader, the champion of many successful campaigns, and an astute politician. Her lavish tomb attests to her status: not only does it contain riches, it even shows humans were sacrificed to serve her in the afterlife!

◀ A statue of Queen Fu Hao outside her tomb

▼ Innumerable slaves and labourers died in the construction of the Great Wall of China. Many of them are actually buried within it, their bones reinforcing the massive structure!

Great Chinese Dynasties

Being a vast land with many ethnic peoples, China was majorly a divided nation. However, there were eight dynasties that united China and gave it a common identity. Some of them ruled for more than 100 years.

Xia Dynasty

The near-mythical first dynasty of China ruled for almost 500 years. Under the reign of about 17 emperors, lots of silk was said to be produced during this period. While ancient Chinese historians, like Sima Qian (145–86 BCE) substantially talked about the Xia dynasty, modern historians struggle to discover tangible evidence. A couple of ambiguous excavations, such as, bits of pottery and shell, are all we have today.

◄ *Painting of Yu the Great, founder of the first Chinese dynasty*

Zhou Dynasty

This was the longest-running dynasty of China (about 790 years). Iron was introduced in China during this period. This led to increased food production as the iron ploughs were stronger and more durable. **Taoism, Confucianism**, and the **Yin and Yang** philosophy developed at this time.

◄ *The Yin and Yang symbol illustrates that each side has an element of other at its core. Thus, neither of the side is superior or inferior to the other.*

c. 2000–1600 BCE	c. 1600–1046 BCE	c. 1046–256 BCE	c. 221–206 BCE

Shang Dynasty

The Shang dynasty bore nearly 30 emperors who together ruled for about 600 years. One of the best discoveries from this dynasty is the **oracle** bones. These bones serve as the historical hints of the way people lived during this period. There are records written on bones, turtle shells or cattle shoulders by ancient people.

▲ *Oracle bones with carved inscriptions*

Qin Dynasty

This is when the Chinese civilisation came under unified Imperial rule. The Qin dynasty made many changes and improvements such as setting up a standard currency system, standard wheel axle size, and standard seal script which are still used by the Chinese. The Qin dynasty set the laws for all the people under their rule. The previous dynasties had built fortifications between warring states. During the Qin dynasty, all the fortifications in the northern area were connected with a 2000 kilometre wall. The main intention was to block the entry of barbarians. The wall served as a precursor to the Great Wall of China.

▼ *The Great Wall of China is not a continuous line of wall. There is discontinuity where mountains or lakes lie to offer protection*

Han Dynasty

This is one of the most important dynasties of ancient China. Many modern Chinese people identify themselves as belonging to the Han **ethnicity**. During this period, the government started conducting imperial exams to select deserving candidates in a fair trial, to work as government officials.

The loom, cast iron, steel, hot-air balloons, and the seismograph (a tool that measures earthquakes) were all discovered or invented at this time. Also during this time, Buddhism spread among the people and the Silk Road helped in building trade relations.

▲ *A Chinese earthen glazed pot made during the Han dynasty*

Incredible Individuals

Lao-Tzu is a semi-legendary Chinese philosopher who lived sometime between the 4th–6th century BCE. He is said to be the author of *Tao Te Ching*, a book that gave rise to the philosophy of Taoism. He famously said, 'the journey of a thousand miles begins with a single step'. Lao Tzu, also called Laozi (the wise old man of China) is worshipped as a deity by many. He is most often painted as riding a bull.

Ming Dynasty

The Ming dynasty came to power by defeating Mongols, who had seized control of China and ruled from 1206–1308. They completed the construction of the Great Wall of China. The best architecture of this period is the Forbidden City, the emperor's grand home in the capital city, Beijing.

▶ *Kiln ceramic ware from the Ming Dynasty*

▼ *The Forbidden City Palace with an amazing lion sculpture*

c. 206 BCE–220 CE | **c. 618–907 CE** | **c. 960–1279 CE** | **c. 1368–1644 CE**

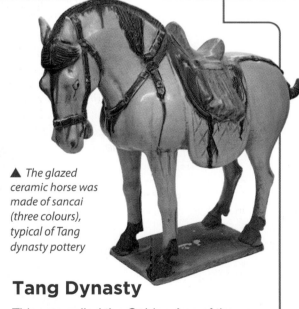

▲ *The glazed ceramic horse was made of sancai (three colours), typical of Tang dynasty pottery*

Tang Dynasty

This was called the Golden Age of the Chinese civilisation. Buddhism and trade flourished during this period. Art, science, and technology also improved. China became the most populous and one of the most prosperous countries in the world.

Song Dynasty

This dynasty rose to power after a period of unrest following the demise of the Tang dynasty. It brought peace and prosperity back to China. Gunpowder and the mariner's compass were invented during this period.

▲ *Ancient Chinese coin of the Song dynasty*

▶ *An antique pagoda built during the Song Dynasty*

The Lost Valley

In the 19th century, a number of explorers stumbled across the remains of an ancient city in Harappa, in what was then northwestern India. In 1920–1921, the Archaeological Survey of India began excavating this site in earnest. What they came across were the astonishing ruins of an ancient yet remarkably advanced civilisation. They named it the Harappan civilisation.

▲ *Harappan cut brick*

The Indus Valley Civilisation

Soon, other sites belonging to the same culture began to be discovered along the Indus River. They stretched westwards as far as Sutkagen Dor, just off the Arabian Sea; and in the east to the Yamuna River basin just north of Delhi. It is thus the most wide-ranging of the three oldest civilisations (Mesopotamia and Egypt being the other two). Most important among these sites is Mohenjo-Daro, now a UNESCO World Heritage Site.

A Civilisation Is Found

It is called the Indus Valley civilisation because it was born in the cradle of the Indus-Sarasvati River basin, also known as the Ghaggar-Hakra Basin. It existed from 3000–1300 BCE and is broadly divided into three phases—the Early Harappan Phase (c.3300–2600 BCE), the Mature Harappan Phase (c.2600–1900 BCE) and the Late Harappan Phase (1900–1300 BCE). Around 1800 BCE, the civilisation began to dwindle and decline. Many archaeologists think it happened due to climate change or because of the Sarasvati River drying up or changing its course. Many believed that the entire civilisation was dead after this, but as per new studies, they went to different places to settle down instead.

▲ *A replica of the so-called Priest King from the Indus Valley civilisation*

Life in the Indus

The people of the Indus Valley had an economy based on agriculture and trade. They were great craftsmen and ship builders too. They were experts at mathematics and geometry.

They were among the first to develop a system of uniform weights and measures, even the bricks they used were all made in an exact ratio of 1:2:4. They made specially rounded bricks to build circular structures like wells.

▼ *An excavated well of the Indus Valley built using special bricks which are broader at one end and taper towards the other*

City Planning

The cities of this civilisation were very well planned. A city was divided into two parts, the **citadel** built on a higher platform and the town. Every street had a good drainage system, the roads were wide and entire towns were protected by huge defence walls. Cities like Lothal had docks for ships. They also built public utility places like the Great Bath at Mohenjo-Daro, irrigation panels, and granaries.

◄ *The Great Bath of Mohenjo-Daro was a public bath with changing rooms surrounding it*

 ## Trade

Now, you may question how do we know they traded with other civilisations? It is because archaeologists found many ornaments, seals, pottery, etc., of Indus Valley during excavations at other places and many objects belonging to these civilisations in the Indus Valley. This indicates the exchange of goods. The ancient Mesopotamian texts call Indus Valley 'Meluhha' or a land of exotic goods.

▲ *Several seals were found at the Mohenjo-Daro and Harappa sites. They used the images of people and animals like unicorns, bulls, elephants etc.*

 ## Burial Rituals

The Harappans believed in life after death as they buried their dead with items, both worn and in jars, in cemeteries. Normal people were buried more simply, while richer or more powerful people had fancier graves. Indus Valley people were good **metallurgists** and had developed techniques to obtain copper and bronze. Hence, archaeologists found tools and figurines made from metals at the Harappa site.

▲ *Scene of a human burial from Indus Valley placed in a museum in India*

Ancient Indian Civilisations

Ancient India saw two urbanisations. The first was during the Indus Valley civilisation on the banks of the Ghaggar-Hakra with bronze metal technology. The second was observed in the Ganga-Yamuna **doab** when iron technology was introduced.

▲ *Nalanda University was one of the first in the world, and ran between 427-1197 CE*

Second Urbanisation

The second civilisation, also known as the second urbanisation, in Ancient India saw many advances in agriculture, trade, science, and technology. It was also a period of great accomplishment in art, architecture, literature, education, philosophy, religion, economy, writing systems, language, and administration.

▶ *A Brahmi inscription at the Ancient Indian caves at Kanheri, India*

Golden Period of Ancient India

▲ *Gold coin from Kushana dynasty*

The second urbanisation is rich in history. This was when Chandragupta Maurya—the first ruler of the Mauryan Empire (c. 321–185 BCE)—dominated the politics of his region. He learned from Kautilya (or Chanakya), the author of the *Arthashastra*, a guide on how to run an empire. Kushana and Gupta rulers famous for their administration and gold coins ruled during this period. The period saw great development in the Sanskrit language and ancient scripts such as Brahmi and Kharosthi which are considered as the 'mother' of the current languages and scripts used in India.

⊛ Incredible Individuals

Alexander the Great wanted to advance his kingdom to India. In c. 326 BCE, the famous battle between Alexander and Indian king Porus was fought and won by Alexander. Porus was retained to govern the kingdom under Alexander's thumb. However, by 325 BCE, Alexander was defeated and returned to the west.

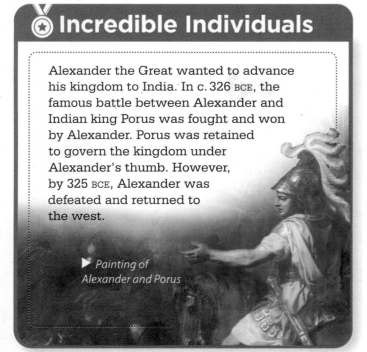

▶ *Painting of Alexander and Porus*

Notable Events

It was during the second urbanisation that metal currency like punch-marked coins and cast copper coins were introduced. The beautiful gold coins of Kushana and Gupta rulers are traced back to this period.

Religion

▲ *Ancient Buddhist sculpture*

It was also during this period that Buddhism, Jainism, and Hinduism saw many developments. Though Chandragupta Maurya was a Hindu, he converted to Jainism later in life. His grandson was Ashoka who focused his kingdom's resources into promoting Buddhism. The majority of their subjects practised Hinduism, Jainism, or Buddhism.

Mesoamerica:
Chocolate, Vanilla, & Art

The Mesoamerican (modern day-Mexico and Central America) civilisation and the Andean civilisation (c. 1500 BCE–1521 CE) are new world civilisations. Till about 500 BCE, Mesoamerica was divided into many small kingdoms. It was unified under the Olmec civilisation which consisted of the Maya, Aztec, Zapotec, Totonac, and Teotihuacan civilisations.

 ## Andean Advances

The Andean civilisation was mainly a village agricultural economy which developed around 2500 BCE. Around 1800 BCE, the Chavin civilisation came into power, which had complex social orders and distinctive styles of arts, architecture, and metallurgy. This culture later, split into smaller civilisations such as the Moche, Early Lima, and Nasca.

Olmec Civilisation

It is the first pre-Columbian civilisation that can be linked to Mesoamerica. It is also believed to be the 'parent' civilisation of the Mexican, Central American, and American Indian civilisations that followed. The examples of these include the Aztec and Maya cultures. These cultures produced amazing objects of art, right from the small jade figurines to huge stone statues of heads. They introduced writing to the new world.

Toltec Civilisation

Toltec in their language 'Nahuatl' meant 'reed people'. Tollan means 'place of the reeds'. They were named after the urban city of Tollan or Tula which is around 80 km from Mexico. They were the successors of Mayan people. They ruled from 10th–2nd CE, but they were defeated by the Aztec Nomads.

▲ *Huge stone head carved and placed in forests*

Chavin Culture

Chavin culture is considered to be the mother culture of all Andean civilisations. The name Chavin is derived from a ruined temple complex in Peru called Chavin de Huantar. This culture is famous for its typical pottery style. They used lots of gold to make beautiful jewellery and artefacts.

◀ *Pottery buried with the skeleton might have been a ritual to comfort the spirit of the dead*

▶ *Toltec warriors carved out of huge stone blocks*

Nasca Culture

The remains of Nasca culture are found in Peru. This culture developed from the earlier Paracas culture which existed in Peru. The Paracas culture was quite famous for its beautiful textiles found in cemeteries. The Nasca culture was famous for their beautiful polychrome pottery, textiles and geoglyphs (large designs or motifs) on the desert land famously known as ' Nazca Lines'.. This culture existed together with, and was followed by, various smaller cultures like Moche (c. 1–700 CE), Tihuanaco (c. 400–1000 CE), and Chimu (c. 1050–1470 CE).

The Mayans

In 2012, some people believed that the world would come to an end. This was based on the Mayan calendar that prophecised that Earth would be destroyed when planet 'Niburu' will collide with it. The planet Niburu does not exist. The Mayans, however, definitely existed in the ancient world.

▲ *Ancient Mayan hieroglyphs*

Who Were the Mayans?

The Mayans were one of the many indigenous cultures that existed in parts of Mexico and central America (hence Meso-middle America). They developed to be culturally rich especially with regards to arts and living conditions, but fell prey to the Spanish conquerors in the 16th century.

Mayan Step-Pyramids

Pyramid-like structures have existed outside Egypt, and some of the largest were made by the Mayans. The most famous Mayan step-pyramid, which still exists today, was a temple to Quetzalcoatl, a deity from the Mesoamerican cultures. He is called Kukulkan and hence this step-pyramid is called the Temple of Kukulkan. The temple was built as a stepped triangle.

Other important constructions were the *stelae* or 'Tetun' which means 'tree stones'. These were carved stone slabs which recorded information about the rulers, their families, and their victories in hieroglyph scripts.

👤 In Real Life

The Mayans were said to be the first to use vanilla. They added it to beverages which used a mix of vanilla, spices and cocoa. However, the beverages were only served to royalty or divinity.

◀ *Vanilla orchid and pod*

Writing Systems

Mayans had a fully developed writing system. It is the only known writing system of the new world. This writing system was made of hieroglyphs (just like the Egyptians) but the symbols used were different. They were quite good at architecture, astronomy and mathematics too. Their economy was largely dependent on agriculture and maize was their main crop.

▼ *The Temple of Kukulkan was designed to act as a physical calendar. Built to perfectly align with the Sun, each of the four sides has 91 steps. Combined with the one step at the top, that works out to 365 steps*

The Aztecs

The word 'Aztec' is derived from the word 'Aztlan', which means either 'white land' or 'land of white herons'. The Aztecs were nomadic people who conquered and ruled most of Mexico and the surrounding regions during 13th century CE.

Agriculture

In 1428 CE, the Aztecs emerged as the strongest power of the region after conquering Azcapotzalco, the capital of Tepanec. They improved techniques of agriculture, architecture, art, writing systems, metallurgy, and administration. They were great at farming and utilised almost all available land for agriculture. They even cultivated the swamps for agriculture! The Aztecs were also known for their irrigation practices.

Religion

The Aztecs had very interesting gods and religious practices. Most of their gods were nature deities such as Tlaloc, the God of rain, and Quetzalcoatl, a feathered serpent God. They believed that chocolate was a gift from Quetzalcoatl. They also worshipped Huitzilopochtli, the God of war.

The Aztecs famously prayed to Tonatiuh, the Sun God. They performed human sacrifices and offered the hearts to Tonatiuh. Sacrifices usually came in the form of people from other tribes, captured during wars and raids. It is even believed that they also ate the sacrificed flesh.

▲ *Tonatiuh, the Sun God*

In Real Life

Montezuma II was the ninth king of the Aztecs (c. 1466–1520 CE). He extended the empire as an able commander of the army. He was famous for his confrontation with the Spanish conqueror Hernan Cortes, and for 'Montezuma's revenge'. It is a term used for foreigners suffering from diarrhoea caused by drinking local water to which they are not immune.

When Cortes came to the Aztec Empire, Montezuma welcomed him as a guest. He offered him presents as well as a chocolate and vanilla beverage reserved for elites. Cortes, however, captured Montezuma and held him captive till his death.

▼ *Portrait of Aztec King Montezuma*

Calendar

The Aztecs developed an elaborate calendar made of a solar year (of 365 days) and a sacred year (of 265 days), based on religious rituals and ceremonies. The Aztec Empire came to an end when their ninth emperor, Montezuma II, was captured by the Spanish explorer Hernan Cortes in the 15th century CE.

▶ *Ancient calendar of the Aztecs*

Incan Civilisation

The Incans controlled the largest empire of the new world. It lasted between 1400 and 1533 CE. The Incans were sophisticated compared to earlier civilisations. Peru, Bolivia, Ecuador, northern Chile and some parts of Argentina were part of the Incan civilisation. All these are now countries, so it can be well imagined how huge the civilisation was.

▶ *A trio of Incan statues*

The Incas

The Incas had a great administrative system. They divided their empire into administrative districts till the lowest local level. Thus, it became easier for them to control the empire. They built roads, bridges and palaces that are some of the best in the world. They also built the famous citadel of Machu Picchu, on a mountain **ridge** nearly 2,430 metres above the mean sea level.

Like the Egyptians, the Incas mummified their rulers once they had passed. These mummies were kept in temples. They were brought out during ceremonies and were offered food and drinks. They even sought advice and opinions from mummies!

Quipu

Today, we record the spoken words by making symbols on paper, i.e., we write. The Incas recorded their information using *quipu*, which was made up of various types of knots made on strings. The size of the knots, the way they were tied, their colours, etc., denoted what the person was trying to say. They used this system to keep tax records, to tell stories and for other communication.

▲ *Colourful quipu*

Quechua Culture

Most of the new world civilisations are lost today. We know them through their art, architecture, inscriptions, or objects obtained during excavation. But that is not the case with the Incan civilisation. The Inca culture and language is still preserved as the Quechua culture.

▼ *Machu Picchu, an Incan citadel built on the ridge of a mountain*

Polynesia:
Land Inside a Triangle

The name Polynesia finds its root in two Greek words—'poly' meaning many and 'nesoi' meaning islands. Thus, Polynesia literally means 'many islands'. Polynesia is a group of islands in the Pacific Ocean which cover a huge triangular area.

▼ *Huge sculptures of ancient warriors on the Easter Island*

🛖 Where is Polynesia?

The apex of the triangle is home to the Hawaiian islands in the north, with New Zealand in the west, and Easter Island in the east at its base. It also consists of many other islands such as the Cook Islands, Samoa, Tonga, Tahiti, and Gambier Island. There are hundreds of islands that are a part of Polynesia and were formed due to volcanic activity.

🛖 Navigation

Imagine searching the ocean for land in small wooden boats with no tool for navigation or for ascertaining the distance and direction, sounds very dangerous, doesn't it? Polynesians were great sea voyagers who travelled the sea in canoes in search of land to settle. They had no navigation system except the position of the Sun and the stars to guide them. The Polynesians mostly relied on marine wealth for livelihood. Fishing and palm tree farming were their main sources of income.

👤 In Real Life

Hawaii is one of the major regions belonging to the Polynesian civilisation. Descendants of the Polynesians have preserved some of the ancient culture that was in danger of being lost when Europeans captured the land. Hawaii faced its darkest period during World War II. The USA had a naval base called Pearl Harbour on the island of Honolulu in Hawaii. On 7 December 1941, the Japanese launched a surprise attack on Pearl Harbour killing almost 2,500 people, wounding 1,000 and destroying 20 American ships and 300 airplanes. US President Franklin Roosevelt declared war on Japan. Thus, USA entered World War II. During the war, the US dropped the first nuclear bombs on Hiroshima and Nagasaki, two cities of Japan, destroying them completely.

🛖 Religion

Polynesians believed that every living as well as non-living thing has a supernatural power called 'mana'. This power could be affected by the bad actions of 'tapu' (which means taboo).

The Polynesians worshipped spirit gods. They prayed to them using chants, songs, and by performing animal and human sacrifices. Each Polynesian island had its own developed art form and architectural style. After the Europeans discovered Polynesians, the culture changed dramatically due to the increased trade practices. It was impacted by both slavery and Christian missionary activities. Eventually, very little remained of the Polynesian culture: some dance forms (like the Hula), the language Rapa Nui, and certain traditions such as Maori battle warfare.

◄ *Wooden carvings in Hawaii*

Ancient Rome

'Rome was not built in a day'. According to Roman mythology, Rome was built by Romulus and Remus, the twin sons of Mars, the God of war. It was, in fact, war that turned Rome from a small town on the banks of River Tiber (in the 8th century BCE) into a vast empire. At its height (in 2nd century CE), it straddled Europe, the Middle East, and northern Africa.

▲ The Colosseum is the largest amphitheatre in the world. It has 80 entrances and can hold around 50,000 spectators!

🏛 Roman Government

For around 400 to 500 years, Roman people had a republic government where officials were elected by people for a limited term. They also had a senate. This system forms the basis of the modern parliamentary system. This came to an end when Julius Caesar declared himself the sole dictator of the empire in 46 BCE. In 27 BCE, Caesar Augustus became the first Roman emperor.

▲ Emperor Augustus

🏛 Roman Trade

The Roman civilisation flourished due to extensive trade relations with other civilisations. The Romans were great soldiers but when it came to arts and architecture, they borrowed inspiration from the Greeks. Romans borrowed Greek gods too, but they changed their names. The Greek God Zeus became Jupiter, Hera became Juno, and Ares became Mars. The tragic half-god hero Hercules, famous for his strength, was adapted from the Greek hero Heracles.

This does not mean that the Romans only borrowed. They gave some amazing gifts to the world. The Latin language of Rome became the basis of many European languages like Italian and Spanish. Its script is still used to write these languages. Tacitus, a Roman historian, wrote *The Annals*, which taught the world how to write about history.

⭐ Incredible Individuals

The Pantheon is a marvel of Roman architecture. It was built by Marcus Vipsanius Agrippa. He was a close friend and confidante of the first Roman Emperor Augustus. A politician, soldier, and administrator, he was a good architect too. Though he borrowed many elements from the Greeks, he made many improvements to the technique. Many important buildings of the Roman Empire were built by Agrippa. The best known constructions are the Baths of Agrippa and **aqueducts**.

▼ Entrance to the Pantheon, Rome

▼ The splendour of the ancient city of Rome is still seen through the ruins of the Roman Forum

Greece:
The Land of Democracy

The Greeks conceived the Olympic Games. They held it in the ancient city of Olympia every four years. As per a mythical story, these games were started by Hercules. The Greek civilisation is said to be one of the most advanced civilisations of the ancient world. They influenced many other civilisations, especially Roman, when it came to building huge monuments. The Greeks were very efficient in administration and military.

▲ *The ruins of the ancient Acropolis of the early Greeks*

 ## Minoans and Mycenaeans

The first Greek civilisation is considered to be of the Minoans, named after their king Minos. They lived on the island of Crete between 2200 BCE and 1450 BCE. After the Minoans came the Mycenaean civilisation. They were the residents of mainland Greece. They fought the battle of Troy. We know about this civilisation and its stories through Homer.

▲ *Homer, a Greek poet who wrote the Iliad and the Odyssey*

▲ *A scene painted on Ancient Greek pottery showing a centaur and a warrior with a typical helmet*

Isn't It Amazing!

During the Trojan war, the Greeks used the great Odysseus's idea to gain victory over their enemies, the Trojans. Greek soldiers pretended to run away from the war. Then they hid in a huge wooden horse near Troy. One of their friends deceived the Trojans saying that the horse was an offering to Goddess Athena left by the Greeks. Once the horse was brought inside Troy, the Greeks jumped out and opened the gates to let in more soldiers and defeat the Trojans.

▶ *Trojan Horse at Troy*

The Classical Age

After the Mycenaean civilisation, we do not know much about Greek civilisation. Perhaps this is why it is called the Dark Ages. However, slowly after nearly 300 years, the Greek civilisation emerged as a phoenix in 800 BCE. Around 480 BCE, Greek civilisation reached great heights. Hence, this period is rightly called the Classical Age.

Huge buildings, temples and stadiums were built; the most famous of these must be the Parthenon. This age bore great poets, playwrights, historians, philosophers, and mathematicians, such as Plato, Socrates, Archimedes, Aristotle, Euripides, and Pythagoras.

Greeks to Remember

Ancient Greece was a land of scholars. It was where great philosophers, playwrights, poets, historians, scientists, mathematicians, and leaders were born. All these great people are still remembered as their inventions and discoveries are still useful in the modern world.

🏛 Greek Philosophers

Socrates, Plato, and Aristotle are three major philosophers from Greece. Socrates is called the founder and father of western philosophy. Plato was his student. Plato wrote many books as dialogues between himself and Socrates. Aristotle was Plato's student and teacher to Alexander the Great.

◀ *Plato was also a soldier in his youth, and he also taught royalty*

▶ *Aristotle was the founder of zoology and had the nickname 'the man who knew everything'*

▶ *Socrates was not a fan of religion, and he was openly bisexual*

⭐ Incredible Individuals

Archimedes was born in 287 BCE. He was a Greek mathematician and inventor. He was asked by the king to check if the new crown was made of pure gold. He kept on thinking how could it be detected.

Tired, he decided to take a bath. When he stepped into the tub of water, some of the water spilled out. This is when he realised that the water that spilled was equal to the weight of his body and so the weight of a pure gold crown would also be more than the fake one. Vitruvius, a Roman architect noted that Archimedes was so overjoyed that he ran naked through Syracuse shouting 'Eureka! Eureka!' which in Greek means 'I have found it'.

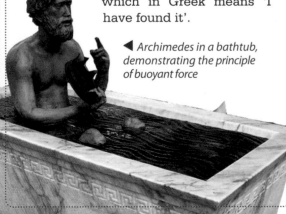

◀ *Archimedes in a bathtub, demonstrating the principle of buoyant force*

🏛 Greek Historians and Scientists

Herodotus is called the father of history. He recorded the Persian wars. Then there was another Greek historian named Thucydides, famous for his precise and fact-filled writing. He wrote about the war between Sparta and Athens. Archimedes, Aristarchus, Euclid, Hippocrates, and Pythagoras are just some of the important scientists and mathematicians of ancient Greece.

Aristarchus was the first to suggest that Sun is the centre of the universe and not Earth, as was believed. Euclid, the father of geometry, wrote the famous mathematical textbook *Elements*. The Pythagoras theorem is used to this day. Hippocrates is known as the father of Western medicine. He was revered for his ethical standards. Although he was an important figure of the Classical Greek era, our knowledge of his life is a mix of fact and fiction. For instance, he is known for the Hippocratic Oath, which doctors around the world take before they begin to serve patients, but it may not have actually been written by him.

▲ *Statue of Hippocrates*

Greek Playwrights and Poets

Aeschylus was a playwright. He was known as the father of tragedy. Euripides was also a Greek playwright who mostly wrote tragedies. He always portrayed women and slaves as strong and intelligent, while others wrote of them as weak and stupid. The playwright Aristophanes was called the father of comedy. Most famous was the poet Homer whose epics *Iliad* and *Odyssey* are still popular.

◀ *A bronze bust of Aeschylus, the father of tragedy*

▼ *Euripides went against the norms in his literary works*

▼ *Aristophanes, the father of comedy*

Greek Leaders

Of all the leaders of Greece, Alexander is perhaps the most famous of all. The greatest military commander of his time, he was said to have never lost a battle. Another famous leader of Greece is Pericles who was a great advocate of democracy and wanted people to live freely. He built many monuments in Athens that still stand today. He was called the first citizen of democratic Athens by historian Thucydides.

👤✓ In Real Life

The death penalty was introduced by Draco under Pericles's famous Draconian law, obviously named after him. These laws were so bad that sometimes even the smallest offences were made punishable by death. While most of the Draconian laws are no longer in use, the death penalty is still debated by countries around the world.

◀ *Bust of Pericles wearing the typical Greek helmet*

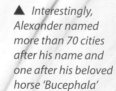

▲ *Interestingly, Alexander named more than 70 cities after his name and one after his beloved horse 'Bucephala'*

MIDDLE AGES

THE MIDDLE AGES

The fall of the Roman Empire marks the beginning of the European Middle Ages. This period lasted roughly from the 5th century to the 15th. The empire in Western Europe split into a number of kingdoms that would eventually give rise to our modern nations. This was, however, a time of poverty, disease, and religious wars like the Crusades. Eastern Europe flourished under the Byzantine and later Islamic empires. Further to the east, Asia had its own progressive civilisations. However, people enjoyed religious freedom only under some rulers. Vigorous international trade flourished alongside art, science, and exploration in Asia. In this sense, the gloomy Middle Ages is a uniquely Western way of viewing the world.

▲ *An illustration from the medieval French epic Song of Roland, written as a chanson de geste (song of heroic deeds), one of the oldest forms of French literature*

The Barbarian Invasions

Between the 4th and 8th centuries, Europe witnessed the Migration Period. German tribes moved west and east across Europe in search of new and fertile lands. They called it Völkerwanderung, meaning 'wandering of the peoples'. This led to many wars with the Roman Empire, which occupied these lands. Ultimately, the Germanic invasions led to the fall of the Empire and the onset of the Middle Ages.

 ## The First Phase (300–500 CE)

In 367 CE, tribes called Picts, Scots, Saxons, and Franks attacked the Roman Empire. In 376 CE, the Visigoths—fleeing another aggressive Germanic tribe called the Huns—burst on to eastern Roman lands. Displeased, the Romans launched several battles against them. The Goths finally crushed the Roman army at Adrianople in 378 CE. An uneasy alliance was formed. The Germans (Goths) were given a place to live as long as they protected the borders from further invasions. The truce did not last long. The Goths rebelled and invaded Italy, **sacking** Rome in 410 CE and settling down in the **Iberian peninsula**. Over 406-07, other tribes fleeing the Huns invaded **Gaul** and reached as far as Spain. They included Vandals, Alani, Suebi, and Burgundians. The Vandals later crossed Africa and set up, in Carthage, the first independent German state on Roman soil.

▶ *In 410 CE, under the leadership of Alaric, the Visigoths sacked Rome. By this time, the Italian city of Ravenna had replaced Rome as the capital of the Western Roman Empire*

▼ *In 455 CE, Rome was sacked again, this time by Vandals; shown in art by 19th century Russian painter Karl Briullov*

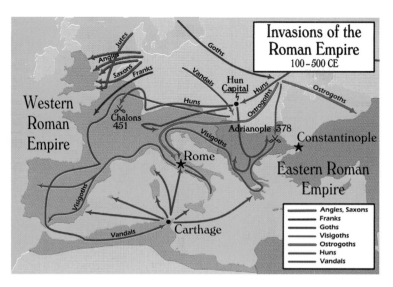

▲ *A map of major invasions of the Roman Empire (100–500 CE), by the Angles, Saxons, Jutes, Franks, Goths, Visigoths, Ostrogoths, Huns, and Vandals*

The Second Phase (500–700 CE)

Tribes of people called Slavs settled in Central and Eastern Europe during this period. The Bulgars, a now-Slavic group, had lived in Eastern Europe since the 2nd century. They conquered parts of the Byzantine Empire in the 7th century. The Lombards, another Germanic tribe, occupied northern Italy and gave it the name we still use today—Lombardy.

▲ *This gold bracteate (a medal worn as a jewel) belongs to the Migration Period. It is carved with what is possibly the Germanic God Odin*

⊙ Incredible Individuals

A feared military general, Attila (406–53 CE) led the Hun Empire at its peak. He was a fierce threat to the Roman Empire, ruthlessly plundering great parts of Central and Western Europe, including Gaul and Italy. The only battle he ever lost was the Battle of the Catalaunian Plains in 451 CE. The story goes that Attila the Hun, the Scourge of God, died the night of his wedding to Ildiko, from excessive drinking! Others say he was killed by his wife Gudrun. His empire died soon after.

▲ *The Feast of Attila shows a crowned Attila and his son Ellack being entertained by singers*

The Fall of Rome

In 476 CE, Ostrogoth general Odoacer (c. 433–93 CE) toppled Emperor Romulus Augustus and became king of Italy. Historians mark this date as the official fall of Rome. By this time, Vandals governed Africa, Visigoths ruled Spain, and Gaul was divided between various tribes, notably the Franks and Burgundians. However, the Eastern Roman Empire (Byzantium)—with its capital in Constantinople—continued until 1453!

▶ *Romulus Augustus gives up his crown to a victorious Odoacer*

Feudal Europe

The unified government of the Roman Empire was gone. Its land was divided up and ruled by Germanic lords and ladies, from manors and castles. **Serfs** and peasants farmed the land and served their lord. In return, the lord and his knights protected the people from invading forces. The lords owed allegiance to kings. This system of governing the land and its people is called feudalism. The kings vied for dominance with the Church. Merchants and craftsmen banded into professional groups called **guilds**. The scientific curiosity of ancient Rome was lost. It was replaced by blind faith in religion, specifically, in **patriarchal**, Catholic Christianity.

▲ *The feudal castle of Bouillon looms over a small town by the River Semois. In 1082, Godfrey of Bouillon sold the eerie fortress to raise money for the Crusades. He eventually became the first ruler of the Kingdom of Jerusalem*

💡 Isn't It Amazing!

Medieval knights had to follow a code of chivalry, which made them noble! They were loyal to one's lord, courteous to ladies, and upheld the Christian faith. Enemy knights were well-treated and exchanged for ransom, not killed outright. While chivalry was a wonderful idea, few knights truly followed it. It was popularised by wandering troubadours (musicians), whose ballads of heroic knights were immensely popular.

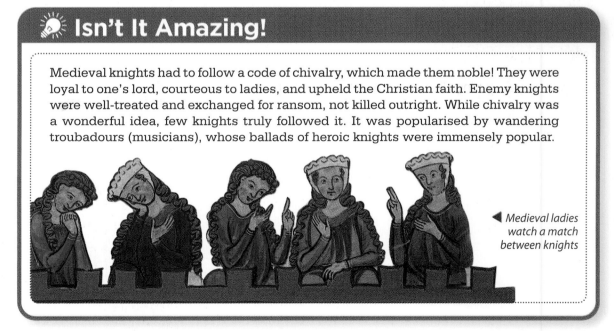

◀ *Medieval ladies watch a match between knights*

Medieval Women

Under Catholicism and feudalism, European women had almost no rights. A noblewoman was expected to obey her husband, bear children, and run the manor. She was rarely allowed a proper education and had no control over her money. Despite this, the Middle Ages witnessed exemplary women, like Empress Matilda (1102–67), who fought for the throne of England, and her daughter-in-law Eleanor of Aquitaine (c. 1122–1204), who joined the Crusades. The military genius Matilda of Tuscany (1046–1115) protected her lands (and the Pope) from the Holy Roman Emperor. Hildegard of Bingen (1098–1179) was a German **polymath** and Aethelflaed (c. 870–18 CE) was the influential Queen of Mercia.

▶ *Matilda was a powerful female ruler of Tuscany*

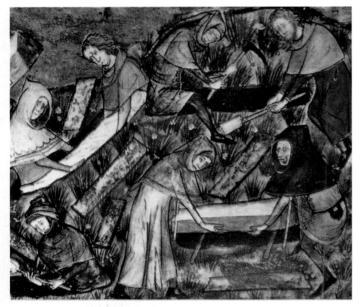

▲ *The people of Tournai bury victims of the Black Death, c. 1353*

The Black Death

Medieval medicine was a mix of folk remedies and faith. There was little science to it and doctors often caused more harm than good. An already poverty- and disease-ridden Europe was therefore decimated when the bubonic plague swept through it in the 14th century. It most likely came from Asia, travelling west on trading ships. Plague, aka the Black Death, caused red swellings that turned purple-black and oozy from thick, dark, smelly blood. So many died of it and so fast, that they couldn't all be buried, and corpses had to be piled up and burnt in pits. People thought it was a punishment from God. It was only in the 19th century that scientists realised plague was a bacterial infection and invented a vaccine against it.

The Little Ice Age

Around 1300, the planet began to cool, starting off a mini Ice Age that lasted till 1850. Changing climate led to bad harvests. People died from cold and famine. As populations fell, trade suffered leading to further poverty and many riots and rebellions.

The Peasants' Revolt of 1381

In England, young King Richard II was taken by surprise when—for the first time—farmers, labourers, and artisans rebelled against heavy taxes and low wages. Led by Wat Tyler, they marched to London, where they massacred Flemish merchants and destroyed a royal duke's palace. Forced to negotiate, the king promised them many things, including the abolition of serfdom. However, Tyler was later killed and the rebellion was mercilessly quashed.

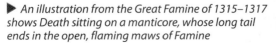

▶ *An illustration from the Great Famine of 1315–1317 shows Death sitting on a manticore, whose long tail ends in the open, flaming maws of Famine*

The Byzantine Empire
(c. 330–1453 CE)

While the Roman Empire in the west was destroyed by Germanic tribes, it continued in the east with its capital at Constantinople. This Eastern Roman Empire came to be known as the Byzantine Empire. A centre of learning and trade, Constantinople was the largest and wealthiest city of Europe during its time.

◀ *A mosaic at Hagia Sofia in Constantinople shows the Virgin Mary and Christ. To their right stands Emperor Justinian I, with a model of the church; to the left is Emperor Constantine I, the founder of Constantinople in 306 CE*

East-West Schism

Over the 5th–11th centuries, the Byzantine church grew apart, over religious and political issues, from the church in Rome. They finally split in the **Schism** of 1054, forming the Eastern Christian churches (led by the patriarch of Constantinople, Michael Cerularius) and the Western church (led by Pope Leo IX). Both popes excommunicated each other. It was only in 1965 that Pope Paul VI and Patriarch Athenagoras I met in Jerusalem and lifted the excommunications!

In Real Life

The official language of the Byzantine Empire was Latin until 700 CE, when Emperor Heraclius changed it to Greek.

Empress Theodora (c. 497–548)

Born the daughter of a circus bear-keeper, talented, strong-willed Theodora married Justinian in 523 CE. When he was crowned emperor in 527 CE, he made her joint ruler. Theodora's skill in governance soon became apparent. In 532 CE, she helped quell the **Nika riots** and saved the empire. She also convinced Justinian to create laws upholding women's rights. This included giving women the right to make choices about their own bodies; the right to property in marriage, divorce, and widowhood; the right to justice against crime and violence, and a voice for the poor and downtrodden women.

▼ *Empress Theodora and her attendants are represented in beautiful mosaics completed a year before her death in 248 CE at the Church of San Vitale in Ravenna*

The Holy Roman Empire

The Franks were western Germanic tribes that entered Roman lands gradually, in relative peace, over the 5th century. They were first united by King Clovis (r. 481/82–511 CE), who founded the Merovingian Dynasty and established its capital in Paris. The Merovingians officially ruled till 751, but by the 720s, they were only figureheads and the true power had been snatched away by a new family— the Carolingian Dynasty. The most famous Carolingian king is undoubtedly Charlemagne (c. 747–814). He was crowned the first emperor of what eventually became the Holy Roman Empire of the Middle Ages.

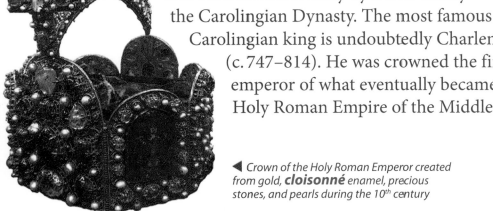

◀ Crown of the Holy Roman Emperor created from gold, **cloisonné** enamel, precious stones, and pearls during the 10th century

🐎 Carolingian Heirs

King Charles I is better known as Charlemagne, meaning Charles the Great. He became king of the Franks in 768 CE and king of the Lombards in 774 CE. In 800, he became the first emperor of what would later be called the Holy Roman Empire. Charlemagne was the son of Pepin the Short, who began the official rule of the Carolingian Dynasty. After Charlemagne, his empire was divided, between three heirs, into the lands of West Francia, Lotharingia, and East Francia. The Holy Roman Empire began when Otto I of East Francia became emperor in 962.

🐎 A Servant of the Crown

Pope Leo III wanted the church, and not the king, to be the top power in the land. He, therefore, hatched a plan to bring Charlemagne under the church's authority. On Christmas day, in 800 CE, he asked the king to kneel with him in prayer. As hundreds of people watched, Charlemagne knelt. Pope Leo silently placed a crown on his head and proclaimed him the first Holy Roman Emperor! The people cheered, considering this to be a great honour. But Charlemagne knew better. The title gave him no power or land, but made him a servant of the church. He never used the title and preferred to be called Emperor of the Franks and Lombards.

◀ Coronation of Charlemagne as Holy Roman Emperor

▶ Stained-glass window portraying Otto I, the first ruler of the Holy Roman Empire, which lasted until Napoleon Bonaparte brought it to an end in 1806

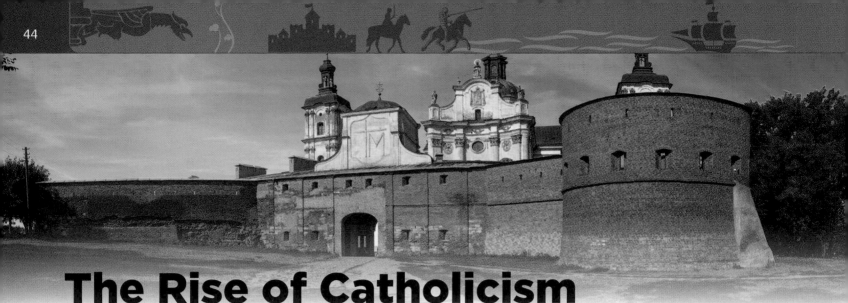

The Rise of Catholicism

With support from monarchs like Constantine I and Charlemagne, the Catholic Church soon gained enormous power. At its centre was the Pope, who oversaw an army of cardinals, bishops, monks, and priests. They told the kings, nobles, and commoners what God wanted. People in the Middle Ages feared God so much, that they often did just as they were told, by their religious leaders.

▲ Monasteries like the Abbey of Monte Casino, originally built by St. Benedict, were self-sufficient places where monks worked on fields, took care of cattle, and even made wine and cheese

▲ The son of a Roman senator, Pope Gregory I (c. 540–604) was a great early administrator of the Catholic Church and famously sent missions to convert England to Christianity

 ## Monasticism

A monk is someone who lives his life in austerity and prayer. In 520 CE, Benedict of Nursia (c. 480–547 CE) stated that a priest could not marry, could not own goods, and had to obey his **abbot**. St. Benedict is considered the father of Western monasticism. Women who followed such rules became nuns. They lived in convents overseen by an **abbess**. Monks wore coarse brown robes and shaved their heads. Nuns wore a gown, a veil, and a white cloth—called a wimple—around their neck and face.

 ## The Wealthy Church

Life was hard during the Middle Ages. People came to believe that if you followed certain rules, you would be safe and could even go to heaven. One of these rules involved donating land, jewellery, and money to the church, to make up for your sins. This was called 'buying an indulgence'. Such penance made the church rich. In fact, the church became so wealthy, that many nobles saw it as a good profession. Soon, it became common for leaders of the church to be aristocrats, who often put the interests of their powerful families before the interests of God and the common people. As the church became increasingly corrupt, the indulgence was used for nefarious purposes. The church even pardoned sins committed in its service, assuring God-fearing extremists that they would have a place in heaven!

◄ A manuscript from the 1490s condemns the church's distribution of indulgences (a way to reduce the punishment for your sin by paying the church) by associating it with Satan

The Inquisition

The Catholic church believed it was responsible for interpreting the word of God. Anyone else who tried to do so was considered as being tempted by the devil and was branded a heretic! To ensure that people obeyed the church, it set up the Inquisition. Priests of the Inquisition found and destroyed anyone who spoke against the church. The heretics were often mercilessly tortured and even burnt at the stake. It was one of the cruellest tools of subjugation in medieval times.

⊙ Incredible Individuals

The brilliant poet-philosopher Dante Alighieri (1265–1321) was a rare light in the literary gloom of the European Middle Ages. His epic *Divine Comedy* was written in Italian at a time when Latin was considered the language of the educated. The poem is a journey through the Christian afterlife. It moves through three parts—Inferno (Hell), Purgatorio (**Purgatory**), and Paradiso (Heaven).

◀ *Dante Alighieri ruminates over a copy of his masterwork, The Divine Comedy*

▲ *The Inquisition prepares to burn heretics at the stake, c. 1493–1499*

St. Francis of Assisi

Friars were monks who travelled under vows of poverty, begging for food and shelter. The most famous was St. Francis of Assisi (1182–1226), who joined the Crusades with the hope to conquer the Muslim people with love rather than war. He was famous for his love of animals. Among his miracles is a story of him saving a village by taming a wolf. In 1220, Francis set up the first known **Nativity** scene to celebrate Christmas.

The Western Schism

Over 1378–1417, the Catholic Church had two, sometimes three, popes at the same time! The French kings, who wished to influence the Church, had French popes who held court in Avignon. This schism ended in 1417 at the Council of Constance. The popes John XXIII and Gregory XII resigned. A third pope, Benedict XIII, was excommunicated. And a fresh, single pope, Martin V, was finally elected for all Catholics everywhere.

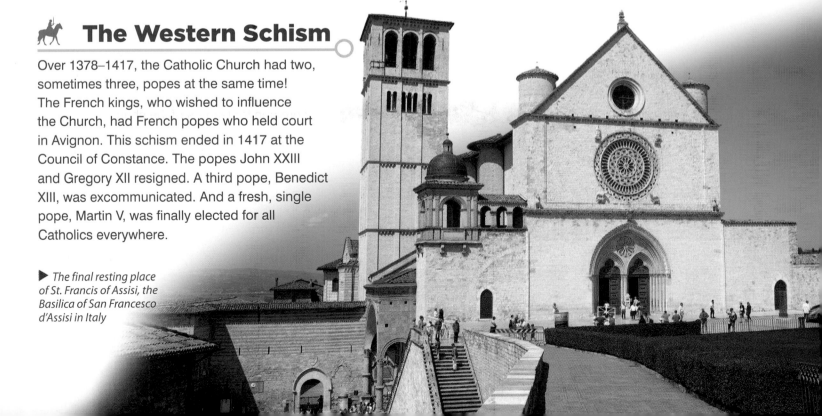

▶ *The final resting place of St. Francis of Assisi, the Basilica of San Francesco d'Assisi in Italy*

This Quran at the University of Birmingham is one of the oldest in the world, and dates to 568–645 CE

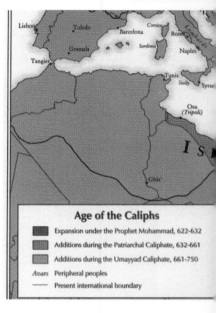

Age of the Caliphs

- Expansion under the Prophet Mohammad, 622-632
- Additions during the Patriarchal Caliphate, 632-661
- Additions during the Umayyad Caliphate, 661-750
- *Avars* Peripheral peoples
- Present international boundary

▲ *Expansion of Islam under the early Caliphs*

The Rise of Islam

Islam is a word meaning 'submission to God's will'. The followers of Islam are called Muslims. The religion was founded in Arabia in the early 7th century by Prophet Muhammad (570–632 CE). Followers of Islam believe in one God, Allah, and in his divine words as given in their holy book, the *Quran*. After the Prophet passed away, Islamic scholars gathered his actions and sayings into additional texts known as the Hadith.

The Rashidun Caliphs (632–661 CE)

After the Prophet's death, Islam came to be ruled by **caliphs** who were elected, or who took over by force. The first four caliphs were called Rashidun, meaning 'rightly guided'. First, there was Abu Bakr (573–634 CE) who had been Muhammad's father-in-law. He had the Prophet's teachings written down in the *Quran*. He was succeeded by Caliph Umar (c. 586–644 CE), another father-in-law of Muhammad's. Under Umar, Muslims conquered the greater part of the Byzantine Empire. Administrative offices were set up and Islam became a true nation. Its Arab armies conquered Mesopotamia, Syria and moved towards Persia and Egypt. Umar also established the Muslim calendar. He was, however, assassinated in 644 CE and Uthman, Muhammad's son-in-law, took over. In 656 CE, Uthman too was killed. His passing led to the First Fitna (Islamic civil war). Muhammad's cousin and son-in-law, Ali (c. 600–661 CE), was selected as the next caliph. He oversaw a tumultuous time for Islam. Despite this, Arab Muslims conquered large regions in the Middle East, including modern-day Iran and Iraq. Islam also spread across great swathes of Europe, Africa, and Asia.

◀ *The amazing Dome of the Rock in Jerusalem was first completed in 691–692 CE at the order of Umayyad Caliph Abd al-Malik, during the Second Fitna. The dome collapsed in 1015 and was rebuilt in 1022–1023*

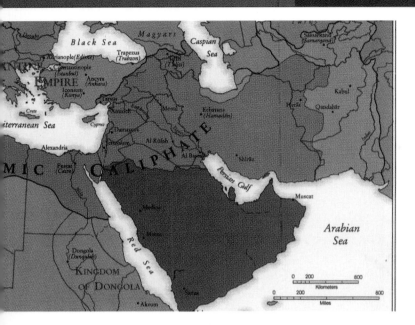

🐎 The Umayyad Caliphate (661–750 CE)

Ali and his supporters were eventually overthrown by Mu'awiya, governor of Syria and a relative of Uthman's. He established Damascus as the capital of the first Islamic dynasty, the Umayyad. With this, the caliph was no longer elected by his peers. The position was passed on within the family. The Umayyad Dynasty ruled from Damascus until 750; and later established another kingdom in Cordoba, Spain.

▲ *Siege* of Baghdad by Hulagu Khan shows the conquest and end of the Abbasid Caliphate at the hands of the Mongols

🐎 The Abbasid Caliphate (750–1258 CE)

The last Umayyad caliph was overthrown by a successful revolt that arose in Persia in 747 CE. It was led by descendants of al-Abbas, an uncle of the Prophet's. Unlike the Umayyads, who were interested in Africa and the West, the Abbasid caliphate—with its Persian sophistication and long history of empire building—looked eastwards. Baghdad, on the River Tigris, became the new capital. Over the next century, the empire grew into an international entity, powerful in commerce, industry, arts, and science. It was supported by strong caliphs such as al-Mans'ur (c. 709–75), Harun al-Rashid (c. 763–809), and al-Ma'mun (786–833). By the 10th century, Islam had spread across great swathes of land, stretching beyond Baghdad in the east, Cairo in the south-centre, and Cordoba in the west.

⭐ Incredible Individuals

The wonder and opulence of Harun al-Rashid's Baghdad is well known to us through the amazing book of Arabian fantasies, *A Thousand and One Nights*. Many details in these stories reflect the splendour of the Muslim court. This period was marked by peace and affability on the part of the caliphates. Harun al-Rashid had such international fame, Charlemagne's biographers record the mutual respect which was shared by the two emperors when they exchanged gifts.

▲ *Caliph Harun al-Rashid receives gifts at his court in Baghdad*

▲ *Arabic text of the fabulous A Thousand and One Nights*

The Golden Age of Islam

While medieval Europe succumbed to superstition, poverty, and disease, the Islamic world flourished with attention given to trade, research, sciences, arts, and philosophy. The period between the 8th and 14th centuries is its golden age. It began with the reign of Harun al-Rashid and his House of Wisdom in Bagdhad—a gathering place for scholars who brought ancient knowledge from across the world, translated and studied it, and increased discoveries and inventions for the benefit of humanity.

◀ *Sabuncuoğlu Şerafeddin (1385–1468), an Ottoman surgeon and physician, is most famous for his book Imperial Surgery, the first-ever illustrated surgical atlas*

🐎 Leading Lights

Ibn-Sina or Avicenna (980–1037) was a doctor, philosopher, scientist and author of 450 books! Most famously, he wrote *The Book of Healing* and *The Canon of Medicine*. He is considered as the Father of Modern Medicine. Al-Razi or Rhazes (c. 854–935) was another great doctor and philosopher. He discovered sulphuric acid, allergic asthma, and established the use of alcohol in medicine. The amazing Al-Biruni (973–1050) excelled in physics, mathematics, astronomy, natural sciences, history, and languages. He was sought by many rulers for advice and to conduct research. Ibn-Rushd or Averroes (1126–98) was a judge and court doctor well versed in philosophy, theology, medicine, astronomy, physics, law, and languages.

▼ *An illustration from Al-Biruni's writings on astronomy explains the different phases of the moon*

ПОЧТА СССР 1973

6к

Абу Рейхан Бируни
1000 лет со дня рождения

▲ *In 1017, Al-Biruni travelled to India, explored Hinduism and authored a study of Indian culture*

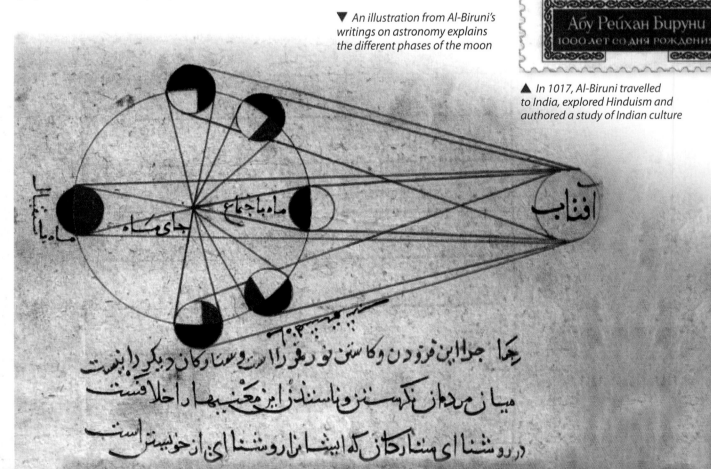

Muslims of Ghazni

Ghazni is a city, beside the River Ghazni, on a high plateau in Afghanistan. During the 10th century, its Muslim rulers, who belonged to an aggressive Turkish dynasty, raided land around Peshawar and even threatened India. Most dreaded among them was Mahmud (971–1030), whose 33 year long reign saw some 12–17 Indian campaigns that destroyed temples and plundered Hindu treasures. After his death, his empire in Afghanistan and eastern Persia fell to a new wave of Turkish tribesmen—the Seljuks.

▶ *The painting shows an Indian raja being captured and presented before Sultan Mahmud of Ghazni*

The Seljuk Turks

In the late 10th century, a group of Turkish tribes, led by a chieftain called Seljuk, swept down the northern borders of the Persian Empire. They converted to Islam and set about conquering an empire for themselves. In 1040, Togrul Beg, a grandson of Seljuk, took Ghazni from Mahmud's son Masud. By 1055, he had conquered the Iranian plateau and Baghdad. The new empire reached its peak around 1092 under Beg's grand-nephew Malik Shah. It stretched from Afghanistan to the Mediterranean, with some Turkish tribes finally occupying the area that would become Turkey one day.

▲ *The Great Seljuk Empire at its peak, upon the death of Malik Shah I in 1092*

The Hashshashin

Soon after Malik Shah's death, Persia was pushed into chaos by a sinister new group called the Hashshashin, or Assassins. These are more correctly known as the Nizari Ismailis. They came into power in the 11th century by seizing fortresses in Persia. In particular, they took over the formidable stronghold of Alamut. By the 12th century, they were also secure in Syria. Rather than battling armies, the Assassins used a vast network of spies and terrorists to infiltrate and destroy enemy camps. This troublesome sect was finally quashed between two great rival powers of the 12th century—the Mamluk sultans of Egypt and the Mongol hordes of Hulagu Khan.

▶ *Rudkhan Castle in Iran was once an Assassin stronghold*

Saxons and Normans

After the ancient Romans left, the British Isles were ruled by tribal chieftains who vied with each other for power. The Anglo-Saxons dominated England from 550–1066. They confronted **Celtic** chiefs in Wales. In the 5th century, the semi-historical **Niall of the Nine Hostages** established the kings of Ireland. In Scotland, the Picts and Scots came together under a king during the 9th century.

Alfred and the Norsemen

In the 9th century, England faced repeated raids from sea-faring Vikings who swept down from Scandinavia. Over 865–876 CE, the Great Danish Army invaded England and defeated the kingdoms of East Anglia, Mercia, and Northumbria. Alfred of Wessex (849–99 CE), later known as Alfred the Great, rallied Saxon forces and forced the invaders back to a region called Danelaw. England finally united under Alfred's son (Edward the Elder) and grandson (Æthelstan).

▲ The Norman Conquest is recorded in the Bayeux Tapestry, commissioned by Bishop Odo of Bayeux, half-brother to William the Conqueror

▲ To establish the Kingdom of England, Alfred the Great built up the borders; established laws, education, and a navy; and reformed the English economy

The Norman Conquest

In 1066, William, the fearsome Duke of Normandy (in France), landed on English shores, determined to take the throne. He defeated the newly crowned Harold Godwinson at the Battle of Hastings and captured the city of London. On 25th December, William was crowned as the king of England. He controlled his new kingdom by building strategically placed castles and giving power to his Norman followers. William the Conqueror is the founder of the current line of British monarchs.

Isn't It Amazing!

The Saxons got their name from their short sword, the scramasax. Saxon lands were divided into shires, which were further divided into 'hundreds'. The peacekeeping officer of a shire was called the shire reeve. This later became our modern word sheriff.

▼ An Anglo-Saxon village

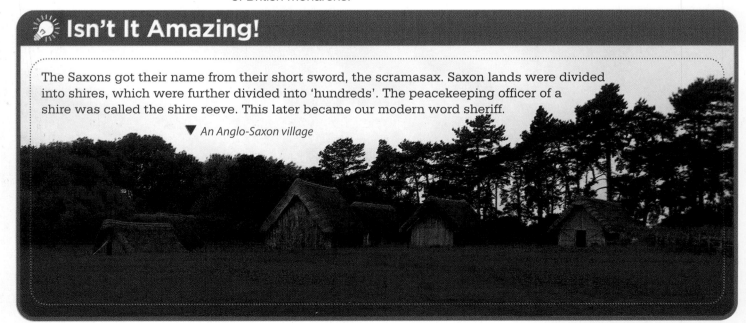

Norman Rule

In 1085, William ordered a full survey of England. His men travelled the kingdom, recording who owned what property—land, livestock, farm equipment, mills, and so on. The findings were entered into the *Domesday Book* which William used to tax and control the people. William's heirs focussed on conquering Wales, Scotland, and Ireland. Henry II (1133–89) set up English administration in Dublin, Ireland. Wales was suppressed by Edward I (1239–1307) in the late 13th century. Scotland, however, remained independent, until its King James VI (1566–1625) inherited the English throne after the famous Queen Elizabeth!

▲ *In 1215, the unpopular King John (1166–1216) was forced to sign the first charter of rights, the Magna Carta. Among many rights that it offered, the promise of swift justice and protection of barons from illegal imprisonment were the popular ones*

▲ *Over the late 13th and early 14th centuries, Scotland fought against English dominance in a series of military campaigns that saw heroes such as Sir William Wallace (c. 1270–1305) and King Robert the Bruce (1274–1329)*

 ## The War of the Roses

Over 1455–87, two sides of the royal family fought for the throne leading to civil war in England. It began after the death of Henry V, the hero of Agincourt, when his successor proved to be mentally ill. The House of Lancaster was represented by a red rose and the House of York by a white rose. The wars ended when Henry Tudor defeated Richard III at the Battle of Bosworth on 22 August 1485. Henry was a grandson of Catherine (widow of Henry V) and her second husband, the Welshman, Owen Tudor. After being crowned as Henry VII, he married Elizabeth of York, thus, uniting the Lancastrian and Yorkist lines. His Tudor Dynasty marks the end of English Middle Ages. In the following years, his son and granddaughter—Henry VIII and Elizabeth I—oversaw England's Golden Age.

◀ *The Battle of Bosworth, the last significant battle in the Wars of the Roses, was fought on 22 August 1485. Henry Tudor's Lancastrian forces overthrew King Richard III, who became the last English king to die in battle*

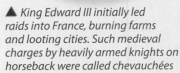

▲ King Edward III initially led raids into France, burning farms and looting cities. Such medieval charges by heavily armed knights on horseback were called chevauchées

◄ The English longbow could fire faster and farther than the French crossbow. It was greatly responsible for the English victory at the Battle of Crécy (and later at Agincourt)

The Hundred Years' War

Over 1337–1453, French and English kings fought to control land that is now part of France. When Charles IV of France died childless, Edward III of England demanded the French throne as his closest living relative. The French, however, refused to have a foreign king and crowned a cousin of the old king's who later became Philip IV of France. Edward responded by going to war!

 ## Early English Victories

With 17 million people, and support from Scotland, France was stronger than England from the start. Yet, the English won the naval Battle of Sluys in 1340. All wars after this were fought on French soil. Under the leadership of Edward III's son—Edward, the Black Prince—England won the 1346 Battle of Crécy and the 1356 Battle of Poitiers. The prince even captured King John II of France!

 ## Battle of Agincourt

The most famous battle of the period was fought in 1415 by 8,000 Englishmen (led by Henry V) against 36,000 trained French soldiers (belonging to Charles VI). Despite the odds, the English decimated the French army! When the battle began, the heavily armoured French knights found their horses slipping in mud because it had rained the previous night. The English archers rained down arrows upon them and used pointed stakes hammered into the ground to injure the charging cavalry. Some 6,000 French soldiers died and one-third of their nobility was killed or captured.

Incredible Individuals

After Agincourt, France was rescued from her terrible state by St. Joan of Arc (1412–31). A young peasant girl, who was inspired by a divine vision to lead the French army and drive the English out of France. Sadly, she was abandoned by the French king after she helped him gain the crown. Joan was eventually betrayed and captured and sold to the English, who burned her at the stake.

◄ She was known as The Maid of Orléans, and died at the age of 19

Medieval Africa

African history of the Middle Ages has been passed on in folklore rather than being written down. Egypt (in North Africa) is, of course, an exception. Fortunately, Muslim travellers like Ibn Batuta (c. 1304–68) left records of their journeys to Africa. Medieval Africa was a vibrant network of kingdoms where goods and ideas were exchanged. Arab scholar al-Bakri wrote admiringly of Ghana in the 11th century and Ibn Khaldun investigated the history of Mali in the 14th century.

Islamic Africa

Merchants travelling down the Red Sea and eastern coast spread Islam to Africa. Ruins of an 8th century wooden mosque can be seen as far south as Kenya, along with Persian pottery and Chinese stoneware. In the 11th century, a Muslim dynasty ruled along the coast of modern Tanzania. Its coins named the ruler as 'the majestic Sultan Ali Bin al-Hasan'. Ibn Batuta wrote about this prosperous sultanate with its vast trade in gold and slaves. Merchants travelling along the oasis routes of Sahara in search of gold, ivory, and salt also spread Islam to western Africa. Its first Muslim ruler was the early 11th century king of Gao. Ibn Batuta, visiting Mali in 1352, expressed mixed feelings about African practices, such as masked dancers and scantily clad women, mingling with Islamic ones.

▲ It was common practice for kingdoms to fight wars using slaves as soldiers. Amazingly, some mamluk (slave) generals used their power to set up the formidable Mamluk Dynasty that ruled Egypt and Syria from 1250 to 1517

▶ Spanning nearly 30 years, the Moroccan scholar-explorer Ibn Batuta visited the Islamic nations, and even non-Islamic lands in India and China

Incredible Individuals

It is said that the richest man on earth during the Middle Ages was Mansa Musa (c. 1280–1337), the ruler of Mali in West Africa. He was famous throughout Europe and the Middle East. He was also famous for his pilgrimage to Mecca in 1324–25. His caravan of over 60,000 people included 500 slaves—each with a gold staff—and 100 camels bearing great mounds of gold dust. Mansa Musa freely gave away so much gold that the precious metal became cheaper, and it was many years before gold increased in value again!

The Crusades

The High Middle Ages was a time when European Christians launched a series of religious wars against Muslims to capture the holy city of Jerusalem. These were called the Crusades. Historians recognise eight major Crusades between 1096 and 1291.

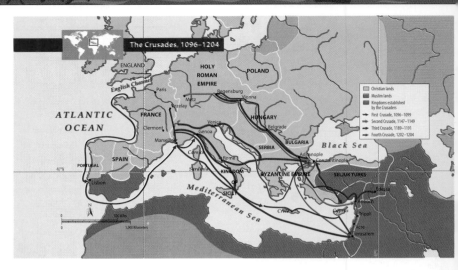

Going to the Crusades was referred to as 'taking the cross' and Crusaders marched wearing a red cross on their clothing and banners

The First Crusade

In 1095, Pope Urban II called on all Christians to rise against the Islamic forces of the Seljuk Turks and recapture the Holy Land. The response was tremendous! Thousands of ordinary citizens, trained knights, and noblemen joined the martial pilgrimage. Four armies were formed under the leaders Raymond of Saint-Gilles, Godfrey of Bouillon, Hugh of Vermandois, and Bohemond of Taranto. A more haphazard band of knights and commoners set off under the command of the preacher, Peter the Hermit. They were called the People's Crusade.

✠ 1095–1099

💡 Isn't It Amazing!

Over 1097–98, the Crusaders and Byzantines marched through Seljuk lands in Anatolia (Turkey) and Syria, capturing key cities like Antioch and the Seljuk capital Nicea (modern-day Iznik). To govern the vast territory, four large Crusader states were established in Jerusalem, Edessa, Antioch, and Tripoli.

▲ *The capture of Jerusalem during the First Crusade was accompanied by the massacre and burning of many innocent Muslim and Jewish defenders of the city*

✠ 1147–1149

The Second Crusade

In 1144, the Seljuk general Zangi recaptured Edessa (in modern Turkey), stunning the other Crusader states. Pope Eugenius III announced the Second Crusade. It was led by King Louis VII of France and King Conrad III of Germany. After a series of defeats, Louis and Conrad attacked Damascus with 50,000 men. Damascus's ruler called Zangi's successor, Nur al-Din, for aid. Together, they sent the Christian army packing.

▶ *Conrad III (1093–1152) was the first King of Germany from the Hohenstaufen Dynasty*

The Third Crusade

In 1169, Nur al-Din's forces—under the command of General Shirkuh and his nephew Saladin—seized Cairo, Egypt. Soon after, Saladin became Sultan and began retaking the Crusader states and Jerusalem. His troops won a decisive battle at Hattin in 1187, which sparked the Third Crusade. The Christian hero this time was King Richard I of England. In 1191, Richard the Lionheart won against Saladin in the Battle of Arsuf, recaptured the city of Jaffa and re-established some degree of Christian control. In the end, Richard was unable to conquer Jerusalem.

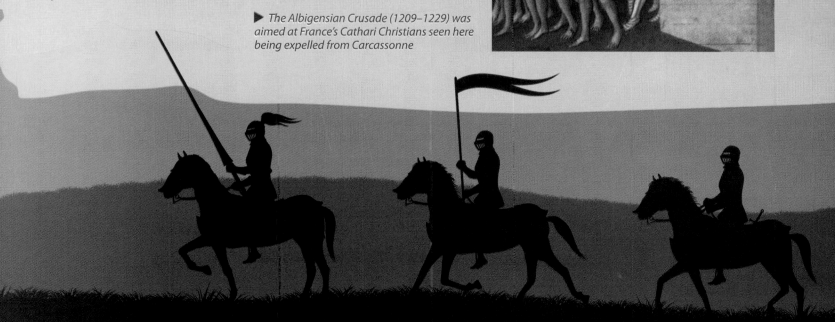

◀ *Saladin spares the life of Guy of Lusignan the King of Jerusalem, after the Battle of Hattin*

The Fourth Crusade

Formed by Pope Innocent III, the Fourth Crusade never even made it to the Holy Land! The Crusaders ended up looting their Christian allies in Constantinople instead. Many stayed on to set up Crusader states in Byzantine territory.

▲ *Crusaders lay siege to Constantinople in 1204*

✚ **1187–1192**   ✚ **1202–1204**   ✚ **1208–1271**

The Final Crusades

The later Crusades met with no success. Some were even aimed at (non-Catholic) Christians! In 1212, a group of children, women, elderly, and poor began a Children's Crusade that didn't get far. Pope Innocent III launched the Fifth Crusade in 1216 against Egypt. The land-and-sea conquest ended with the Crusaders surrendering to Saladin's nephew, Al-Malik al-Kamil, in 1221. In the Sixth Crusade (1229), Emperor Frederick II acquired Jerusalem from al-Kamil through diplomacy. When their treaty expired, the Muslims took back the city. Over 1248–54, Louis IX of France took the Seventh Crusade to Egypt, but the battle met with failure. Louis launched the Eighth Crusade in 1270 after the Mamluk Sultan Baybars demolished Antioch. The mission never reached Syria and Louis died in Tunis, Africa. In 1291, the city of Acre fell to the Mamluks. Historians mark this as the end of the Crusader states.

▶ *The Albigensian Crusade (1209–1229) was aimed at France's Cathari Christians seen here being expelled from Carcassonne*

Boyars and Magyars

In medieval Russia and many Eastern European countries like Bulgaria, boyars were members of the ruling nobility. They held important posts in the military and formed a council to advise the Tsar (emperor of Russia). The Carpathian regions belong to the Romanians. Their boyars comprised of judges and leaders who were duly elected until the role became hereditary. The ethnic people of Hungary are called Magyars. They have occupied the Hungarian land for most of the second millennium.

▶ The funeral of a Rus chieftain on a ship, as described by the Arab traveller Ahmad ibn Fadlan in the 10th century

🐎 Medieval Hungary (896–1526)

The Magyars established Hungary in 896 CE. Their leader Prince Arpad established the first royal house. In 1000 CE, the country became a kingdom with the crowing of its first king, Saint Stephen. Tatars (Mongols) attacked the lands in 1241 and the house of Arpad was wiped out in 1301. One of the greatest kings in the following years was Matthias Corvinus, who protected Hungary against Ottoman aggression. A decade after his death, the Ottomans split Hungary in the Battle of Mohács (1526). The western and northern areas remained under the occupancy of Hungary; the southern lands fell to the Ottomans; and the eastern regions became semi-independent as the Principality of Transylvania.

💡 Isn't It Amazing!

The land south of the Carpathians and north of River Danube became a state called Wallachia. Its most famous ruler was Vlad III (1431–76), gruesomely called Vlad the Impaler because impaling those who offended him on a stake was his favorite mode of punishment. He often arranged groups of staked bodies in favorite patterns, such as a ring outside of the city. The Romanians called him Dracul, meaning the devil.

▲ Vlad Tepes's bloodthirsty life inspired Irish author Bram Stoker to pen his Gothic masterpiece, Dracula

 ## Kievan Rus

The powerful empire called Kievan Rus centred around the city of Kiev during the Middle Ages. In coming times which would eventually form Russia and Ukraine. Its people were originally Vikings who migrated to Eastern Europe in the 9th century. They established a kingdom under King Rurik whose dynasty ruled Rus for 900 years! In 880, King Oleg made Kiev his capital and set out in expanding the empire. He even raided Byzantium and Constantinople, but finally made peace with them.

◀ *A monument to princes Rurik and Oleg in Old Ladoga, Russia*

Golden Age of Kievan Rus

The rule of Vladimir the Great (c. 958–1015) and Yaroslav the Wise (c. 978–1054) marked the Golden Age of the empire. Vladimir united many of the Slavic states under his rule and converted to Christianity. This strengthened his ties with Constantinople, which, in turn, increased the flow of trade and knowledge. Kievan Rus reached its peak under the rule of mighty Yaroslav the Wise, whose wise administration policies induced the strength of military and gave boost to the cultural development. Yaroslav codified the laws, built a library, and promoted education. After his death, the Mongols invaded the land, bringing an end to the unity of Rus.

In Real Life

The boyars were at the height of their power in the Middle Ages. Tsar Ivan the Terrible brought them to heel in the 16th century. Tsar Peter the Great further curbed their powers by abolishing the council of advisors in 1711.

▶ *Tsar Ivan the Terrible (1530–1584)*

◀ *Vladimir considered many religions before choosing Christianity! Ivan Eggink's painting shows him listening to the Orthodox priests, while the papal envoy stands aside in discontent*

Mongol Hordes

The Mongolian steppes were home to nomadic empires such as the Xiongnu (3rd century BCE–1st century CE), Xianbei (c. 93–234 CE), Rouran Khaganate (330–555), Turkic Khaganate (552–744) and others. In Central Asia, the Khitan group established the Liao Dynasty (907–1125), which ruled Mongolia and parts of Russia, Korea, and China. The various tribes finally united in 1206 under a man named Temujin (1162–1227), who was renamed Genghis Khan and was elected on the banks of the Onon River. Genghis Khan's army of warriors is remembered today as the Mongol horde!

▲ *A 14th century portrait of Genghis Khan, the fearsome founder of the Mongol Empire*

The Khan's Empire

Genghis Khan became the ruler of a huge sweep of land which extended from Asia to the Adriatic sea. His descendants expanded the empire, conquering places as far-flung as Poland and Vietnam. At its height, the Mongol Empire was about the size of Africa! Though Genghis Khan is chiefly remembered for the terror of his invasions, he was also a good ruler to his subjects. He allowed religious freedom, abolished torture, encouraged trade, and set up the first international postal system. He died in 1227 during a campaign against the Chinese kingdom of Xi Xia.

The Khatuns

Genghis Khan's vast empire was ruled by women—by the Khan's aunts, daughters, and consorts! Throughout his life, he had been protected and enabled by women. He trusted them to rule well and not betray him. Defeated kings were forced to join the horde to conquer other parts of the world. Meanwhile, the Khan women were brought in to administer the land, sign treaties, suppress rebellions, and pass judgements. Genghis Khan's daughters ended up controlling the valuable Silk Route. They gave him aid for his campaigns in China and Persia. His daughter Altani was even made 'Hero Ba'atur', a title given to military and political champions. Sadly, after the Khan's death, his heirs neglected his legacy.

◀ *Gold dinari from Genghis Khan's time struck at Ghazni in 1221–1222*

Members of various tribes bow to Genghis Khan as he is elected ruler of the Mongols

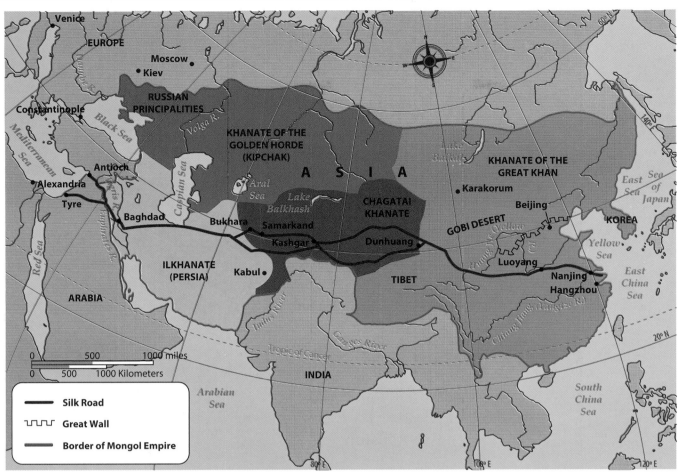

▲ *The Silk Road in the Mongol Khanates in 1294 CE*

🐎 The Mongol Khanates

The great conqueror's grandchildren settled in three increasingly independent regions. Kublai Khan, as the Great Khan, had the grandest realm. His brother Hulagu ruled the Ilkanate lands of Persia and Mesopotamia. His cousins, the brothers Batu and Berke, moved with the Golden Horde to Polish and Russian territories. The horde's name here seems to have come from the golden tent used by Batu. In Central Asia, Genghis's second son ruled a fourth realm called Chagatai Khaganate.

🐎 The Yuan Dynasty of China

From 1252 onwards, Kublai Khan pressed southwards through mountains to China. In 1264, he became the Great Khan, which gave him more resources to conquer China. In 1271, he moved the imperial capital to Beijing and built a magnificent city. Mongols called it Khanbaliq—the city of the Khan. From this base, he overwhelmed the Song Dynasty and became the first Mongol-Chinese emperor of the new Yuan Dynasty. His reign and empire became famous through the writings of the Italian merchant Marco Polo, who spent many years in the Mongol court.

👤 In Real Life

Over the 14th century, Mongol power all but disappeared. The last Il-Khan died in 1335. The Yuan Dynasty fell to the Ming Dynasty in 1368. In 1380, the grand prince of Moscow defeated the Golden Horde in a battle on Kulikovo Plain. The Mongols hung on for another two centuries, but they were now competing with many rising rivals.

▼ *Kublai Khan, wearing Mongol-style furs over Han Chinese silk brocades, out on a hunting expedition*

The Kingdoms of China

▲ *Eighty-seven Celestials, the draft painting of a fresco by master artist Wu Daozi (c. 685–758)*

At the start of the Middle Ages, the Chinese lands were split into many kingdoms. This was called the period of the Northern and Southern Dynasties. The man who reunited China in 589 CE established the Sui Dynasty. He took the title Wen Di (Cultured Emperor). The dynasty was overthrown in 618 CE by one of the emperor's high officials. He established the Tang Dynasty, which oversaw a dynamic Golden Age for China.

◀ *Yang Di, the second Sui emperor, famously constructed the Grand Canal—the longest and oldest artificial river in the world*

Incredible Individuals

Wu Zetian (c. 625–705) was the only woman to rule China in her own right. A concubine of the powerful Emperor Taizong, she later became empress to his more feeble heir, Emperor Gaozong. After his death, she became the sole ruler of the Zhou Dynasty, which began and ended with her. Empress Wu had a large and loyal network of spies who enabled her to rule successfully. A ruthless empress, she employed talented people and made smart decisions.

▲ *The Fengxian cave of the Longmen Grottoes, commissioned by Wu Zetian, who made Buddhism the state religion*

Tang Dynasty (618–907)

Chinese culture under the Tang Dynasty reached new heights, particularly in ceramics and literature. The Japanese adopted the Chinese way of writing at this time, modifying the characters to suit their own language. Imperial China controlled all land from the northwest desert oases of the Silk Road to parts of Manchuria in the northeast and Vietnam in the south. Princes as far off as Bukhara and Samarkand recognised the emperor's sovereignty. The dynasty weakened after the devastating **An Lushan Rebellion** (755–763). Later many more rebellions followed. Most shockingly, in 878–79, a rebel army trying to overthrow the Tang massacred tens of thousands of people in the port city of Guangzhou.

▶ *The Tang period is famous for its sancai (three-colour) ceramics, as seen in this fierce tomb guardian*

🐎 Song Dynasty (960–1279)

After the Tang, China split into many states. This was the Five Dynasties and Ten Kingdoms Period (907–960). It ended when a warlord took over and established the Song Dynasty. Paper money, which had come into use shortly before, became a familiar currency during the Song rule. The emperors encouraged civilian administrators and reduced the power of military lords. Over time, Song rule made the nation most sophisticated. However, it also weakened China. The Songs were finally overthrown by Kublai Khan and his Mongol Yuan Dynasty.

▶ *The design of the Chinese sailing ships (called junks) was perfected during the later Song period. Its pioneering features such as the bulkhead, the sternpost rudder, watertight hulls and multiple masts were copied around the world*

🐎 The Ming Dynasty (1368–1644)

Kublai Khan's grandson and successor managed to keep order in the Yuan Empire. But a number of disasters in the early 14th century made it weaker. There were serious issues that sprouted such as a war between rival Mongol princes, widespread famine, and disastrous floods, that ultimately resulted into a massive rebellion. In 1368, Zhu Yuanzhang, a Buddhist monk and rebel leader, captured Beijing and sent the Mongols flying back to their native grasslands. He called his new empire, Ming (brilliant). Chinese explorations under Ming reached as far west as Africa and the Middle East. They are to be credited for building the famous Forbidden City of Beijing. China became famous for its exquisite porcelain, lacquer, silks, gold, silver, and medicines.

◀ *A troop of pike-wielding Ming soldiers ferry across a river*

Medieval India

The collapse of the Gupta Empire (480–550 CE) marks the start of the medieval period in India. This was marked by wars among the regional kingdoms and a series of invasions by the Afghans and Turks.

🐎 The Fight for Kannauj

The Pratihara Dynasty ruled most of India over the 6th–11th centuries. Their capital was at Kannauj. The empire reached its peak under Mihira Bhoja (836–85) and Mahendrapala I (885–910). The empire's expansion triggered a three-way power struggle with the Rashtrakuta Empire (from the south) and Pala Empire (from the east) for control of the Indian subcontinent and of Kannauj over the 8th–10th centuries.

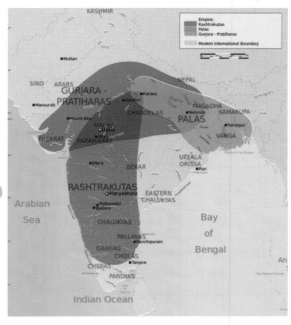

▲ The tripartite fight for Kannauj and the Gangetic Plains in the early medieval period

🐎 Chola Champions

One of the longest-ruling dynasties in history, the Cholas became a military, economic and cultural power under Rajaraja Chola I, his son Rajendra Chola I, and their immediate successors. Their mighty kingdom traversed from up east to the Ganges and across the oceans to Southeast Asia. The Chola fleet represented the height of medieval Indian sea power.

◀ Sala (founder of the empire) fighting the tiger is the emblem of the Hoysala Empire (10th–14th centuries). They were known for exquisite architecture as seen here in Chennakeshava Temple, Belur

▶ Early medieval India saw the rise of Rajput clans like the Gurjara-Pratihara, who are most famous for temples such as the one at Khajuraho, now a UNESCO World Heritage Site

The Delhi Sultanate

For 320 years, the Delhi Sultanate stretched over large parts of India. The period saw five dynasties—the Mamluk (1206–90), Khilji (1290–1320), Tughlaq (1320–1414), Sayyid (1414–51), and Lodi (1451–1526). Qutb ud-Din Aibak, a former *mamluk* (slave) of Muhammad Ghori, became the first sultan of Delhi. His Mamluk Dynasty is not to be confused with the other powerful Mamluk Dynasty of Egypt.

⊛ Incredible Individuals

The Delhi sultanate enthroned one of the few female Islamic rulers, Razia Sultana (ruled 1236–40). She was five when Aibak died and her father Iltutmish took the throne. Finding that none of his sons measured up to his daughter, Iltutmish became the first sultan to appoint a woman as his heir. The Persian historian Minhaj-i-Siraj recorded that Razia Sultana was a just monarch cherished by her subjects. Sadly, she was overthrown and killed by her brother Bahram.

◀ *Coin from Razia Sultana's time*

▲ *Aibak famously commissioned the exquisite tower, the Qutb Minar, which was completed by the Khiljis*

The Vijayanagara Empire

Based in the Deccan Plateau, the Vijayanagara Empire was established by brothers Harihara and Bukka Raya in 1336. The empire warded off Islamic invasions, brought new technologies in water management, established a dynamic sea trade and evolved Carnatic music to its current form. It is famous today in the folktales of King Krishnadevaraya and his witty court poet Tenali Rama.

▲ *The ruins at Hampi, Vijayanagara's capital city*

Samurai and Shogun

Japan's first emperor, Jimmu Tenno, came to power way back in 660 BCE. Medieval Japan is marked by the shifting of power from the emperors to military warlords called Shoguns. It also saw the rise of a warrior class called Samurai and clans of spies called Ninjas.

▲ A silver Wadokaichin coin

Asuka Period (c. 538–710 CE)

Power was centred in the Asuka region. At this time, the Chinese writing system was adopted in Japan. Buddhism was introduced from China via the Korean peninsula. In 708, a mint was set up in the province of Omi. It made coins that became the first Japanese currency.

◀ *Prince Shotoku (574–622), a semi-legendary regent of the Asuka period who is venerated even today for his virtuous and non-violent administration*

Nara Period (710–794 CE)

Empress Gemmei (660–721) set up a new capital in Nara, modelled on the Tang capital in China. This was a period of slow development. The emperor's family fought for power with Buddhists and other groups. Towards the end of the 8th century, Dokyo, a powerful priest-minister rose to the forefront. Fearing the dominance of priests, a family of nobles called Fujiwara rebelled. They crowned a new emperor, Konin. His successor, Emperor Kammu shifted the capital again—first to Nagaoka, and in 794 to Heian (present-day Kyoto). This helped sever connections with the temples of Nara and re-established government under the emperor's will.

▲ *The famous Daibutsu (giant Buddha) at Todai-ji, one of the Seven Great Temples of the Nara period*

Heian Japan (794–1185)

Imperial Japan reached its peak during the Heian period. Court life was noted for its art, poetry, and literature. The first known novel—*Genji Monogatari (The Tale of Genji)* was published in 1010. Its author was the court lady Murasaki Shikibu.

◀ *A 17th century sculpture of Murasaki Shikibu at her desk. She was a Japanese novelist, poet, and lady at the Imperial court during the Heian period*

During the Heian era, the emperor disbanded his army. Gradually, his power declined. Royal descendants, such as the Fujiwara, Taira, and Minamoto families, took the chance to set up rival regimes. They hired guards, police and soldiers for their provinces. Other nobles began to follow their example. Soon, Japan had private armies that did not report to the emperor. The ensuing rebellion established the samurai warrior classes as a force to reckon with.

Rise of the Shogun

Over the 12th century, a series of battles took place between the noble families of Japan. This destroyed the Fujiwaras and culminated in the Genpei Wars (1180–85) between the Taira and Minamoto clans. When the Taira clan fell, Minamoto Yoritomo became the first Shogun (military ruler) of Japan.

The Kamakura Period (1185–1333)

▲ *Minamoto Yoritomo, the first Shogun*

Minamoto's headquarters in Kamakura gave the first Shogunate its name. Civil, military, and judicial matters were in the hands of the Shogun and a system of feudalism—much like the one in Western Europe—was established. Two new Buddhist sects—Jodo and Zen—arose at this time.

▲ *A wooden Kongorikishi, a muscular guardian of the Buddha, from the 14th century Kamakura Shogunate*

Isn't It Amazing!

Over 1274–81, the Japanese faced a few invasions by Mongols. In the end, the Japanese were saved by the weather. Kublai Khan's 600 ships and 23,000 troops were destroyed by typhoons! Shinto priests called this phenomenon *kamikaze*—divine wind!

The samurai Suenaga facing Mongol and Korean arrows and bombs

The Muromachi Period (1336–1573)

The emperor's power was briefly brought back during the Kenmu Restoration. However, his allies, who brought down the Kamakura Shogunate in 1333, were ambitious warlords. The Ashikaga Takauji (1305–58) finally drove the emperor from his court and supported a new emperor who, in turn, installed Ashikaga as the new Shogun. The third Ashikaga Shogun shifted his residence to Muromachi, which gives its name to this historical period.

▶ *China's Ming Dynasty sought help from the Muromachi Shogun to suppress Japanese pirates along coastal China*

RENAISSANCE

RENAISSANCE

In Western Europe, the Middle Ages gradually came to an end in the 15ᵗʰ century. The period coincided with the rise of progressive philosophers, extraordinary artists, brilliant scientists, and inventors. This period is known as the Renaissance. The term means 'rebirth'. It began in Italy, with a renewed interest in the knowledge of ancient Greece and Rome. Over the 16ᵗʰ and 17ᵗʰ centuries, it spread to the rest of Europe. The Renaissance coincided with the Age of Discovery, when Europeans discovered trade routes, lands were conquered, and colonised both the **Old World** and the New World! Great strides in ship-building, navigational tools, and the use of gunpowder powered their advances. This was also the time when religious reformers tried to cleanse the Catholic Church of corruption, which led to the rise of the Protestant movement.

▼ Early Renaissance blossomed under the patronage of the Medici family. Three of its most influential members are depicted in the fresco, Procession of the Youngest King, painted by Benozzo Gozzoli around 1459. The young boy in the blue-gold hat riding a horse is a young Lorenzo Medici, later nicknamed Il Magnifico (the Magnificent).

Quattrocento

The Italian term for the 15ᵗʰ century is **Quattrocento**. It marks the first phase of the Renaissance. Until then, **Constantinople** had been the centre of scholarship and culture. In 1453, when Constantinople was conquered by Turkish armies, many of its scholars fled to Italy. They brought **Classical** knowledge to cities like Florence, Rome, Milan, and Venice, which led to the rise of the Renaissance. So what was happening at this time in the other parts of the world?

▶ Around 1401, Lorenzo Ghiberti (see pp. 18–19) won a commission to create a set of bronze doors for the Florence Baptistery. Historians mark this event as a start of the Renaissance. Ghiberti's doors remain one of the most valued treasures of the period

1419
Architect Brunelleschi designs the first famous Renaissance dome for the Florence Cathedral.

1420
After 115 years in Avignon, France, the Pope returns to Rome, bringing prestige and wealth back to the city.

1434
The Medici family become leaders of Florence.

1440
Oba Ewuare seizes power in West Africa's Benin City and turns it into the thriving and highly developed Benin Empire.

1443
The Buddhist Zhihua Temple was built by the Ming dynasty in Beijing; King Sejong the Great of the Joseon Dynasty creates and publishes the Hangul, the Korean alphabet.

▶ In 1469, Lorenzo de Medici, the 'Magnificent', becomes First Citizen of Florence. His patronage of the city's artists and scholars led to the high point of Florentine Renaissance

1494–1559
The Italian Wars lead to the downfall of the Italian **city states**. Artists and scholars leave to find safer places to live, taking the Renaissance to other parts of Europe.

1494–1497
The firebrand priest Girolamo Savonarola becomes ruler of Florence and burns its treasures of art and literature in the Bonfire of Vanities.

◀ On 23 May 1498, Borgia Pope Alexander VI excommunicates Savonarola, who is hanged and burned the following year

1490–92
Martin Behaim creates the Erdapfel, the oldest extant globe showing Earth.

1486
Renaissance nobleman Pico della Mirandola publishes his 900 **treatises** on religion and philosophy. He is condemned by the Catholic Church but saved from **execution** by Lorenzo de Medici.

◀ Behaim's globe, the Erdapfel

Birth of Leonardo da Vinci, the genius and **polymath** who is considered the defining Renaissance man.

▶ *In 1495, Leonardo da Vinci painted his masterpiece, The Last Supper, on a wall at the Convent of Santa Maria delle Grazie*

1440–69

Under Moctezuma I, the Aztecs become the dominant power in central America, historically called Mesoamerica.

1450

Johannes Gutenberg invents the printing press, making it easy for more people to acquire books and publish their ideas and beliefs.

▲ *In 1454, Johannes Gutenberg published the Gutenberg Bible using the new printing press. Forty-nine copies of this valuable edition are still around*

1452

1453

The Ottoman Empire seizes Constantinople, marking the start of the Ottoman Classical Age, which lasts until the death of Suleiman the Magnificent (1494–1566).

Birth of Guru Nanak, the founder of the Sikh religion in India.

1467–1615

Japan's Sengoku period is a time of violent civil war, ending in the country's unification.

1485

Thomas Malory publishes *Le Morte d'Arthur*, the best-known tales of King Arthur to this day.

1481

Spanish Inquisition begins its practice of *auto-da-fé*—public penance for condemned heretics, which includes burning them alive!

1471

Sixtus IV becomes Pope. He commissions major Renaissance projects such as the Sistine Chapel, but is also infamous for corruption and favouritism.

1469

The marriage of Ferdinand II of Aragon and Isabella I of Castile leads to the unification of Spain. Being devout Catholics, the royal couple begin the wars of Spanish Reconquista—to expel Jews and Muslims from Spain—and set up the horrific **Spanish Inquisition**.

1469

▶ *In 1492, Boabdil, the last Muslim ruler in Spain, surrendered to Ferdinand and Isabella, bringing an end to the Spanish Reconquista*

The Cinquecento

The 16th century (Cinquecento) saw the rise of the Western world through naval conquest, trade, and colonisation. Wars were now fought with gunpowder and cannon. Bloody conflicts between **Catholics** and **Protestants** dominated this era. Despite all this, science and art flourished, and the Renaissance spread across Europe. Elsewhere in the world, the Ottoman Empire reached its zenith, China ended its naval explorations, Japan suffered through the Warring States period, and India saw the rise of the Mughal Empire.

The powerful Safavid Dynasty begins unifying Iran, eventually turning it into one of the greatest empires of Islam.

◀ *The Safavid Dynasty reached its height under Shah Abbas the Great (1571–1629), the empire's fifth and possibly its strongest ruler*

1501 ❯ 1503 ❯ c. 1505 ❯ 1506 ❯ 1507 ❯

1503
Leonardo da Vinci begins work on the *Mona Lisa*, completing it three years later.

◀ *The Mona Lisa, famous for her mysterious smile, is thought to be a portrait of Lisa del Giocondo, a noblewoman of the Gherardini family of Florence and Tuscany*

c. 1505
Sultan Trenggana builds the first Muslim kingdom in Java called Demak.

1506
Following a series of drought, famine, and plague catastrophes, over 2,000 **Marranos** (converted Jews) are killed and burned in Lisbon by Christians seeking God's mercy!

China's Ming Dynasty bans foreign trade and shuts all seaports in response to Wokou (pirate) wars.

1507
The first known smallpox **epidemic** of the **New World** devastates the indigenous people of a Caribbean island.

1600 ◀ 1578 ◀ 1558 ◀ 1556–1605 ◀ 1550–51 ◀ 1548

1578
Mongol leader Altan Khan recognises Sonam Gyatso as a reincarnation of two previous lamas (teachers). He is given the title Dalai Lama—becoming the third incarnation of that line.

1558
Queen Elizabeth I is crowned at age 25, marking the start of the Elizabethan era—the golden age of English Renaissance.

1556–1605
Akbar the Great (born 1542) expands Mughal control over India with a series of conquests.

1550–51
The Valladolid Debate—on the human rights of Native Americans—is seen as the first moral debate in the history of European colonisation.

▲ *'Wild men,' shown on the facade (exterior) of the Colegio de San Gregorio, where the Valladolid Debate was held*

1600
The Battle of Sekigahara marks the end of Japan's Warring States (Sengoku) period and puts the military leader Tokugawa Ieyasu in power. Queen Elizabeth I allows the British East India Company to advance upon Asia.

Copernicus publishes his theory of Heliocentrism; says 'the Sun lies at the centre of the solar system'.

◀ *Statue of Copernicus with his model of Heliocentrism, in Poland*

Italian diplomat Niccolo Machiavelli writes *The Prince*, a book of political philosophy for ambitious rulers.

▲ *Statue of Niccolo Machiavelli, Renaissance historian, philosopher, politician, humanist and writer, at the Uffizi Gallery in Florence, Italy*

| 1508–12 | 1512 | 1513 | 1516–17 | 1518 |

Michelangelo paints his famous *Genesis* fresco on the Sistine Chapel ceiling.

▲ *The fresco on the ceiling of the Sistine Chapel was commissioned by Pope Julius II, also nicknamed as the Warrior Pope*

▶ *Babur crossing the River Indus in the heat of battle, a painting commissioned by his grandson Akbar, c. 1589*

The Ottomans defeat the Mamluk Dynasty and acquire Egypt, Syria and Arabia.

The Turco-Mongol leader Babur defeats Ibrahim Lodi, Sultan of Delhi, in the First Battle of Panipat and establishes the Mughal Empire.

The bizarre, month-long Dancing Plague is seen in Strasbourg, where hundreds of people dance without rest for days! Many die of heart attack, stroke or sheer exhaustion.

| 1547 | 1531–32 | 1527 | 1526 | 1523 |

Ivan IV, nicknamed as the Terrible, unifies Russia and is crowned its first tsar.

King Henry VIII breaks away from the Roman Catholic Church and becomes head of the Church of England.

The **Sack of Rome** by the troops of Charles V, Holy Roman Emperor, marks the end of the Italian Renaissance. The movement continues to spread outside Italy.

The cocoa bean is introduced to Spain by explorer Hernán Cortés, and chocolate enters the global stage!

◀ *Charles V on horseback, 1548, painted by the famous Venetian artist Titian*

The Italian Renaissance

At the beginning of the Renaissance, Italy was divided into many city states, each with its own government. The Kingdom of Naples in the south, Sicily, and the Papal States (with its capital in Rome) were in decline. In contrast, centres like Florence, Vienna, Genoa, and Milan were flourishing, with a growing class of merchants and powerful noblemen. The Renaissance began in Florence under the patronage of an influential family of merchant-bankers called the Medicis.

The Spirit of Humanism

One of the best changes seen during the Renaissance was a change in general attitude, brought about by the philosophy of Humanism. This is a belief system—a way of thinking—that had existed in many forms throughout the world in ancient times. The Italian poet Petrarch (1304–74) discovered (and further developed) this philosophy through the letters of Cicero, an ancient Roman statesman. Humanism teaches that each person has the right to live with dignity; that all humans deserve access to knowledge and the means to break free from religious orthodoxy. It is a belief in a scientific and rational outlook. Through Humanism, people began to see that life was not just about fighting wars or working hard, but that it could be comfortable and enjoyable too.

▶ *The front page (c. 1340) of one of Petrarch's manuscripts shows the imagined figure of the ancient Roman poet Virgil, who greatly inspired Petrarch*

Renaissance Guilds

During the Middle Ages, people of specific trades such as merchants or craftsmen came together to form professional groups called guilds. When the Great Plague struck in 1348, it halved the population of many city states. People were plunged into poverty. At this time, certain guilds were able to bring stability in cities like Florence and Venice. Soon, they rose to power and became as wealthy as—some wealthier than—the nobility. Their patronage of art, literature, science, and architecture became the driving force of the early Renaissance.

◀ *The Four Crowned Martyrs is a Renaissance sculpture commissioned by the Guild of Stone and Woodworkers. It shows the guild's patron saints, who, legend says, were masons from ancient Roman times. Ordinary masons and woodworkers appear at the base of the sculpture*

The Medici Influence

Followers of Humanism, the Medicis were wealthy bankers who encouraged art and science. Most famous among them was Lorenzo (1449–92). As the First Citizen of the Republic of Florence, he turned the city into a spectacular centre of the Renaissance. His example was followed across Italy. The Sforzas of Milan, the Montefeltro dukes of Urbino, the Orsinis and Colonnas of Rome, and the Bentivoglios of Bologna were some of the other patrons of the Renaissance. Their families produced some of the most influential cardinals, popes, and **condottieri** in Italian history.

▶ *Painted by the brilliant Botticelli (1445–1510), the Madonna del Magnificat shows the poet and political adviser Lucrezia with her children. A young Lorenzo is holding the inkpot*

The Renaissance Leaves Italy

The end of Italy's Renaissance came slowly, with the discovery of new east-west trade routes the Italian port-cities were replaced as major trade routes. Religious fervour rose again when the monk Girolamo Savonarola took control of Florence over 1494–98. This culminated in the horrific Bonfire of Vanities—the public burning of great works of scholarship, poetry, and art. In the same period, Italy also faced a series of foreign invasions. In 1527, the armies of Charles V, Holy Roman Emperor, looted and destroyed Rome. The Sack of Rome greatly reduced Papal power. Many Renaissance masters left to find patrons in other cities. Thus, the Renaissance spread its wings to Europe.

▲ *A Majolica (tin-glazed earthenware) plate from c. 1540 shows a scene from the 1527 Sack of Rome*

▲ *Girolamo Savonarola by Renaissance artist Fra Bartolomeo, c. 1498*

👤 In Real Life

The Vatican City is the world's smallest, fully independent nation. Set within medieval and Renaissance walls, it is also the only country to be a full UNESCO World Heritage Site.

▲ *The iconic St Peter's Basilica at the heart of the Vatican City*

◀ *The Medici family gave France two of its most influential queens. Catherine de'Medici (1519–89), on the far left, married Henry II of France and gave birth to three of its later kings—Francis II, Charles IX, and Henry III. Marie de'Medici (1575–1642) married Henry IV of France and ruled the country after his death with great political acumen. She was immortalised by the genius Rubens in a series of 24 amazing paintings*

The Italian Wars

During the Renaissance, small feudal princedoms in Western Europe fused together to form great competing monarchies. At the end of the 15ᵗʰ century, the most notable were Spain, France, England, and the Holy Roman Empire. For the next 150 years, they quarrelled, made friends, and then quarrelled again. The Italian Wars (1494–1559) were a series of battles that were fought to control the independent city states of Italy.

French Ambitions

In 1494–1495, King Charles VIII of France invaded Italy. Assisted by Ludovico Sforza, the Tyrant of Milan, he seized Naples. In response, Venice, Mantua, and Rome allied with Spain and the Holy Roman Emperor to drive him away. In 1499, Charles VIII's successor, Louis XII, captured northwest Italy, including Milan and Genoa. Louis then schemed with Ferdinand V of Spain to conquer Naples and divide it between themselves. But they couldn't agree on how to split it fairly. By 1502, the French and Spanish parties were in open war! Louis was eventually forced to sign the Treaty of Blois (1504–1505). He kept Milan and Genoa, but promised to hand over Naples to Spain.

▲ *The courageous Chevalier de Bayard fought in the Battle of Garigliano (1503) and ensured the safe retreat of the French army by defending a bridge against the enemy*

▲ *Kings of France: Charles VIII (1470–1498) and Louis XII (1462–1515)*

Incredible Individuals

The marriage of Ferdinand of Aragon and Isabella of Castile in 1469 led to a unified Spain that grew rapidly through trade, conquest, and colonisation. By the early 16ᵗʰ century, their grandson Charles V, the Holy Roman Emperor, ruled the most powerful empire in Europe and the New World. He was also head of the rising House of Habsburg, who would rule most of Europe in the coming centuries.

▶ *Marriage portrait of Ferdinand and Isabella*

The Republic of Venice

Venice tried to extend its territories by exploiting the tensions between the mighty empires. But in 1509, it was crushed by a new alliance of France which comprised of Spain, the Holy Roman Empire, and Pope Julius II. Shortly after, the Pope made peace with Venice. They formed a Holy League with other powers to expel France from Milan. In 1513, Swiss mercenaries of the League routed the French at Novara. They took control of Lombardy (northern Italy) and held it until 1515, when Louis's successor, Francis I, defeated them. The peace of Noyon (1516) gave Milan back to France, while Naples remained with Spain.

The Battle of Pavia

After Charles V became King of Spain (in 1516) and later Holy Roman Emperor (1519, in Germany), he and his allies expelled the French from Milan in 1521. Francis I, King of France, made new attempts to recapture the city, but was defeated, and captured in 1525 during the Battle of Pavia. France was compelled to sign the Treaty of Madrid (1526), renouncing its Italian claims and even giving up Burgundy.

▲ Maximilian I (1459–1519), Holy Roman Emperor, in his armour; painted by Peter Paul Rubens nearly 100 years after the monarch's death

The Sack of Rome

As soon as he was released, Francis I broke the treaty. He formed the League of Cognac with Venice, Florence, Pope Clement VII, and Henry VIII of England. Outraged, Charles V sent his troops to punish the Pope. They sacked Rome for a full week in May 1527.

▲ The Sack of Rome, by Dutch Golden-Age painter Johannes Lingelbach

▲ At the Battle of Pavia, the Imperial army (under statesman Charles de Lannoy and commander of the Pavia garrison, Antonio de Leyva) attacked the French army (under the command of Francis I) on the hunting grounds of Mirabello, outside the city walls. Within four hours, the French were defeated. Their king was captured and imprisoned

Habsburg Victories

The French did not meet with lasting success. The flourishing port of Genoa, with its naval fleet, sided with Charles V in 1528. The emperor also restored power to the Medicis, making them princes of Florence. In 1529, France signed the Treaty of Cambrai, once more giving up on Italy. Two later French wars (in 1542–1544 and 1556–1557) also ended in failure. Francis died in 1547, after signing a third treaty, at Crepy, renouncing Naples. His successor Henry II did not fare much better against the Habsburg emperor.

▶ Charles V (1500–1558) and Philip II (1527–1598), both portraits by Renaissance master-painter Titian

Renaissance Art

During the Middle Ages, art in Western Europe was restricted to Christian subjects and icons.
The images were flat and evenly coloured. A great deal of Renaissance art was also religious. But it
also explored Classical mythology and daily life. Most importantly, for the first time, art began to
look three-dimensional and realistic. The architect Brunelleschi (1377–1446) described the rules
of **perspective,** which helped create amazing compositions. Artists developed techniques like
sfumato and **chiaroscuro**, which gave paintings soft lines, delicate shading, and compelling
light-and-shadow effects. Oil painting and a new type of fast-drying **fresco** came to the forefront
at this time.

▲ In 1486, Sandro Boticelli completed The Birth of Venus, a masterpiece of
Florentine Renaissance. Under the influence of Savonarola, Boticelli burnt
some of his precious paintings in the Bonfire of Vanities (see p. 9)

▲ Judith Beheading Holofernes is a Biblical story painted over 1599–1602
by Caravaggio using a technique called chiaroscuro, which is a way of
creating bold contrasts between light and dark

🕐 The Renaissance Triumvirate

The three most famous masters of the Italian Renaissance are Leonardo da Vinci (1452–1519), Michelangelo (1475–1564)
and Raphael (1483–1520). They studied human anatomy so they could accurately portray movement of muscle, bone and
expression. Da Vinci dissected some 30 corpses and made about 13,000 pages of drawings on animals, nature, humans,
and even featured scientific inventions, war machines, and city defences.

▲ The School of Athens, an amazing fresco by Raphael, depicts Classical scholars with the faces of
Renaissance geniuses. The central figure with the flowing beard is the great Greek philosopher Plato,
modelled after Leonardo da Vinci. Michelangelo is drawn as the Greek philosopher Heraclitus sitting
alone, brooding, in the foreground (both men were loners)

▲ Da Vinci's Mona Lisa was created using
sfumato, a technique that uses varying
shades of colours to build up an image
(no lines are drawn)

▲ *Michelangelo imbued his paintings with muscular power and contained turbulence, as seen in his incredible Genesis fresco, The Creation of Adam, on the Sistine Chapel ceiling in Rome*

Flemish and Dutch Art

Northern painters showed a great deal of interest in nature and real life. The works of Pieter Bruegel the Elder (c. 1525–1569) capture the magic of the age in vivid colours and a multitude of figures. A unique artist of this time was Hieronymus Bosch (1450–1516), who painted complex, dreamlike canvasses that often evoked fear and confusion.

▲ *The Peasant Dance by Pieter Brueghel the Elder*

Titian

The greatest painter of Renaissance Venice was Tiziano Vecellio (c.1488–1576), known to English-speakers as Titian. He developed a system of colour painting that had three main guidelines—limit the number of colours, choose the richest and purest form of those colours, and create a simple harmony with colour. This contrasted with the established Renaissance practice of using a great variety of colours.

▲ *Bosch's imaginative Hell, a panel from his* **triptych**, *The Garden of Earthly Delights*

▲ *Titian's amazingly rich colour work in The Assumption of the Virgin (1516–1518) caused a sensation when it was first unveiled*

▲ **Tintoretto's** *luminous masterpiece, Presentation of the Virgin in the Temple (1551–1556)*

▲ **El Greco's** *The Burial of the Count of Orgaz (1586–1588) is a harmony of earthly and heavenly figures in saturated hues and brilliant contrasts*

Song and Verse

With the invention of the printing press, the ideas of Humanist scholars and Protestant reformers filled books and pamphlets, marking a new age of literature. Playwrights and poets reached a wider audience, since their most popular works weren't limited to performances, but could be printed and distributed. Most importantly, writing was no longer limited to 'scholarly' languages like Latin. Speakers of Italian, German, English, etc., wrote in their own languages. Before this period, people spoke in a number of regional dialects and spellings varied tremendously. With the new books, editors and authors began to make the first attempts at standardising spellings, grammar, and other aspects of languages.

▲ An 18th century illustration of Prince Hamlet startled by his father's ghost, from the famous opening act of Shakespeare's play Hamlet

▲ William Tyndale, who published the first English translation of the Bible, was strangled, and then burnt on the orders of King Henry VIII; a 1563 woodcut from the Book of Martyrs by Protestant historian John Foxe

Vernacular Literature

In 1400, there was no standard form of English, French, German, Portuguese, Spanish, or Italian. But as Renaissance authors wrote and published their books, editors and officials began to take a leaf from the works of masters to form the basis for their national language. Martin Luther's German translation of the *Bible* in the early 16th century sold over half-a-million copies in that century. This is simply amazing, given that most people in that age didn't know how to read! Luther's East Middle-Saxon manner eventually became standard German. Italian was largely founded on the works of three authors—the poet Dante (1265–1321), the philosopher Petrarch, and the Humanist writer Boccaccio (1313–1375). Sixteenth century writers adopted their Tuscan way of writing for all of Italy. William Tyndale's English *Bible*, the 1611 King James's *Bible*, and William Shakespeare's masterful works deeply influenced English writers. Spain adopted the Castilian style after Miguel de Cervantes (1547–1616) published his brilliant book *Don Quixote*.

◀ The reconstructed Globe Theatre; William Shakespeare built the original in 1599 to stage his plays

▶ Our phrase 'tilting at windmills', meaning 'attacking imaginary enemies', comes from the scene of the misguided Don Quixote tilting (fighting) at windmills, imagining them to be fierce giants!

▲ Dante Alighieri

▲ Francesco Petrarch

▲ Giovanni Boccaccio

Music

Around 1330, an Italian school of music developed in northern cities of the region. This included Padua, Verona, Bologna, Florence, and Milan. The verses were often in Italian. Leading composers such as Leonardo Giustiniani (1398–1446) and Marsilio Ficino would make verses as someone played the lute. Such experiments led to the invention of *contrapuntal* music—music that hinged on the pleasing interplay of two melodic lines. The Flemish composer Josquin des Prez (c. 1440–1521) was considered the greatest of the age. He wrote masses, **chansons**, and **motets**. The works of Giovanni Pierluigi Palestrina (c. 1525–1594) and Orlando di Lasso (1532–1594) represent the zenith of Renaissance music.

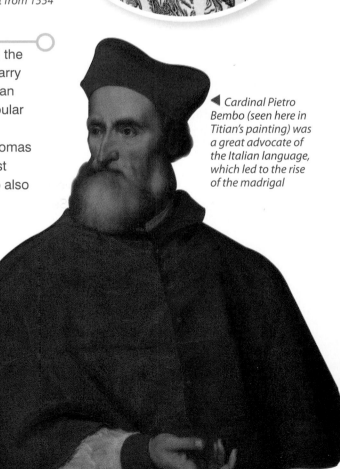

▶ *Palestrina presenting his masses to Pope Julius III, a woodcut from 1554*

The Madrigal

The Renaissance saw the development of a special kind of song called the Madrigal. It was sung by small groups of people. Each person would carry a different part in the song. Occasionally, the lines would be played by an instrument. Madrigals were adored across Europe. By far the most popular one was *The White and Gentle Swan* by the Flemish composer Jacob Arcadelt. English composers who excelled at the madrigal included Thomas Weelkes, William Byrd, Thomas Morley and Orlando Gibbons. The most accomplished Italian madrigal composer was Claudio Monteverdi, who also developed the first major operas.

◀ *Cardinal Pietro Bembo (seen here in Titian's painting) was a great advocate of the Italian language, which led to the rise of the madrigal*

◀ *A portrait of Monteverdi by Bernardo Strozzi*

Sculpture

Italian sculptors of the Renaissance were often multi-talented, working as smiths and carvers of a variety of materials. The period is often considered to begin with the famous competition for the doors of the Florence Baptistery in 1403.

▲ The brilliant late-Renaissance sculptor Benvenuto Cellini (1500–1571) created Perseus with the head of Medusa, one of the masterpieces of 16ᵗʰ century Florentine art

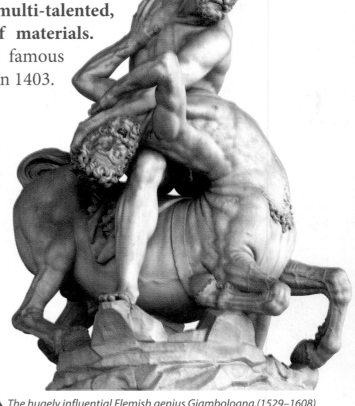

▲ The hugely influential Flemish genius Giambologna (1529–1608) specialised in bringing Classical stories to life, as with Hercules and Nessus (seen here) and Samson Slaying a Philistine

🕐 Lorenzo Ghiberti (1378–1455)

The son of a goldsmith, Lorenzo Ghiberti is best known for the Florence **baptistery's** eastern doors, named the 'Gates of Paradise' by Michelangelo. Each door is carved with five scenes from the *Old Testament*. Ghiberti used a painter's point of view to give the illusion of depth to each panel carving. He created sculptural illusion by extending some figures off the panel such that they look closer to the viewer, while portraying others in the background. This unusual perspective made figures less distinct, giving one the optical illusion that they were far away from the viewer.

▲ Panels on Ghiberti's Gates of Paradise

◀ The slender and flowing form of David stands in contrapposto, an asymmetrical pose where the upper body is at an angle to the hip and legs. One leg is usually thrown out at an angle

🕐 Donatello (c. 1386–1466)

A student of Brunelleschi's and an early assistant to Ghiberti, Donato di Niccolo di Betto Bardi (Donatello) was a master sculptor of early Renaissance. His workshop in Florence hosted many students. Donatello was inspired by Classical sculpture and expressed himself with stone, bronze, wood, clay, wax, and **stucco**. He is considered the first Renaissance sculptor to celebrate the human body. His most famous work is the amazing life-size figure of David—the first-known free-standing nude statue made in Western Europe since ancient times.

Michelangelo (1475–1564)

The brilliant Michelangelo expressed his talent by painting and designing buildings. But it is his awe-inspiring sculptures that leave the greatest impression on the viewer. These are works of immense muscular power and profound emotion. Like Donatello, Michelangelo was enraptured by the human form and took pains to study it. An early example can be seen in his *Battle of the Centaurs*, which shows a multi-dimensional tangle of writhing bodies. In the more mature *Pieta*, he uses multiple contrasts to enhance the drama and pathos of Virgin Mary holding her dead son. A masterpiece of the same period is his heroic, gigantic *David*. Michelangelo's most refined style is seen in the *Moses*, he created for the tomb of Pope Julius II.

▶ *Michelangelo's David statue shows extraordinary musculature and power*

▲ *The unfinished Battle of the Centaurs (1492)*

▶ *Michelangelo moulded the Pieta (1498–1499) to show various contrasts—man and woman, vertical and horizontal, dead and alive, clothed and bare*

French Sculpture

Renaissance influence was first seen in French sculpture in Tours. Its main proponent was the amazing Michel Colombe (1430–1515). His 1508 relief sculpture of St. George and the Dragon was made for the high altar of the Chateau de Gaillon. It blends a Gothic theme with Italian modelling. Under Queen Catherine de'Medici (1519–1589), the royal house of France brought greater Italian influence into French art. The three great sculptors of this time were Pierre Bontemps (c. 1505–1568), Jean Goujon (c. 1510–c. 1568), and Germain Pilon (1535–1590).

▶ *Relief sculpture of nymphs by Jean Goujon at a fountain in Paris called Fontaine des Innocents*

Spanish Sculpture

The period 1530–1570 marked the zenith of Spanish Renaissance sculpture. This era was led by the amazing Alonso Berruguete (1488–1561) whose works show deep, religious emotions. Berruguete was a student of Michelangelo's. His most important works are the **retable** of the Mejorada, the retable of San Benito de Valladolid, the choir-stall reliefs in Toledo Cathedral, and the fantastic tomb of Cardinal Tavera.

▶ *The retable of San Benito de Valladolid*

Architecture

Renaissance architects of Italy revived Classical Roman and Greek designs for buildings. Classicism focussed on set ideas of harmony, symmetry, and proportion in all structures, whether it was a single building or an entire city. The earliest innovators of Renaissance architecture were engineers like Filippo Brunelleschi who worked in Florence. The High Renaissance found its home in Rome, with geniuses like Donato Bramante, who served as chief architect in the construction of St. Peter's Basilica. Over the 15th and 16th centuries, Renaissance architecture spread to the rest of Europe, where it combined with native styles to produce entirely unique buildings.

▲ *The Ideal City, painted c. 1480–1484, depicts the ideal Renaissance town with its triumphant archway, Roman colosseum and octagonal baptistery surrounded by dignified homes. The entire space is broken up according to mathematical principles*

🕐 Identifying Renaissance Architecture

Renaissance architecture followed mathematically calculated rules of geometry and proportion. On the outside, buildings looked austerely beautiful with repeated rows of columns, round arches, blind arches, medallions, and sometimes, even statues. Three types of Classical columns—Doric, Ionic, and Corinthian—were popular. Statues were used to decorate nooks and rooftops. Town plans radiated from a central point that had important buildings like a baptistery and **colosseum**.

DORIC   IONIC   CORINTHIAN

◀ *The Doric, Ionic, and Corinthian styles for columns; the styles could be mixed to make composite columns*

▶ *Repeating rows of arches and columns topped by statues at the National Library of St. Mark, designed by Renaissance architect Jacopo Sansovino*

Filippo Brunelleschi (1377–1446)

A talented and technically skilled architect, Brunelleschi is best known for his amazing dome at the Duomo di Firenze (Cathedral of Florence). It is the first octagonal dome in history. Brunelleschi invented some of the machines that helped construct the dome. Brunelleschi is also famous for re-inventing the rules of perspective, which allowed artists to realistically portray three-dimensional spaces and objects on flat, two-dimensional paper.

▶ *Cathedral of Florence with Brunelleschi's octagonal dome and Giotto's harmonious campanile (bell tower)*

Grand Country Homes

Many wealthy Renaissance families ruled their lands from villas on vast country estates with beautifully designed gardens. The fabulous Villa d'Este is one such estate in Tivoli. It has playfully exaggerated, late-Renaissance (Mannerist) buildings; innumerable grand fountains; and terraced gardens that overlook the city of Florence. The architect Pirro Ligorio created it for Cardinal Ippolito II d'Este. The villa's famous gardens are set on a steep slope of the Sabine hills. A river plunges down the slope. Its waters are channelled into a spectacular variety of water features, including the remarkable 'water organ'. The stream runs around the garden, ostentatiously creating a forceful, theatrical effect.

▶ *Fountain and garden at Villa d'Este, Tivoli*

Donato Bramante (c. 1444–1514)

One of the masters of the Italian High Renaissance, Bramante brought the unique architecture to Rome when, under orders from Pope Julius II, he designed the Tempietto (small temple) of San Pietro in 1502. Surrounded by slender columns and mounted by a dome, the small building is almost like a sculpture. Yet, it has all the grandeur and correct proportions of Classical construction. Within a year of its completion, the impressed Pope asked Bramante to undertake the grandest architectural work of 16th century Europe—the complete rebuilding of St. Peter's Basilica.

▲ *Commissioned by Ferdinand and Isabella of Spain, the Tempietto marks the spot in Rome where, according to legend, Saint Peter was crucified*

▶ *The amazing dome of St. Peter's Basilica in Rome was created by Michelangelo*

Science and Technology

After the dogma and superstition of the Middle Ages, Western Europe opened its mind to science once more during the Renaissance. This was caused by the rise of Humanism, the discovery of new lands, and increased trade. The increase in exploration and commerce brought in the knowledge of the Islamic East and also revived an interest in Classical scholarship. In this fertile soil, the seeds of scientific investigation were first planted. The increased use of gunpowder in wars fuelled technologies in both offence and defence. These went on to have wide-ranging applications in all walks of life.

▲ Mathematician and astronomer Nicolaus Copernicus (1473–1543) put forth the theory of Heliocentrism, the idea that the Sun, not the Earth, was at the centre of the universe

▲ The Danish astronomer Tycho Brahe (1546–1601) observed the night sky before the telescope was invented. His studies of a comet and a supernova showed that the universe beyond the solar system was not as unchanging as was popularly believed

▲ English physician William Harvey (1578–1657) was the first man to describe our circulatory system in detail. He showed how blood was pumped by the heart, to the brain and the body

Galileo Galilei (1564–1642)

A mathematician and astronomer, Galileo questioned a great many things that people took for granted as the work of God—like the occurrence of tides, the mechanics of objects in motion, and the movement of heavenly bodies. He pioneered many practical tools of science, like the telescope. His telescopic observations gave the first verifiable evidence in support of Heliocentrism (see p. 7). In 1610, Galileo discovered the four largest moons of Jupiter. He named them in honour of four Medici brothers, one of whom—Grand Duke Cosimo II—later became his patron.

▲ Galileo was tried and condemned for heresy by the Roman Inquisition for his support of Heliocentrism

▲ Galileo shows the Doge (duke) of Venice how to use a telescope

◀ As a child, Johannes Kepler (1571–1630) saw the Great Comet of 1577. He later formulated the laws of planetary motion that laid the foundation for Newton's discoveries on gravity

The Scientific Method

How is science conducted? The first real answer to this came during the Renaissance, when a method for science was established. It was based on observation and gathering data. Do you have questions about the world around you? For instance, 'Why is chocolate sweet?' A scientist would observe what goes into making chocolates and theorise that 'chocolate is sweet because of one or more of its ingredients'. He would test his theory—in this case, by tasting all the ingredients. The test would tell him that sugar in chocolate is sweet. Based on this result, the theory would be modified to reflect the newfound truth—that 'chocolate is sweet because it has sugar'. Most importantly in science, other people should be able to test a theory. If they come to the same conclusion that you did, then you gave a good, strong theory that many people will accept as truth.

▶ The English statesman Francis Bacon (1561–1626), one of the greatest Renaissance thinkers, developed the investigative method of science. It is named the Baconian Method in his honour

Leonardo da Vinci

Though he is best known for his paintings, Leonardo da Vinci was first and foremost a scientific mind. He observed and drew thousands of figures from nature, including details of human and horse anatomy. His discoveries extend into the field of acoustics and geology. He experimented with water flow, medical dissection, mechanics, and aerodynamics. Da Vinci was even hired to engineer cannons, bridges, siege engines, and defensive fortifications.

▲ Da Vinci created a coloured map of Imola as part of his plans to fortify the town. This is one of the earliest examples of a city map, drawn from a bird's-eye view

▲ In the 1470s, Renaissance Italy gave us the earliest-known parachute design. Around 1485, Leonardo da Vinci took it a step further. The Venetian inventor Fausto Veranzio (1551–1617) further modified da Vinci's parachute sketch with a bulging sail-like piece of cloth (as seen here) that was more effective at slowing down a fall

The Printing Press

The spread of knowledge during the Renaissance was fuelled by the invention of the moveable printing press by a German goldsmith, Johannes Gutenberg (1398–1468). The mechanical device could produce 3,600 pages in a working day. No longer were books luxury items that had to be laboriously copied by hand. By the start of the 16th century, over 200 European cities had printing presses. People could now read the *Bible* in their own language. They became aware of the corruption in the Catholic Church. This fuelled the Protestant Reformation (see pp. 22–23).

▶ The printing press, arguably the single most influential event of the Renaissance

Exploration and Reformation

The Renaissance coincided with two other European phenomena: the Age of Exploration (roughly 1450–1600) and the Reformation Period. The former refers to the European discovery of the Americas and of new trade routes to Africa and Asia. Great strides were made in navigational tools, ship technologies, and map-making. At the same time, a great religious and political upheaval took place at home. Led by the German monk Martin Luther, this was called the Protestant Reformation. The Catholic Church ceased to be the sole form of Christianity in the West.

▲ The map of the world as given by 2nd century BCE Roman mathematician and astronomer Ptolemy was finally discarded during the Age of Discovery! New and increasingly accurate maps were made during the 15th–17th centuries

1415
The Portuguese seize the Muslim port-city of Ceuta in northern Africa. This inspires Prince Henry—known as Henry the Navigator—to initiate the Age of Discovery with explorations of trade routes along West Africa.

1492
Christopher Columbus lands in the Caribbean. He misguidedly believes it to be Asia and claims it for the Spanish crown!

1497
Under the banner of Henry VII of England, Italian adventurer John Cabot lands on the east coast of North America. He too mistakes it for Asia and claims it for England!

▶ Vasco da Gama lands at Calicut, India; c. 1880 by Ernesto Casanova

1498
Vasco da Gama reaches India by rounding the tip of Africa, thus discovering a new route to Asia.

1509
The Portuguese win the Battle of Diu against an alliance of the Sultan of Gujarat, the Mamluk Sultan of Egypt, and the Zamorin of Calicut, marking the onset of Portugal's dominance of the Indian Ocean spice trade.

1600
English merchants found the East India Company and set out to exploit trade in Asia and India.

1562–98
The French Wars of Religion take place between Catholics and Huguenots (French Protestants) and end when Henry IV grants religious rights in the Edict of Nantes.

1558
Queen Elizabeth I restores religious tolerance in England.

1554
Queen Mary enforces Catholicism in England, executing and burning her subjects for heresy. They name her Bloody Mary.

1545–63
At the Council of Trent, the Catholic Church puts Counter-Reformation activities into motion to counter the Protestant movement.

◀ This painting by the Huguenot Francois Dubois depicts the 1572 St. Bartholomew's Day Massacre in which Catholic mobs slaughtered thousands of their Protestant countrymen. The massacre went on for weeks!

◀ The Council of Trent, 1588, by Italian painter Pasquale Cati

Martin Luther posts his 95 Theses on the door of a church in Wittenburg, Germany, igniting the Protestant Reformation.

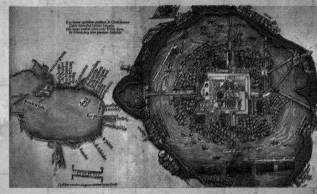

◀ Map of the island city Tenochtitlan and the Mexican gulf, made by one of Cortes's men

▲ The church doors on which Luther posted his reforms were destroyed in a fire. In 1857, King Frederick William IV of Prussia ordered their replacement. Luther's words are now engraved onto this door

Spanish **conquistador** Hernan Cortes's horrific assault on the Aztec capital of Tenochtitlan inspires other Europeans to conquer the Americas.

1509–11	1517	1519	1521

The most influential Dutch humanist Desiderius Erasmus (1466–1536) publishes In Praise of Folly—an attack on European orthodoxy and superstitions.

Explorer Ferdinand Magellan sets out to journey around the world. Three years later, his ship Victoria completes the first circumnavigation of the globe.

Luther appears at the **Diet** of Worms before Charles V, Holy Roman Emperor, on charges of heresy. He is excommunicated by Pope Leo X.

▶ Luther at the diet (imperial council) in the city of Worms

Henry VIII separates the Church of England from the Catholic Church of Rome.

1541	1534	1532	1526	1522

Francisco de Orellana encounters and explores the Amazon River.

Francisco Pizarro leads the Spanish conquest of the Incan Empire.

William Tyndale publishes the English Bible.

Luther begins translating the Bible into German. For the first time, ordinary Germans could read the word of God.

◀ In 1533, Pizarro executes the last Incan emperor

Islamic Eurasia

At the start of the Renaissance, Muslim lands were prosperous. The major Islamic empires had become more centralised. The Ottomans controlled vast domains in southeastern Europe, Turkey, northwest Africa, Egypt, and Syria; and the Safavids ruled Iran and Iraq. By the end of the period, however, these empires were rapidly shrinking and giving way to Western expansion and colonisation.

Ottoman Empire

In 1453, Sultan Mehmet II captured Constantinople. Renaming it Istanbul, he turned the city into the Ottoman capital. It became the seat of one of the most powerful empires ever seen. Ottoman territory and culture reached its height under the rule of Suleiman the Magnificent (ruled 1520–1566). His people called him the Lawgiver. He sent governors—called Pashas or Beys—to rule the many nations that came under Ottoman sway.

▲ The Timurid Empire stretched beyond Persia, modern Afghanistan and Central Asia. However, it shrunk rapidly after the death of its founder, Timur, in 1405. By the early 16th century, the original empire was extinct

▲ Francis I and Suleiman the Magnificent agree to a Franco-Ottoman alliance; c. 1530, believed to be painted by Titian

The Safavid Empire

The Safavids were rulers of Persia (Iran) over the 14th–18th centuries. The state was founded not by warriors but by a medieval holy man named Shaykh Safi al-Din (c. 1252–1334). At the start of the 16th century, his followers defeated the rulers of northern Iran. Their teenage leader Ismail I (ruled 1501–1524) proclaimed himself Shah, using the ancient title for Persian rulers. Ismail united all of Iran for the first time since the 7th century! The Safavids fought with the Ottomans for the fertile plains of Iraq. The warring lasted for more than 150 years and Baghdad changed hands numerous times.

▶ The Safavid's most notable ruler was Shah Abbas I (1571–1629). Europeans were amazed by his capital city of Isfahan, with its innumerable parks, libraries, schools, shops, and public baths

⊛ Incredible Individuals

Suleiman's favourite wife, Hurrem Sultan, rose from being a slave to the most influential woman of the empire. She took an active part in state affairs, which was unheard of in that male-dominated world.

▲ Titian's c. 1550 painting titled La Sultana Rossa is thought to be a portrait of Hurrem Sultan

The Tsardom of Russia

Mongol power in Russian lands declined after a united army, led by Prince Dmitry Donskoy of Moscow (1350–89), defeated the Mongol-Tatars in the 1380 Battle of Kulikovo. Over the 15th century, Moscow absorbed neighbouring states such as Tver and Novgorod. Ivan III (1440–1505), dubbed the Great, finally brought all of central and northern Rus under Moscow's control. He became the first Grand Duke of Russia. His grandson, the infamous Ivan the Terrible, took complete hold of the **boyars** and Russian territories. In 1547, he was crowned the first Tsar ('Caesar') of Russia.

▲ *A 19th century painting at the Grand Kremlin Palace, Moscow, shows Prince Dmitry Donskoy in the Battle of Kulikovo*

Ivan the Terrible (1530–84)

The nickname 'Terrible' meant terrifying and awe-inspiring. The early part of Ivan's rule was marked by glorious leadership. Later in life, he descended into madness and became a cruel despot. Over his life, Ivan nearly doubled the size of Russia. He introduced the printing press, revised the laws, limited the power of the Church and created a standing army. He encouraged the expansion of trade, making Russia rich and multicultural. But after the death of his beloved wife, Ivan became sick and disabled. His secret service network—the Oprichnina—became increasingly ruthless, murdering thousands of people to satisfy the paranoid and unbalanced monarch. On his death, Ivan left behind a ravaged nation, a broken government, and an unfit heir.

▲ *In a fit of maniacal rage, Ivan the Terrible killed his own son. Russian artist Ilya Repin painted a grief-stricken Tsar cradling his mortally wounded son. Ivan's other son, who inherited the throne, was mentally unfit to rule*

From Rurik to Romanov

The death of Ivan's sons marked the end of the Rurik Dynasty in 1598. It was followed by the Time of Troubles, which saw severe famine and civil war. A number of pretenders tried to take the throne. This ended in 1613, when the council of ministers made Michael I the tsar. He established the Romanov Dynasty, the last royal family to rule Russia.

▲ *Among the pretenders to the throne was False Dmitri I (ruled 1605–1606). His short rule ended when he was captured and killed by a mob of boyars*

▲ *Sixteen-year-old Michael is offered the crown at the Ipatiev Monastery in 1613*

Isn't It Amazing!

Owing in part to the widespread, hygienic practice of banya—a wet steam bath—Russia suffered fewer losses during the plague outbreaks over 1350–1490 than the rest of Europe.

▲ *A traditional banya, painted by Russian artist Tichov (1876–1939)*

Mughal India

The Mughal Empire ruled great swathes of the Indian subcontinent from 1526–1858. At its height, in the early 18th century, the empire stretched over modern-day Afghanistan, Pakistan, Myanmar, and almost all of India. The dynasty was founded by a descendent of Timur called Babur. In 1526, he defeated Sultan Ibrahim Lodi of Delhi at the First Battle of Panipat. This was the first time gunpowder was used in India. After his death, the empire went to his heirs, Humayun (1508–1556), Akbar (1543–1605), Jahangir (1569–1627), Shah Jahan (1592–1666), Aurangzeb (1618–1707), and then a series of increasingly powerless rulers.

🕐 Akbar the Great

By far the most charismatic and broad-minded Mughal ruler, Akbar the Great was enthroned when he was just 14 years old. The empire was on shaky grounds at this time. Delhi itself had been conquered by a minister called Hemu. Akbar's armies met and defeated Hemu at the Second Battle of Panipat, securing the throne for the Mughal ruler. Akbar continued to expand his territory—first under the guidance of his chief minister Bairam Khan and after 1560, on his own. His military conquests gained him a sprawling empire that killed thousands. But he also tried to rule his subjects justly. He bridged religious barriers and supported scholarship and art. Stocky and only five feet and seven inches tall, with a 'lucky' wart on his nose, Akbar was alert, physically tough, and energetic. He could not read or write, but he loved art, poetry, debate, music, and philosophy. He oversaw a golden age of Indian art and culture. Unfortunately, his enlightened policies were reversed under the rule of his great-grandson, Aurangzeb.

▲ This c. 1811 painting shows Akbar the Great on the Peacock Throne, the legendary jewelled throne of the Mughal emperors that was actually commissioned later, in Shah Jahan's time

▼ The pinnacle of Mughal architecture, the Taj Mahal was built over 1630–1653 by Emperor Shah Jahan as a tomb for his beloved wife Mumtaz Mahal

The Nine Gems

The court of Akbar the Great attracted numerous talents. Most famous among them were the group of men called the Nine Gems. Tansen (c.1500–1586) was a gifted singer who revolutionised classical music with his compositions. The wise and witty Birbal (1528–1583) was appointed in court as a favoured counsellor and eventually bestowed the title Raja. Abul Fazl (1551–1602) was Akbar's historian. Over time, he painstakingly documented the monarch's life and rule in the amazing book, *Akbarnama*. The poet Faizi (1547–1595) was a genius at composing Persian verses. He became most famous for his translation of a 12th century book on mathematics called *Lilavati*. Akbar made him tutor to his son. Todar Mal handled the empire's finances as its *diwan*. He introduced standard weights and measures, and created a systematic approach to revenue collection. Man Singh, the Raja of Amber, was Akbar's trusted lieutenant who led many successful campaigns. The poet Abdul Rahim Khan-I-Khan was the son of Bairam Khan. Fagir Aziao Din and Mullan Do Piaza were two other important advisors.

▲ *Akbar receives the poet Abdul Rahim Khan-I-Khan, son of Bairam Khan*

▲ *Abul Fazl presents the Akbarnama to Emperor Akbar*

▶ *Raja Birbal, a 19th century painting*

Religion

Under Akbar, religious tolerance became the norm. The *jizya*—a tax on non-Muslims—was dropped. The Muslim lunar calendar gave way to the more practical solar calendar. Akbar even developed a religion by mixing the best of Hinduism, Islam, and Christianity. He called it Din-i-Ilahi. His descendant Aurangzeb, however, was a devout Muslim who imposed Islamic law and treated his non-Muslim subjects harshly. In response to the strong Islamic presence, Hinduism experienced a resurgence, called the Bhakti movement. At the same time, a new religion called Sikhism was founded by Guru Nanak.

▶ *Guru Nanak (1469–1539)*

▶ *Babur and his followers visit a Hindu temple, an illustration from the emperor's biography, Baburnama*

Imperial China

At the start of the 15th century, the Ming Dynasty ruled China. The Yongle Emperor (1360–1424) put down his rivals and solidified his power, both in court and with neighbouring states. He lay down the foundations for the fabulous imperial residence, the Forbidden City. Literature and art blossomed in Beijing. China funded far-flung naval explorations. The exquisite blue-and-white Ming porcelain became a highly sought-after treasure. Eventually, corruption and infighting brought down the Ming Empire. Rebellions broke out across the land. When an army of Manchus invaded, the Ming could not repel them. In 1644, the Manchus set up the Qing Dynasty—the last imperial dynasty of China.

▲ A blue-and-white Ming-period dish painted with a dragon

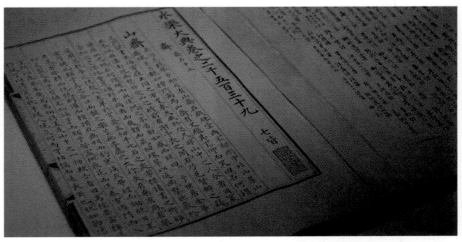

▲ The Yongle Dadian was a massive encyclopedia—22,000 chapters long! It is one of the most important Chinese literary works from the time of Emperor Yongle. Sadly, only about 800 chapters remain today

🕐 Engineering an Empire

In the early 15th century, the Mongols rose briefly to harass China's borders. In response, Emperor Yongle moved his capital to the more defensible city of Beijing in 1421. He spent a great deal enlarging the city and securing it with a 10 m high wall that ran around Beijing for 15 km! To meet the new city's food demands, he rebuilt the Grand Canal, so grain ships could reach the capital. He also repaired the Great Wall of China to strengthen the northern borders.

▲ The Zijincheng (Purple Forbidden City) covers 7.2 km² and has thousands of rooms, carefully laid out according to the traditional Chinese view of the world. There is even a river running through the estate. At the heart of the complex, on the most elevated site, is the Hall of Supreme Harmony, where imperial receptions were held

👤 In Real Life

Like many governments today, Ming China was run by civil servants. A job with the civil service was highly coveted. Applicants sat for difficult exams. The men who scored the highest got the best jobs. Men studied for years to pass the exam and earn a prestigious position.

▶ Civil-service candidates waiting for their results, c. 1540, by Qiu Ying

Women in Ming China

The stability and increased wealth of the Ming period led to a sharp rise in the population. As cities grew, women from the richer families began to gain more freedom. They owned businesses in their own name and could trade as merchants. They were even allowed to be professional artists. Sadly, other laws—such as a widow's right to inherit her husband's property—were unavailable/lacking at this time. Indeed, widows were expected to follow their husbands in death!

▶ By the Ming period, young girls from all walks of life would have their feet tightly—and cruelly—bound to keep them small throughout their life. Special 'lotus shoes' like this Qing-period shoe were embroidered for feet, which were supposed to be no larger than 10 cm!

Zheng He (c. 1371–1433)

The greatest explorer of the period was the military general and diplomat Zheng He. A Muslim by birth, Zheng He was only 10 years old when he was forced to join the Ming army. He soon made powerful friends at court. When the emperor wanted to conquer the 'Western Oceans', he chose Zheng He to lead the navy. Zheng He undertook seven voyages—with hundreds of ships—and explored Asia, India, the Middle East, and East Africa.

◀ After visiting Somalia in Africa, Zheng brought back a giraffe for Emperor Yongle!

Rise of the Qing Emperors

In 1644, a rebel army under the command of Li Zicheng (1605–1645) attacked Beijing. When it entered the city in April, the last Ming emperor—Chongzhen (ruled 1611–1644)—hung himself. An army commander called Wu Sangai heard this news while he was fighting Manchu troops in northeastern China. He thus, quickly made peace with them and requested their help. The Manchus obliged. But once they had put down the rebellion, they decided to stay on as rulers! Li Zicheng was killed by peasants and the Manchus established the Qing Dynasty, which ruled for almost three centuries.

Isn't It Amazing!

Though he did much good for China, Yongle Emperor was also immensely cruel at times. On taking the throne, he killed most of the preceding emperor's servants. In another horrific event, he ordered 2,800 concubines, servant girls and guards to a slow-slicing death! His successor freed many of the survivors.

▲ Yongle Emperor on the Dragon chair

▲ Qing Dynasty's fourth monarch, the Kangxi Emperor (1654–1722), who completed the Manchu conquest of China

The Unification of Japan

At the start of the 15th century, Japanese states had an imperial figurehead but were actually ruled by military warlords (Shogun) of the Ashikaga family. The Shoguns of the first half of this period faced severe famines and civil war, which culminated in the Onin War (1467–1477). After this war, the local leaders *(daimyo)* of individual states became so powerful, they broke free from the Shogun's rule. Having so many military leaders led to a time of violence and discord called the Sengoku—the Warring States Period. The men who unified Japan again were Oda Nobunaga and—after his death—Toyotomi Hideyoshi and Tokugawa Ieyasu. The Sengoku ended with the formation of the phenomenal Tokugawa Shogunate, which lasted until the late 19th century.

▲ *The armour of Oda Nobunaga*

▲ *Oda Nobunaga watches a Sumo (wrestling) tournament*

Oda Nobunaga (1534–1582)

From the bloody struggles of the Sengoku *daimyo* rose an unexpected leader. He was the head of a small province called Owari. No one expected Oda Nobunaga to become the powerful leader of Japan. Yet, he succeeded in occupying the capital. Oda was a military genius who successfully adapted firearms to Japanese warfare. He also developed military infrastructure like ironclad ships, a network of roads, and formidable castles. His armies could thus move at great speed. Most importantly, Oda chose his warriors for their ability, not based on class, rank, or family connections. He suppressed not only the other *daimyos* but also broke the power of warrior-monks. Oda was also a talented statesman, establishing economic and financial laws that made it easier for his people to live in tough times.

Honno-ji Temple

At the height of his power, Oda Nobunaga was betrayed by his general Akechi Mitsuhide. While Nobunaga was resting in a temple, he was surrounded by Mitsuhide and his troops. Nobunaga ordered his **page**, Mori Ranmaru, to set the temple on fire so no one could take his head. He then committed suicide. His devoted page followed soon after.

◀ *Oda displayed his power and prestige by supporting the arts and building amazing gardens and castles. His Azuchi castle on Lake Biwa was covered with gold statues on the outside, while the inside was decorated with exquisitely painted screens and ceilings*

🕐 The Hideyoshi Regime

Oda was betrayed just when he was poised to achieve his goal. His brilliant counsellor Toyotomi Hideyoshi (1537–98) took over the unification of Japan. The son of a peasant, Toyotomi rose to become one of Nobunaga's most powerful commanders. He eliminated many rivals (including the rebel Akechi Mitsuhide) with his shrewd judgment and prompt actions. By 1590, all of Japan was under his control.

▶ *Known as the One-Eyed Dragon of Oshu, the daimyo Date Masamune (1567–1636) was an outstanding military tactician and man of high ethics in a time of war and unrest. He served both Toyotomi and Tokugawa and is venerated as a hero to this day*

▲ *Gazing up Toyotomi Hideyoshi's skinny, lined face, Oda Nobunaga nicknamed him Kozaru, meaning Little Monkey!*

🕐 The Tokugawa Shogunate

Because they were of relatively humble origin, neither Oda nor Hideyoshi took the title of Shogun. After Hideyoshi's death, another Oda ally, Tokugawa Ieyasu (1543–1616), won power at the Battle of Sekigahara in 1600. In 1603, he took the title of Shogun, establishing a period of peace and stability. The rule of his successors Hidetada and Iemitsu saw a rise in the persecution of Christians. Things came to a head in the Shimabara Rebellion of 1637–1638 during which thousands of Christian rebels and sympathisers were executed. Soon after, Japan expelled all foreigners and isolated itself from the world for the next 200+ years!

▲ *Tokugawa Ieyasu, founder of the last Shogunate of Japan*

⭐ Incredible Individuals

Toyotomi was a great supporter of tea master Sen no Rikyu (1522–1591), the man who took the Japanese tea ceremony to new heights. All current tea masters trace their lineage to him. Rikyu was, however, forced to commit *seppuku*—ritual suicide—in 1591, owing to Hideyoshi's contentious actions.

▶ *The original tea-ceremony master Sen no Rikyu in a painting by the great artist Hasegawa Tohaku (1539–1610)*

▲ *Christian prisoners of the 17th century awaiting execution*

REVOLUTION & INDEPENDENCE

THE FALL OF **EMPIRES**

Since the dawn of civilisation, there has been a discrimination between the 'haves' and the 'have-nots.' For the longest time, the have-nots—the poor and the downtrodden—more or less accepted their sorry fate. Barring the occasional revolt and short-lived **republics**, people had little say in how they were governed. Power rested with kings, priests, and aristocrats. This changed in the 18th century with the Age of Enlightenment. The great philosophers of this time spread the idea that all people were equal in the eyes of the law, whether they were rulers or commoners. They called for democracy and came up with new forms of government. The long-oppressed people welcomed these ideals. They fought for freedom from the monarchs and empire builders. Beginning with the American and French revolutions, the struggles for independence forever changed the political and social order of the world.

▼ Washington crossing the Delaware, an 1851 oil-painting celebrating a historic moment of the American Revolution

Enlightenment and Revolution

18th-century Europe saw the rise of intellectuals who embraced the principles of science, rational thought, and personal freedom. This period is called the Age of Enlightenment. Some of its greatest proponents were philosophers in France, like Voltaire and Diderot. Their writings became enormously popular among the common people. Their ideas encouraged people to revolt against the kings and the Church, and established the first modern republics. The Age of Enlightenment was responsible for the American Wars of Independence and the French Revolution. These, in turn, affected movements for freedom across the globe. Such revolutions led to new forms of governance such as socialism, capitalism, and **communism**.

▲ French scholars of the Age of Enlightenment circulated their ideas by spreading printed books **pamphlets**, and by meeting at scientific academies, clubs and **literary salons**. This painting shows a reading of Voltaire's 1775 play L'Orphelin de la Chine—a tragedy about Genghis Khan and his sons— in the salon of Madame Thérèse Rodet Geoffrin (1699–1777), a leading figure of French Enlightenment

▲ Like many leaders of the Enlightenment, the German explorer, botanist and overall **polymath** Alexander von Humboldt (1769–1859) was disgusted by slavery and criticised colonial oppression

Voltaire

Voltaire was the pen name of the French philosopher and writer François-Marie Arouet (1694–1778). A witty, satirical writer, he courageously spoke out against tyranny, bigotry, and cruelty. His opposition of the Church and French monarchy led to his imprisonment and later to his banishment. His books, plays, and histories greatly influenced the French Revolution and the course of European civilisation.

▶ Der Tafelrund (The Round-table) shows famous men of the Enlightenment gathered around Prussian royalty at the Palace Sanssouci. Voltaire, wearing a purple coat, appears third from the left

💡 Isn't It Amazing!

While Enlightenment encouraged the common people to rise and topple monarchies, in some countries, the rulers themselves embraced Enlightenment and made reforms in their governments. Such rulers—like Empress Catherine the Great of Russia (1729–96), King Frederick the Great of Prussia (1712–86), and King Gustav III of Sweden (1746–92)—were called 'enlightened despots'!

▶ As the head of the government of Portugal, the first Marquis de Pombal (1699–1782) was an enlightened despot. His sweeping reforms included abolishing slavery, weakening the Inquisition, creating the foundations for secular public schools, and restructuring the tax system

Diderot

The French philosopher Denis Diderot (1713–84) helped spread the ideals of Enlightenment by writing, compiling, and editing the *Encyclopédie*—the first big encyclopedia that was available to everyone. He was aided by a team of littérateurs, scientists, and even priests. Diderot faced immense criticism and pressure to censor his work and make it more conventional. However, he remained undaunted and eventually published the amazing *Encyclopédie* as 17 volumes of text and 11 volumes of illustrations.

▶ *"If there is something you know, communicate it. If there is something you don't know, search for it."— An engraving from the 1772 edition of the Encyclopédie on which the haloed figure of Truth, in the top centre, is unveiled by the figures of Philosophy and Reason (on the right)*

◀ *The English philosopher John Locke (1632–1704) is called the Father of Liberalism. His ideas influenced the Founding Fathers of America, in particular President Thomas Jefferson. His belief that all humans have a right to 'life, liberty and the pursuit of happiness' appears in the US Declaration of Independence*

◀ *A key figure of the German Enlightenment, Immanuel Kant (1724–1804) wrote three major books in the history of philosophy—Critique of Pure Reason, Critique of Practical Reason, and Critique of Judgement*

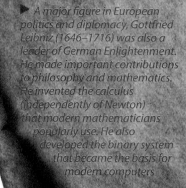

▶ *A major figure in European politics and diplomacy, Gottfried Leibniz (1646–1716) was also a leader of German Enlightenment. He made important contributions to philosophy and mathematics. He invented the calculus (independently of Newton) that modern mathematicians popularly use. He also developed the binary system that became the basis for modern computers*

▲ *One of the Founding Fathers of the USA, Thomas Paine (1737–1809) became famous for his patriotic pamphlet called Common Sense, which deplored English control over the American colonies. His other amazing works were The Age of Reason—a criticism of the Bible, and The Rights of Man—which defended the French Revolution*

◀ *The economist and philosopher Adam Smith (1723–90) wrote the Wealth of Nations, in which he famously argued that wealth was not money! He believed wealth came from capital and labour. His theories greatly influenced the way Western businesses operate, including how they interact with governments and compete with other businesses*

The Haskalah Movement

In the late 18th century, the Jewish population of Europe began to absorb the values of Enlightenment. They also integrated with neighbouring gentiles (non-Jews), adopting many of their manners, technologies, crafts, and aspirations. This time of Jewish Enlightenment came to be known as Haskalah. It led to a study of the Talmud—Jewish laws and legends—in a manner opposed to superstition, fanaticism, and orthodoxy. One of its leading figures was Moses Mendelssohn (1729–86), a Jewish philosopher of Dessau, Germany. He is held to be responsible for the renaissance of the House of Israel.

▶ *A painting of an imagined meeting between Moses Mendelssohn (right), the leading Enlightenment dramatist Gotthold Lessing (standing), and the Swiss theologian and poet-philosopher Johann Kaspar Lavater (left). The enduring friendship between the Jewish Moses and the gentile Lessing was a high point of the Haskalah. Lavater held greatly publicised debates with Moses, for whom he had deep respect*

Cromwell's Protectorate and Restoration

Over the 16th–17th centuries, England was plagued by religious strife. The largely Protestant population suffered whenever a Catholic monarch took the throne. Things became more complicated when the Catholic King Charles I quarrelled with his Protestant Parliament, leading to a civil war. King Charles's supporters (the Cavaliers) met the Parliament's soldiers (the Roundheads) in battle and were defeated. King Charles was arrested and found guilty of treason! He was beheaded in 1649. The military and political leader Oliver Cromwell (1599–1658) took over the government and ruled England as its Lord Protector. After Cromwell died, his son Richard came to power. However, Richard was so inefficient, the people begged old King Charles's son to take over. The crowning of Charles II restored the monarchy in Britain.

▶ *And When Did You Last See Your Father? (1878) by William Frederick Yeames shows an imaginary Royalist household during the English Civil War. The Parliamentarians question a boy about his Royalist father while his sisters worry in the background*

▶ *A German print from the time shows the execution of Charles I outside the Banqueting House of the Palace of Whitehall*

🕐 Civil Wars Under Charles I

After Charles I married a Catholic French princess (called Henrietta Maria), he tried to impose elements of Catholic services—such as incense and bells—on the Church of England. This worried his people, who despised Catholicism. Charles then quarrelled with his Parliament over taxes and the grant of certain rights. He even closed down Parliament for 11 years and ruled on his own! Eventually, the Parliament raised an army and fought against the King's troops. It won the first war and King Charles was imprisoned. He escaped, and a second war broke out. This time, when the Parliament won, they put the king on trial and had him executed. Nevertheless, Charles's death did not put an end to the civil war because his son and heir was still alive.

▼ *Led by Thomas Fairfax and Oliver Cromwell, the Parliament's New Model Army won over the Royalist troops (commanded by Prince Rupert) at the Battle of Naseby on 14 June 1645*

Charles II

Charles I's eldest son, the Prince of Wales, fled Britain and set up court in Holland. He called himself King Charles II of England even though he was in exile and had not been crowned. Charles II had a loyal following in Scotland, where he had been born. With their support, he renewed the fight against the Parliamentarians. The Third Civil War (1649–51) ended when Charles II was defeated at the Battle of Worcester on 3 September 1651. Things looked grim, but Charles II managed to disguise himself and escaped the land.

Restoration

The Commonwealth that Oliver Cromwell ruled might have permanently removed royal power from England. But his son, Richard Cromwell, was unable to carry out his father's policies. Richard resigned in 1659. George Monck, Governor of Scotland, established military rule. He then negotiated between Charles II and Parliament to bring back the heir to the throne. Finally, in May 1660, Charles II was welcomed home. At the start of his rule, he punished the men who were directly responsible for his father's death. He even had Oliver Cromwell's body dug up, decapitated and hung in chains! Despite this, he is generally thought of as a fun-loving king who supported the arts and sciences.

▲ *The Proscribed Royalist, 1651, by John Everett Millais, shows a Royalist, fleeing after the Battle of Worcester, being hidden in the trunk of a tree by a young Puritan woman*

▲ *The soldier and statesman Oliver Cromwell was a fervently religious man. In this portrait, he is wearing the medieval armour—a symbol of chivalry, and carrying the baton— symbolic of high military command*

▲ *Charles II, often called the Merry Monarch, in his coronation portrait*

In Real Life

Oliver Cromwell, a zealous Puritan, wanted people to live simple, industrious lives. Music and sports were frowned upon and theatres shut down. In contrast, Charles II pursued pleasure, power, and people of wit and charm.

▲ *Charles II threw open the theatres after Restoration. He was particularly captivated by the English actress Nell Gwyn*

Catherine of Braganza

In 1662, Charles married Catherine of Braganza, a princess of Portugal. As part of her dowry, she brought the wealthy cities of Tangier(in North Africa) and the seven islands of Bombay (in India) to the English throne. Catherine is also credited with introducing the habit of tea-drinking to the island nation.

▶ *Catherine of Braganza, Queen of England, Scotland, and Ireland; painted c. 1665*

Wars of American Independence

The American Revolutionary War was fought between Great Britain and its 13 colonies in North America over 1775–83. The Continental Army—the army of the colonies—was led by George Washington. It ultimately defeated the troops of the British Empire. The colonies became independent and formed the United States of America.

▶ John Trumbull's painting Declaration of Independence shows the five-man drafting committee of the Declaration of Independence presenting their work to the Congress. The painting appears on the back of the US $2 bill

The Red Coats are Coming!

The British government forced its colonies to follow certain laws on trade and taxes. The colonists' protests led to the Boston Massacre of 1770 and events of the Boston Tea Party—a political protest in 1773. In 1774, the British made things worse by signing the Intolerable Acts, which restricted freedom and made trade harder. In 1765, when Britain needed money to fight France, it passed the Stamp Act. This forced the colonists to buy stamps from the King's government for legal papers, newspapers and even playing cards. But colonies refused to do what the King wanted. Finally, the British sent troops (the Red Coats) to control the colonies.

▲ The American silversmith Paul Revere (1735–1818) became a folk hero when he rode through Boston on the night of 18 April 1775 warning the residents that the Red Coats (the British) were coming. His tale was made famous in a poem by Henry Wadsworth Longfellow. Revere also made an engraving of Red Coats firing at civilians in the Boston Massacre

▲ The Boston Tea Party was a political protest in which Americans boarded three ships in Boston Harbour and dumped all its 342 chests of tea into the sea! This caused huge losses for the British who owned the tea and would have sold it to the Americans at very high prices

Lexington and Concord

The first shots of the American Revolutionary War were fired in the battles at Lexington and Concord on 19 April 1775. Some 700 British troops were deployed to find and destroy enemy supplies in Lexington Green. Instead, they encountered 70 **minutemen**, but with superior numbers, the battle only lasted a few minutes. The soldiers then moved on to Concord. This time, they were ambushed by 400 minutemen, and lost 250 men. The British retreated to Boston. The colonists blockaded their exit and began the Siege of Boston, which lasted until George Washington drove out the British in March 1776.

▲ Engraving of the battle on Lexington Green shows British soldiers in military formation firing at the untrained, scattered minutemen. Eight of them were killed while the British lost one man

Battle of Bunker Hill

In an effort to break the **Siege** of Boston, the British attacked the 1,200 strong colonial troops that were occupying the hills around the city. On 13 June 1775, they clashed at Bunker Hill and Breed's Hill. Though the British captured the hills, they lost over 226 men and more than 800 were injured. This battle proved to be a huge morale booster for the colonists as they stood up to trained soldiers.

▲ Artist John Trumbull (1756–1843) saw the death of Joseph Warren, a politician and volunteer in the colonial army, in the defence of Breed's Hill. This became the subject of his iconic painting, The Death of General Warren at the Battle of Bunker's Hill

Battle of Saratoga

The events that took place in Saratoga during the later part of 1777 marked a turning point in the revolution. There were actually two military engagements: the Battle of Freeman's Farm (19 September) and the Battle of Bemis Heights (7 October). Under the command of General Horatio Gates, the Americans attacked the British army led by General John Burgoyne. On 17 October, Burgoyne's army of around 6,000 troops surrendered. The victory caused France and Spain to ally with America.

▲ General Burgoyne surrenders his sword to General Gates

Incredible Individuals

George Washington (1732–99) was appointed the commander-in-chief of the colonial armies in 1775. Washington had to hold together this 'army' of colonial farmers against trained and experienced British soldiers. Despite the odds, he led the colonists to victory over the course of six years. When the Revolutionary War ended, the government asked him to be their ruler. But Washington denied them and went home. Later, in 1789, he was voted in as the first President of the independent United States.

▲ In one of his famous victories, Washington led his troops across the Delaware River on Christmas Day of 1776. His attack surprised the better-armed Hessian (German) troops at the Battle of Princeton and Trenton, New Jersey. Some 22 were killed, 83 injured, and 850 captured with supplies

Southern Battles

In 1779, the fighting moved to Georgia and South Carolina. General Nathanael Greene (1742–86)—Washington's trusted officer—led the rebels. He won many battles against the British. In 1781, George Washington and French general Jean Rochambeau led an offensive battle against British troops in the Battle of Yorktown (in Virginia). This was the last major land battle in the Revolution. The Americans won a decisive victory and the British surrendered.

▲ The Surrender of Lord Cornwallis at Yorktown, 19 October 1781

The French Revolution

The people of France rose against their oppressive monarchy in a fierce and bloody rebellion in 1789. They wrote a new constitution that gave ordinary people a say in their government. It was established on the principles of *'liberté, égalité, fraternité'*, which mean liberty, **equality**, **fraternity**. The revolution ended when Napoleon Bonaparte took power in November 1799.

▲ *A caricature shows the downtrodden Frenchman carrying the Church and Nobility on his back*

▲ *The Romantic artist Eugene Delacroix commemorated the Revolution with his painting Lady Liberty Leading the People*

Storming the Bastille

In May 1789, the people submitted a list of problems they wanted the king to fix. It was called the *Cahiers de Doléances* (*Book of Complaints*). They were supported by the Director-General of Finances, Jacques Necker, who believed the Church and noble families should pay their fair share of taxes. When the rulers did not agree, the people set up their own National Assembly on 10 June 1789. On 14 July, they stormed the Bastille prison, killed its governor and released the prisoners. The National Assembly took control of Paris and its president, Jean-Sylvain Bailly, became Mayor. By the end of July, the revolution had spread all over France.

▲ *The Storming of the Bastille in July 1789—the prison governor, Marquis Bernard-René de Launay, can be seen arrested in the centre. He was decapitated and his head was raised on a stick and paraded around the city*

▲ *On 14 July 1790, one year after the Bastille event, thousands of people gathered in Champ de Mars, Paris, to celebrate. The diplomat Charles Maurice de Talleyrand (1754–1838) led the crowd in a religious mass. The gathering, which included the king and his family, swore loyalty to 'the nation, the law, and the king'*

The Fall of the Monarchs

As the revolution increased in fervour, many aristocrats fled the country. In October 1789, the Palace of Versailles was mobbed by 7,000 women! The royal family tried to escape Paris dressed as servants. Their plans failed. The king and queen spent time in and out of prison over the next two years. The new government failed to curb the people's anger. By 7 September, 1,400 people were dead. The king was accused of plotting with foreign rulers to invade France. In January 1793, Louis XVI was found guilty of treason. On 21 January, the king was beheaded under the **guillotine**. Queen Marie Antoinette followed on 16 October.

▲ The royal family arrested in their attempt to flee

▲ The guillotine beheads King Louis XVI

The Reign of Terror

Though the king was dead, the situation in France did not immediately improve. In June 1793, a revolutionary club called the Jacobins began to rise in power. A Jacobin called Maximilien de Robespierre (1758–94) and eight other members set up the Committee of Public Safety. This group became responsible for the Reign of Terror, which lasted until the spring of 1794. Robespierre believed in keeping people afraid. Anyone who broke his laws—even if it was not proven—could be guillotined. Some 16,594 people were guillotined and around 40,000 may have died in prisons. Eventually, the Committee turned against Robespierre. He and his supporters were executed without trial on 28 July 1974.

Napoleon Seizes Power

A new constitution called the Directoire (Directory) was put in place. However, the people who were in charge—the Directors—were very unpopular. They ignored election results and used the army to control people. Finally, the Corsican general Napoleon Bonaparte used his army to take control. On 9 November 1799, Bonaparte took power. This event is called the **Coup** of 18 Brumaire (a date on the French Republican Calendar). Napoleon set up a new government called the Consulate. He became the dictator and, in 1804, the Emperor of France.

▲ The execution of Robespierre; prisoners were transported from the prisons to the guillotine in a wooden cart called the tumbrel

◀ Napoleon Bonaparte at the Coup of 18 Brumaire

From Slavery to Statehood

The Haitian Revolution of 1791–1804 was the first successful anti-slavery insurrection in the West. Self-liberated slaves overthrew French colonialists in Saint-Domingue (modern Haiti). Led by charismatic ex-slaves like Toussaint L'Ouverture, they founded a free state governed by non-white people and former captives. This was a defining moment in the history of Western racism. Not only did the nation successfully defend its hard-won freedoms, it tore down the long-held European belief that non-white people could not govern themselves.

▶ *Battle of San Domingo, a canvas by January Suchodolski, shows colonial troops fighting the rebels*

Plantation Problems

Along with Jamaica, Haiti was the world's leading producer of sugar. The profit made here exceeded profits from all the 13 American colonies put together! Whereas in France, the wealth was in the hands of a few rich people while the masses suffered poverty and degradation.

▲ *A sugar factory in Saint-Domingue*

Independence

Napoleon's brother-in-law Charles Leclerc restored French rule in Haiti. When it became apparent that they would re-establish slavery, a rebellion broke out once again. The French were finally defeated in 1803. On 1 January 1804, Dessalines, the new leader declared Haiti a free state. He became a self-proclaimed monarch and assumed the title of Emperor Jacques I, but was killed in October 1806.

The Call to Arms

Many slaves ran away from the plantations. They formed gangs, called maroons, and fiercely raided the plantations. The maroon leader François Mackandal was the first to unify black resistance. This amazing **Vodou** priest even set up a spy network among the plantation slaves. His rebellions over 1751–57 created havoc until he was captured and burned at the stake in 1758. On 22 August 1791, some 10,000 slaves plunged the island into civil war. They burned down plantations and killed slave owners and people of mixed ancestry. This uprising went on for 13 years!

ⓞ Incredible Individuals

A black military commander, Toussaint L'Ouverture (c. 1743–1803) was a self-educated former slave. He led the Haitian Revolution and successfully negotiated freedom from the colonialists—for a while. Toussaint ruled the island until Napoleon came to power. In a deceptive plot, Toussaint was shipped off to France and imprisoned in an icy prison, where he died.

▶ *General Toussaint L'Ouverture*

◀ *In November, 1803, Vicomte de Rochambeau led the French colonial army against Dessalines's troops in the Battle of Vertieres. This was the last land battle of the Haitian Revolution*

The Eighty Years' War

In the mid 16th century, the modern-day countries of Belgium, Luxembourg, and the Netherlands were a group of Dutch states called the Seventeen Provinces. They were ruled by King Philip II of Spain. The Dutch War of Independence was spread over 1568–1648. For this reason, it is more popularly known as the Eighty Years' War. It led to the split of the northern and southern Netherlands. The northern region formed the United Provinces of the Netherlands (the Dutch Republic).

▶ *Philip II berates William the Silent before leaving the Netherlands in 1559*

 ## The First Phase

Spain imposed heavy taxes and strict religious restrictions on its colonies. The Dutch even suffered from the horrific **Inquisition**. Their resentment boiled over into the fierce 1556 Beeldenstorm—the 'Iconoclastic Fury'—in which Catholic icons and decorations were stripped from churches. Philip II sent the Duke of Alva, nicknamed the Iron Duke, to suppress the protests. In 1568, the influential **stadtholder** William I of Orange (called William the Silent) tried to drive out the unpopular duke. He failed and was forced to flee. Some of his co-conspirators, like the Counts of Egmont and Horne, were caught and beheaded. The provinces continued their resistance under the exiled William. In 1573, Dutch ships, forming an irregular force called the Geuzen, captured Holland and Zeeland from Spain. In 1581, other states joined them to form the Republic of the Seven United Netherlands.

▲ *The Iconoclastic Fury (Beeldenstorm) of 1556*

▲ *Dutch ships ram into the great Spanish galleys off the coast of Flanders*

 ## The Second Phase

After a twelve-year truce (1609–1621), war broke out again. Initially, Spain had the upper hand. But after 1625, the Dutch leader Prince Frederick Henry of Orange scored several victories. In 1635, the Dutch allied with France and attacked Spanish provinces in Flanders and Wallonia (northern and southern Belgium). In 1648, Spain signed the Peace of Munster, which recognised Dutch independence. This marked the start of the Dutch Golden Age.

▲ *The Surrender of Breda followed a 1624–1625 siege of the city by the brilliant Spanish general Ambrogio Spinola*

▲ *The Peace of Munster, 15 May 1648*

Fall of the Ottoman Empire

With its capital in Turkey, the Islamic Ottoman dynasty ruled over a mighty, multi-cultural empire in Eurasia for some 600 years. The Ottomans made the region secure and stable. They also oversaw amazing accomplishments in the arts, sciences, and society as a whole. But in the 1600s, the empire began to lose its vitality. In 1683, the Ottoman Turks suffered a disastrous defeat in the Battle of Vienna. Over the next century, they continued losing parcels of land. Greece won its freedom from the empire in 1830. In 1878, the Congress of Berlin secured the independence of Romania, Serbia, and Bulgaria. The empire lost almost all its remaining territories in the Balkan Wars of 1912 and 1913. Finally, after World War I, the empire was carved up between the winners—Britain, France, Greece, and Russia. Ottoman rule officially ended in 1922 when the title of its Sultan was eliminated. Turkey was declared a republic in 1923.

▲ During the Greek War of Independence (1821–29), the Greeks used fire ships to burn down Ottoman frigates. Greek independence was affirmed by the Treaty of Constantinople in July 1832

▲ The Russo-Turkish War weakened Ottoman influence over Bulgaria. But it was only in 1908 that King Ferdinand I of Bulgaria was able to proclaim full independence before crowds in the city of Tarnovo

▲ The Serbian Revolution consisted of two main uprisings against the Ottomans. The first uprising (1804–13) was led by Karadorde Petrovic nicknamed Black George (seen here on the left). The second uprising (1815–17) was led by Milos Obrenovic, who became the first prince of a semi-independent Serbia. Full independence came in 1878

▲ The Romanian War of Independence is otherwise called the Russo-Turkish War of 1877–78. Romanian troops in alliance with the Russian army defeated the Ottomans at battles in Grivitsa, Rahova, Vidin and Smârdan. They returned victorious to the capital city of Bucharest, passing under its arc of triumph on 8 October 1878

Isn't It Amazing!

In the 14th century, the Ottomans created a system called Devshirme, in which 20 per cent of the Christian boys in conquered lands became slaves of the state. Many of these slaves were trained in government and military service. As a result, they became powerful and wealthy. In the mid-16th century, they seized Turkish land that was meant to support the Turkish cavalry. The cavalry thus became secondary to the deadly and disciplined military slaves, who were called Janissaries. People now began to pay so as to become part of this elite corps! The Devshirme system was abolished in 1826, after Sultan Mahmud II suppressed a Janissary revolt and executed some 6,000 men.

▲ *The registration of Christian boys for Devshirme, 1558*

▲ *Mustafa Kemal Atatürk, founder of the Republic of Turkey, wearing the traditional Janissary uniform*

The Battle of Vienna

For almost two long months—over July–September, 1683—Grand Vizier Kara ('Black') Mustafa **besieged** the city of Vienna with an army of over 100,000 men. Vienna sent out a plea for help and an extraordinary army of Christian rulers came to its rescue. King John III Sobieski of Poland arrived with 18,000 soldiers; Elector Max Emmanuel of Bavaria with 11,000 men; and Prince George Friedrich von Waldeck with 8,000 Germans. George of Hanover (the future King George I of England) brought a guard of 600 cavalry. John George III von Wettin, the Elector of Saxony, led a troop of 9,000 Saxons. Finally, the Imperial General Lieutenant Duke Charles of Lorraine brought 20,000 Austrians. The Turkish defeat marked the beginning of the Ottoman decline.

▲ *Turkish armies surround the walled city of Vienna*

The Armenian Holocaust

The horrific Armenian Genocide refers to two separate but related events that led to the systematic massacre of millions of men, women, and children, including the elderly and infirm. The first occurred over 1894–97 when Sultan Abd-ul-Hamid II carried out campaigns against the Armenians, destroying over 300,000 lives. The second took place over 1915–16, when the Young Turk government deported and executed over two million Armenians. The ethnic group suffered simply because they held different beliefs and followed a different lifestyle from their overlords and neighbours. To this day, the Turkish government denies the Armenian Genocide ever took place.

▲ *On 24 April 1915, hundreds of Armenian leaders and scholars were rounded up and killed in Istanbul. At the same time, some 5,000 people were butchered in the streets and homes. Nearly 1,750,000 Armenians were kicked off the land. Hundreds of thousands died from starvation, disease or sheer exhaustion on their journey. Several more were massacred by military forces*

The Austro-Hungarian Empire

During 1804–67, Central Europe was ruled by a remnant of the Holy Roman Empire, which Napoleon had brought to an end. This empire was ruled by the House of Habsburg and was called the Austrian Empire. It was a hodgepodge of cultures and peoples that included Germans, Venetians, Hungarians, Slovenes, Poles, Czechs, Slovaks, Romanians, Ukrainians, Croats, and Serbs. Over 1867–1918, the empire also ruled over the kingdom of Hungary. During this period, it was called the Austro-Hungarian Empire. Its capital city was Vienna.

▲ Peasants slaughter the nobility of Austria-owned Galicia (modern-day Ukraine and Poland) in 1846

▲ The 1918 National Assembly in Alba Iulia saw the union of Transylvania with Romania. This was an act of national liberation for the Transylvanian Romanians

Nationalism and the Empire

The 19th century saw a spike in nationalistic fervour. The many ethnic groups of the empire wanted their own independent nations. The empire was also hampered by aggressive foreign rivals and unstable finances. It was not as industrial as other Western countries. Nor did it have strong naval resources or riches from overseas colonies. The Habsburgs depended on their large army and numerous strong forts to keep together an increasingly fragmented empire.

▲ Signing the Treaty of Saint-Germain-en-Laye on 10 September 1919, effectively dissolving the Austro-Hungarian Empire

▶ The revolt of Czech troops in Austria in May 1918 was brutally suppressed under military law

Incredible Individuals

The Austrian statesman Klemens von Metternich (1773–1859) guided the Austrian empire, particularly its foreign policy, under Francis II and his son Ferdinand I. He was so influential, with his network of spies, that this period of 1815–48 came to be known as the Age of Metternich. Under his rule, nationalist revolts in Austria-owned parts of northern Italy and Germany were ruthlessly crushed. At home too, he suppressed all revolutionary and liberal ideals. His Carlsbad Decrees of 1819 limited education, press, and free speech. The empire's stability did not survive Metternich's retirement.

▲ An early diplomatic success of Metternich's was the marriage of Napoleon Bonaparte and Archduchess Marie Louise of Austria in 1810

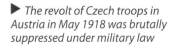

The Spring of Nations

From March 1848 to November 1849, the empire was assailed by nationalist revolutions. Its many ethnic groups demanded **autonomy** or outright independence. Some even sought to take over other nationalities! In the end, there were no clear leaders or unifying goals and the revolutions failed to achieve anything long-lasting.

▲ *Revolutionary barricades on the streets of Vienna, 1848*

▲ *Proclamation of the short-lived autonomous state of Serbian Vojvodina during the 1848 revolutions*

World War I (1914–18)

On 28 June 1914, Archduke Franz Ferdinand, the heir to the empire, was visiting the Bosnian capital of Sarajevo. While he was driving down to visit wounded men at the Sarajevo Hospital, a Bosnian Serb student activist shot and killed him. The assassination led to war between Austro-Hungary and Serbia. The allies of both nations joined in and soon the World War was in full swing. Ultimately, the empire lost the war. The victors supported nationalist sentiments and wanted to break up the empire permanently.

▲ *Illustration of the assassination of Archduke Franz Ferdinand in a 1914 Italian newspaper*

▲ *Duke Franz Ferdinand and his wife about to board their car—a few minutes before the assassination*

The Empire Disintegrates

Almost overnight, the empire broke up. On 28 October 1918, a group of Czechoslovaks in Prague passed a 'law' claiming independence for their state. In Krakow, a Polish committee established free Poland after uniting with Galicia and Austrian Silesia. On 29 October, the Croats in Zagreb declared independence for Slavonia, Croatia, and Dalmatia. On 30 October, German Austria proclaimed itself a free state. As a consequence of losing the war, the empire was forced to move out of its remaining territories. Finally, Emperor Karl I (1887–1922), the last Habsburg ruler of Austro-Hungary, renounced his right to participate in the Austrian government on 11 November and in the Hungarian government on 13 November.

▲ *Coronation portrait of Karl I, the last ruler of the Austro-Hungarian Empire, with Queen Zita and Crown Prince Otto, 1916*

Latin American Wars of Independence

Over 1808–26, South America fought to be free of its European overlords. Spain and Portugal had been ruling this continent for over 300 years. Yet, in these two decades, all of Latin America gained independence, barring the Spanish colonies of Cuba and Puerto Rico.

▲ In early 1817, Generals José de San Martin (left) and Bernardo O'Higgins crossed the formidable Andes Mountains with an army of Argentines and Chileans. On 17 February 1817, they seized the Chilean capital of Santiago. Exactly one year later, on 18 February 1818, Chile declared its independence from Spain

▲ Fought on 9 December 1824, the Battle of Ayacucho secured the freedom of Peru. It is often considered the end of the Spanish-American wars of independence

Creole Concerns

In the middle of the 18th century, the Spanish royal house tightened its control over its South American colonies. Part of this effort involved putting Spanish-born authorities in place of Creole officers. Creoles are people of Spanish or European descent who are born in the Americas. This felt like a slap in the face for the Creoles, who had been loyal to the crown until then. They were angered by the loss of their status, wealth, and power. At this time, the ideals of Enlightenment spread like wildfire through the cities. Many Creoles adapted these ideals to their purpose and sought the right to govern themselves, free from the overseas kings.

English Influence

Around 1795, Spain and England were not on good terms. The powerful English fleet cut off Spain's access to its American colonies. The Creoles were delighted as Spain was forced to loosen its controls. It also sharpened their desire for greater self-determination.

▼ In 1820, the First Chilean Navy Squadron raided Spanish ships in an effort to liberate Peru. The squadron—a fleet of 8 warships and 16 transport ships—was commanded by the British Admiral Thomas Cochrane

Napoleon's Influence

In 1807, when Napoleon began his attack on the Iberian Peninsula, Prince Regent John of Portugal fled on British ships to Brazil. He landed in Rio de Janeiro with 15,000 officials, nobles, and courtiers, transforming the colony into his administrative centre. When Napoleon took the Spanish king and his heir Ferdinand hostage, the leaders of South America fought to fill the power vacuum. Many **juntas** rose and ruled during 1808–10. Men from Spain set up governments in Mexico City and Montevideo that were loyal to Spain. In contrast, Santiago, Caracas, Bogota, and other places saw Creole-controlled juntas.

▲ Portrait of Joseph I Bonaparte of Spain c. 1808 by François Gérard

▲ The Portuguese royal family flees to Brazil, an 1812 painting by Henri l'Eveque

The Final Victory

The liberation of South America rose in two movements. From the north rose Simon Bolivar, who became known as the Liberator. He liberated many regions including Venezuela, Colombia, Ecuador, Peru, and Bolivia. From the south came another powerful force in the more discreet person of José de San Martin. After conquering their home regions, the two movements fought through other territories and met on the Pacific coast. From the Pacific Coast, troops under northern generals finally stamped out the last vestiges of loyalist resistance in Peru and Bolivia by 1826. Brazil had gained its independence and set up a constitutional monarchy in 1822. In the same year, Mexicans also passed a constitutional monarchy and raised their military officer Agustín de Iturbide to the position of emperor. This First Mexican Empire was soon toppled and Mexico became a republic in 1823.

▲ A statue in Ecuador commemorates the historic meeting of Simon Bolivar (left) and José de San Martin (right)

▲ Fought on 24 July 1823, the Battle of Lake Maracaibo is usually seen as the final battle for Venezuelan freedom

▲ On 24 June 1821, Simon Bolivar's troops met Royalist forces in the Battle of Carabobo. Bolivar's decisive victory led to the independence of Venezuela

Decline of the British Empire

Formed over the 16ᵗʰ–18ᵗʰ centuries, the British Empire was the largest in history. Like most colonisers, it did not have a good humanitarian record with its overseas territories. Over the 19ᵗʰ and 20ᵗʰ centuries, most colonies overthrew British rule and became independent. After WWII, Britain left the Indian subcontinent in 1947, Palestine in 1948, and Egypt (specifically, the Suez) in 1956. It withdrew from Africa in the 1950s and 60s, and from various island protectorates in the 1970s and 80s. In 1997, the transfer of Hong Kong to China marked the end of the British Empire.

▼ *British territories in Africa and the years in which they gained independence*

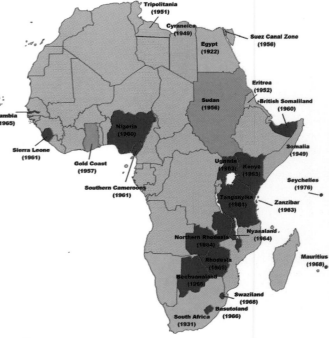

Commonwealth of Nations

In 1867, many British overseas territories were given the status of Dominions. These included Canada, Australia, New Zealand, Newfoundland, South Africa, and the Irish Free State. Together they were known as the Commonwealth. In 1923, Britain recognised their right to set their own foreign policies. The Balfour Declaration of 1926—made legal by the 1931 Statute of Westminster—granted them complete freedom from the UK.

▲ *Flags of the Commonwealth of Nations in Parliament Square, London; many more former British colonies are now part of the Commonwealth*

▲ *A march in support of the Balfour Declaration in 1917, in front of the parliament building in Toronto, Canada. The man in the shiny black top hat is Rabbi Yosef Weinreb, the chief rabbi of Toronto at the time*

Palestine

Following the terrible events of WWII, many Jewish people sought refuge in British-controlled Palestine, then a Muslim land. Here, they fought with the Arabs to create a separate Jewish state. Britain, which had been governing the area since 1922, found it difficult and expensive to maintain a military presence. Over 1947–48, it withdrew from Palestine. The United Nations then stepped in and voted to split Palestine into a Jewish state and an Arab state.

▲ *A Palestinian protest against British policies, 1929*

🕐 British Malaya

Britain had colonised Southeast Asia for its rich sources of rubber and tin. Over 1948–60, it clashed in **guerrilla** warfare against communist troops of the Malayan National Liberation Army. The Muslim people of Malaya supported the British effort to quell the MNLA—on the condition that they would leave as soon as the communist uprising was put down. In 1963, the 11 Malay states along with Singapore, Sarawak, and North Borneo joined to form Malaysia (though Singapore would be ousted in 1965). Brunei stayed a British protectorate and became an independent state in 1984.

🕐 The Indian Subcontinent

The Indian population had been revolting against British policies since the **Mutiny** of 1857, when the Indian troops rebelled against the British for forcing them into religiously intolerable acts. Throughout the following decades, social and religious leaders led vociferous protests against the increasingly violent British rule. Most significant of these was the civil rights leader Mahatma Gandhi, famous for his firm belief in the principle of non-violence. Finally, in 1947, Britain left the subcontinent—after dividing it into a secular India and an Islamic Pakistan. In the following year, Burma and Sri Lanka also gained their independence.

▲ *The Commonwealth's Avro Lincoln bomber dropping bombs on communist rebels in the Malayan jungle, c. 1950*

🕐 Around the Suez

In 1952, British PM Winston Churchill was forced to acknowledge the Egyptian Revolution led by Gamal Abdel Nasser (who eventually became President of Egypt). The following year, British troops withdrew from the Suez Canal zone. In 1956, Sudan became independent, causing British power in the Middle East to weaken. Britain deployed its troops, intervening in Oman (1957), Jordan (1958), and Kuwait (1961). By 1968, however, the financial situation in the UK forced it to withdraw from its bases in the east of Suez. The British left Aden in 1967, Bahrain in 1971, and the Maldives in 1976.

▲ *The Free Officers being welcomed by the crowds in Cairo in the months following the 1952 Revolution. The four men standing in the car are, from left to right: Youssef Seddik, Salah Salem, Gamal Abdel Nasser, and Abdel Latif Boghdadi*

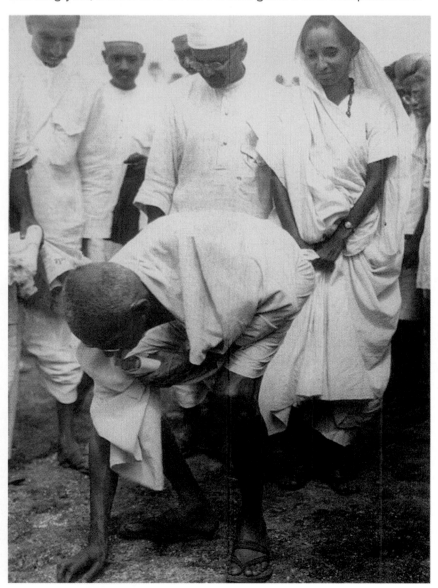

◀ *Mahatma Gandhi led a vast crowd of men and women to pick salt during the Salt Satyagraha, defying the British choke-hold over this necessary commodity*

Women's Suffrage

By the end of the 19th century, most democracies acknowledged that all men had certain inviolable rights. This included the right to vote for their government. Sadly, women were still kept under the thumbs of their husbands or fathers. This changed in the late 19th and early 20th centuries, when women began participating more outside their homes. They showed effective leadership in organising moral reforms. During the war years, they took over important roles that kept the country running. Over this period, women fought for equal civil rights. This began with the movements for suffrage—a term that meant the right to vote in political elections.

▲ The first women's rights convention was held from 19–20 July 1848 at Seneca Falls, New York, and was organised by activists such as Elizabeth Cady Stanton

▲ South Australia granted women the right to stand for Parliament in 1895; the South Australian teacher, journalist and suffragist Catherine Helen Spence stood for office in 1897!

▲ A German election poster from 1919 states, 'Equal rights – equal duties!'

A Voice for Women

In the UK, two main movements sprung up in the campaign for women's rights. Some newspapers belittled the groups with names such as the suffragists and the suffragettes. They wore the colours purple, white, and green. They made banners, badges, and sashes displaying the words 'Votes for Women'. However, the two groups had very different ways of drawing attention to their cause.

▲ British suffragettes with their banners outside Police Court; they are led by Mabel Capper who was imprisoned six times and was force-fed during her hunger strike

Suffragists

Members of the National Union of Women's Suffrage Societies (NUWSS) were called suffragists. At the height of the movement (1890–1919), they were led by the moderate champion Dame Millicent Garrett Fawcett. The suffragists believed in non-violent protests. They sought votes for the middle class, better education for women, and the right for women to own property. Their hard work led Congress to raise many bills in favour of women's suffrage.

▶ The statue of Dame Millicent Fawcett in London

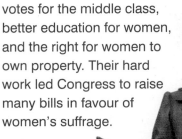

Suffragettes

Emmeline Pankhurst, an NUWSS member, became frustrated with the peaceful approach. She decided to form her own society, which she named the Women's Social and Political Union (WSPU). The club's motto was 'Deeds Not Words'. From 1905 onwards, their campaigns became increasingly violent. They used aggressive tactics—such as hunger strikes, handcuffing themselves at public places, breaking windows, and even planting bombs—to get people to listen.

▲ Emmeline Pankhurst arrested by police outside Buckingham Palace while trying to petition King George V in May 1914

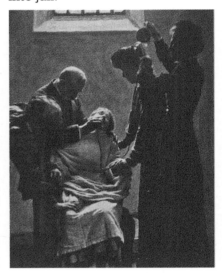
War Efforts

When WWI broke out, able-bodied men were sent away to fight in foreign lands. The role of women in society changed drastically! In addition to cooking, washing, cleaning, and raising their children, they now also did the many essential jobs in society and industry. They even worked in dangerous factories making weapons and explosives for the war!

▶ Women working in a gas-mask factory in Geneva, Switzerland

The Representation of the Peoples Act

After the war ended in 1918, the UK Parliament granted *some* women—that is, women who were at least 30 and owned property—the right to vote. In 1920, the American Congress passed a law granting suffrage. It was only in 1928 that women in the UK received equal suffrage with men. However, the fight for women's rights across the globe was far from over.

▶ In 1918, Irish revolutionary and politician Constance Markievicz (1868–1927) became the first woman elected to the British House of Commons. A year later, she was appointed to the cabinet as Minister for Labour

▲ The first women representatives in Japanese government, 1946

South Africa and Apartheid

The word apartheid means 'apart-hood'. Apartheid was a system of racial separation, where people of colour were forced to live apart and follow different rules from white people. Over 1948–94, it was enforced by the government of South Africa. The country of largely black people and those with mixed ancestry faced harsh inequalities under the rule of white men.

Living under Apartheid

Certain areas of South Africa—including residential neighbourhoods, schools, hotels, restaurants, shops, public toilets and even train compartments—were reserved for white people. Black people were forced to live in strictly watched townships and 'tribal homelands'. They had to carry identification papers wherever they went. It became a crime for black and white people to marry each other. When people of colour broke the law, they were severely punished or jailed. If they protested the atrocities of apartheid, they were branded as communists and put in jail.

▲ *Sign at a public beach declaring the area 'whites-only'*

The African National Congress

In the 1950s, rebellions against apartheid began to gather pace. The protests were called the Defiance Campaign. The most influential group of protesters was the African National Congress (ANC). Young activists like Nelson Mandela, Walter Sisulu, and Oliver Tambo encouraged non-violent mass action to bring down the white supremacy. The ANC was originally formed in 1912, when it was called the South African Native National Congress (SANNC). The movement began with educated and elite black people. In 1919, they sent a petition to London asking for a better deal for South African blacks, but nothing came of it. Gradually, their opposition became stronger, louder and by the 1950s, outright militant!

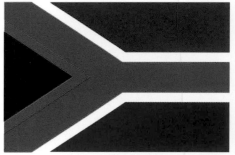

▲ *The multi-coloured flag of South Africa was adopted after the end of apartheid*

The Sharpeville Massacre

On 21 March 1960, thousands of people gathered in the township of Sharpeville to protest the enforced carrying of identity cards. South African police opened fire on the crowd. They killed 69 and wounded 180. All the victims were black. Most had been shot in the back. The horrified country erupted in riots, marches, and strikes. The government declared a state of emergency and jailed black leaders and thousands of others. The ANC now began to take a more militaristic approach against the apartheid government. Its leader Nelson Mandela co-founded the 'Umkhonto we Sizwe', meaning *Spear of the Nation*. The new group was the armed wing of the African National Congress. Its mission was to fight against the South African government.

▶ *Graves of the people killed during the Sharpeville Massacre*

Soweto Uprising

On 16 June 1976, thousands of school students began a peaceful protest on the streets of the Soweto township. Things turned violent when the police set their trained dog on the protesters, who then killed it. The police switched to firing at the children, killing 176 and injuring hundreds more. This day is now marked as a public holiday called Youth Day.

▶ *Among the first to die was a 13-year-old boy named Hector Pieterson. He became a major symbol of the uprising*

International Pressure

The atrocities of the South African government became a subject of international condemnation. In the 1980s, many nations started to pressure South Africa to end apartheid. They cut off business ties and imposed **economic sanctions** against the South African government. Sports teams from the country were barred from international events. Under extreme pressure, the government began to reluctantly relax some of the apartheid laws slowly. It was still not enough. Violence and protests continued throughout the 1980s.

▲ *A 'Boycott Apartheid' bus in London*

Freedom from Apartheid

On 2 February 1990, F. W. de Klerk, President of South Africa, declared the end of apartheid. He lifted the ban on political parties like the ANC. He also released Nelson Mandela from prison. Over the next few years, all apartheid laws were abolished. For the first time in 1994, people of all colour voted in government elections. The ANC won and Nelson Mandela became the President of South Africa.

Incredible Individuals

A lawyer by trade, Nelson Mandela (1918–2013) was one of the firebrand leaders of the ANC. After the Sharpeville massacre, he led military action against the state with a group called the Umkhonto we Sizwe. They even bombed government buildings. Nelson was arrested in 1962. He spent 27 years in jail! During this time, he became a symbol for his people and the figurehead of the anti-apartheid struggle.

▲ *Nelson Mandela, 1994*

In Real Life

The South African stand-up comedian Trevor Noah is the son of a white man and a black woman. His hilarious yet touching book *Born A Crime* tells the most amazing stories about his childhood under the tyranny of apartheid.

▲ *Noah performing his comic routine in 2019*

Imperial and Soviet Russia

Starting in 1917, Russian idealists led the people in a series of violent protests to overthrow the monarchy and establish a new form of government. This was the Russian Revolution. The imperial government of Tsar Nicholas II—the last of the Romanov dynasty—gave way to the Soviet Union. The new state was governed by Vladimir Lenin (1870–1924) and his group of revolutionaries, who were called the Bolsheviks. They followed the principles of communism.

▲ *Vladimir Lenin, the first head of Soviet Russia*

Bloody Sunday

On 22 January 1905, a large body of workers marched to the Tsar's palace demanding better working conditions. Rather than listening to them, the government sent soldiers to shoot down the people. Nearly 200 people died. This horrific day is called Bloody Sunday. It destroyed any reverence the nation had for its ruler. The Tsar had become the enemy of the people!

World War I

In 1914, Imperial Russia forced its masses to join the army and fight against Germany in WWI. The soldiers were neither trained nor equipped with proper weapons. Many didn't even get shoes or food. Nearly two million Russians died in the war; another five million were grievously wounded. The Russian people raged against the Tsar for entering the war and for sending their young men to be killed.

▲ *Rows of soldiers stand by the triumphal arch of Narva Gate and prepare to fire upon the approaching protesters, led by the priest Gregory Gapon*

▲ *Russian troops marching to the war front*

◄ *Russian and German soldiers meet in 'no man's land' (the disputed ground between two armies facing each other)*

▲ *WWI poster from Russia showing the world on fire*

The February Revolution

Tired of war rations and state corruption, on 8 March 1917 (28 February according to the Russian calendar), Russian workers went on strike. Many banded together and started rioting. Once more, the Tsar ordered his soldiers to fire upon the mobs. This time though, the soldiers refused! The army **mutinied** against the Tsar. With no power, the Tsar was forced to give up his throne. A temporary government took over. It was run by two groups—the Petrograd Soviet (who represented the workers and soldiers) and the Provisional Government (the traditional government without the Tsar).

▲ Workers of Putilov factory protesting on 8 March

▲ Surrounded by ministers and generals, Tsar Nicholas II signs his abdication in the royal train

▲ Burning of Tsarist symbols in front of the Annen Palace in St. Petersburg

Red October

One of the main parties of the Petrograd Soviet were the Bolsheviks. They wanted a communist government for Russia. The Bolshevik Revolution of October 1917 gave Lenin full control of the state. He set up the first communist-ruled country in the world. The royal family was placed under house arrest. Red October is the term for the events that took place over this month. Russia signed the Peace Treaty of Brest-Litovsk with Germany and exited WWI. The new government began the industrialisation of the country. It also reformed laws concerning religion and land ownership. Women now had the same legal rights as men.

▲ The Bolshevik, a 1920 oil painting by Russian artist Boris Kustodiev (1878–1927)

Civil War

In July 1918, countries such as the US, UK, France, and Japan sent armies to support anti-Bolshevik groups to overthrow the communist government. This plunged the country into civil war. During 1918–20, the Bolsheviks (Red Army) fought against the anti-Bolsheviks (White Army). Lenin diverted food and supplies to his army. As a result, some 3–10 million people died of starvation. The Bolsheviks won and named the new country USSR (Union of Soviet Socialist Republics). Several countries of the former Russian Empire, such as Estonia and Ukraine, became independent of the new nation.

▶ Posters such as this White Army poster of a white knight destroying the Red Army dragon fired up the people to fight for their cause; they never showed the dead bodies or starved, homeless masses that were the true images of war

China Becomes a Republic

At the start of the 20th century, China was ruled by the Qing dynasty of emperors. Because of a number of natural disasters, famine, internal rebellions, and war with Japan, he empire was weak and the people unhappy. In October 1911, the Wuchang Uprising brought down the Qing emperor and the Republic of China was established.

▲ *Rebels ambush the Imperial army during the Wuchang Uprising; a print created by wartime artist T. Minyano, c. 1920*

▲ *This photo, taken in 1922, shows Puyi (1906–67), the last emperor of China, who was forced to abdicate in 1912*

🕐 Wuchang Uprising

The uprising started out as an accident. At the time, revolutionaries of the New Army were building bombs to use against the Qing government. One of the bombs accidentally exploded. When the police arrived on the scene, the New Army revolted rather than face arrest. The local government panicked and fled. When the Qing emperor failed to respond, the revolutionaries quickly set up a temporary government. Soon, other provinces and revolutionaries followed their example. Over a month, the leaders of these provinces met and declared the Republic of China! Yuan Shikai—a wily minister of the Qing dynasty—persuaded the last emperor, a six-year-old boy named Puyi, to give up the throne. Shikai then took power as President of the Republic of China.

▲ *The revolutionary army attacks Nanking and crosses a stream, a T. Minyano print of an episode in the revolutionary war of 1911*

◀ *President Yuan Shikai in 1915*

▲ *Rebels fire canons in the Defense of Yangxia (18 October–1 December 1911), the largest military engagement of the Wuchang Uprising*

The Early Republic

A popular revolutionary leader at the time was Dr Sun Yat-Sen (1866–1925). He worked towards creating a Chinese government based on Three Principles of the People—nationalism, democracy and the livelihood of the people. Fearing his rise, Yuan Shikai suppressed his political party, the Kuomintang. In 1915, Yuan tried to restore the monarchy and made himself emperor. This was opposed by the revolutionaries and by his own military commanders. Yuan was forced down. A few months later, he died of kidney failure.

◀ *The Yuan Shikai 'dollar' (yuan in Chinese) was first issued in 1914 and became a dominant coin type of the Republic of China*

The Long March

Since 1927, the Kuomintang had been at loggerheads with another political group—the Communist Party. The Communist Army was led by Mao Zedong and Zhou Enlai. In 1934, it was almost completely annihilated by Chiang Kai Shek's troops in southern China. But the communists escaped on a long, circuitous route that ultimately went over some 8,000 kilometres and 370 days. This was a period of great fatigue, sickness, desertion, and loss for the Communist Army. Of the 90,000 strong body, only some 20,000 made it to the final destination in 1935. But this time also allowed the Army to rebuild itself in northern China.

Mao Zedong Takes Over

Following the end of WWII, the Communist Army (later called the People's Liberation Army) returned to fight the Kuomintang. This time, it was victorious. Chiang Kai-shek and the Kuomintang fled to Taiwan, where the party is still active today. On 1 October 1949, Mao Zedong declared a new country, the People's Republic of China (PRC) from Beijing.

The Warlord Era

Yuan Shikai's death left a power vacuum in China. This marked the rise of regional warlords who fought to take over the government in Beijing. Various warlords came and went, but none who could establish a unified China. Meanwhile, Sun Yat-Sen—and then his successor Chiang Kai Shek—gradually won greater and greater territories. Over 1917–27, they united the country and brought an end to the warlord era. In 1928, Kuomintang forces took Beijing and became the recognised national government.

▲ *Sun Yat-Sen (seated) and Chiang Kai Shek*

▲ *Zhou Enlai (1898–1976) was the first Premier of the People's Republic of China, serving as head of government under Chairman Mao Zedong*

◀ *Chairman Mao Zedong (1893–1976) proclaims the founding of the People's Republic of China*

Arab Spring

Beginning in 2010–11, countries in the Middle East and North Africa saw a wave of pro-democracy protests and uprisings. This period is called the Arab Spring. Events began in African Tunisia and spread rapidly to Egypt, Libya, Yemen, and Syria. Major protests were seen in Algeria, Iran, Jordan, Morocco, Sudan, and a number of other places. The resulting riots and civil wars toppled authoritarian regimes. Sadly, they didn't all lead to the establishment of healthy democracies. But it showed people across the globe that millions of people living in Islamic nations wanted free expression and democratic governance.

▶ Protests in Tahrir Square

◀ Zine El Abidine Ben Ali with George W. Bush at the White House in 2004

17 Dec 2010

A 26-year-old vegetable seller, Mohamed Bouazizi, set himself on fire after police seized his stall—his livelihood. Tunisian streets erupted in protests, marking the start of the Jasmine Revolution against the Tunisian government.

14 Jan 2011

After 23 years of iron-fisted rule, Tunisian President Zine El Abidine Ben Ali resigned and fled to Saudi Arabia. The coverage of the protests over social media galvanised the people of neighbouring countries, particularly Oman, Yemen, Egypt, Syria, and Morocco.

25 Jan 2011

Thousands of protesters gathered in Tahrir Square, in the Egyptian capital of Cairo, for 18 days. They demanded the resignation of President Hosni Mubarak.

11 Feb 2011

After 30 years in power, President Hosni Mubarak of Egypt resigned. The Supreme Council of the Armed Forces took over, bringing in a new period of chaos and instability.

Zine El Abidine Ben Ali was sentenced to prison by a Tunisian court.

15 Jul 2012

The Red Cross officially declared the Syrian uprising as a civil war. The following February, the UN gave the death toll of the war at over 70,000.

13 Jun 2012

2 Jun 2012

Hosni Mubarak was sentenced to life in prison.

27 Feb 2012

Ali Abdullah Saleh, dictator of Yemen, resigned. He was killed in 2017, while the country was engulfed in a civil war.

◀ On 24 April 2012, the minaret of the Great Mosque of Aleppo, which was built in 1090, was destroyed in the heavy weapons' crossfire between the Syrian government and rebel forces

▶ Hosni Mubarak

▶ Ali Abdullah Saleh, former dictator of Yemen

In February 2011, demonstrators in many Muslim-majority countries staged a 'Day of Rage' to honour political martyrs, oppose dictatorial governments, and push for democracy

◀ Yemeni protesters with banners and pink bandannas

President Ali Abdullah Saleh of Yemen was injured in a failed assassination attempt.

15 Feb 2011

Protests broke out against the Muammar Gaddafi's authoritarian regime in Libya. The uprising soon turned into the Libyan Civil War.

15 Mar 2011

Pro-democracy rallies began in Syria.

3 Jun 2011

1 Jul 2011

Moroccans passed constitutional changes limiting the power of their monarchy.

20 Aug 2011

In the Battle of Tripoli, rebels captured Libya's capital city of Tripoli, all but overthrowing the dictator Muammar Gaddafi.

◀ Pro-democracy protesters in Casablanca; on 22 May 2011, the police beats thousands of them in Morocco

20 Dec 2011

Egyptian women rose in protest against human rights abuses.

28 Nov 2011

Egypt held its first democratic parliamentary elections. President Morsi was elected in June 2012, but removed in a coup in July 2013.

23 Oct 2011

Tunisia held its first democratic parliamentary elections.

20 Oct 2011

Gaddafi was captured by rebels in the city of Sirte. He was tortured and killed.

▶ Libyan dictator Muammar Gaddafi

WARS

THE WORLD AT **WAR**

The medieval era came to an end with the invention of firearms. Once soldiers could shoot from a distance, pitched battles on the open field between huge armies and cavalry became a thing of the past. Warfare developed new strategies. Manoeuvres like the *tercio*—pike and sword tactics combined with blocks of **arquebusiers**—were developed. War now involved long campaigns and sieges. Battles that were fought on the open field often led to large numbers of wounded and dead. For the first time, nations developed standing armies. These were **battalions** of trained, professional soldiers who were in the government's pay all year long, whether or not there was a conflict. Nations also needed greater treasuries to sponsor war. More money meant better arms and larger armies.

▼ An iconic piece of war art, the *Surrender of Breda*, by the brilliant artist Diego Velazquez, shows Dutch leader Justinus van Nassau relinquishing the key to the city of Breda. Strikingly, the victorious Spanish general, Ambrogio Spinola, treats the opposite party with courtesy, placing a friendly arm on van Nassau's shoulder

The Thirty Years' War

Over 1618–48, German lands became the battlefield for a calamitous war that involved power-hungry European countries such as France, Spain, and Sweden. This Thirty Years' War began as a fight between Catholic and Protestant Christians. The two sects had been at loggerheads since the 16th century. The Catholic Habsburg dynasty and others saw the war as an opportunity to gain more land and influence. Their armies pillaged and burnt towns and villages, over and over again. People were robbed, tortured, and killed. Famine and disease followed poverty in every state that faced battle. Millions of people died and it was the worst war of its century. The war ended with the Treaty of Westphalia, but its shattering effects lasted a long time afterwards.

▲ *The Peace of Westphalia was a series of peace treaties signed over May–October 1648 by 109 parties, including all the major nations of Europe. The map of Europe changed as new boundaries were established. The Peace also gave Catholics and Protestants equal rights*

The Bohemian Revolt (1618–1620)

In 1617, the Holy Roman Emperor Matthias, who had no children of his own, decided to name his cousin Ferdinand of Styria the heir to his Bohemian Kingdom. Ferdinand was a fervent Catholic, while Bohemia had a large protestant population. Some of the Protestants were worried that Ferdinand would take away their religious rights. In 1618, Ferdinand sent two Catholic councillors to Prague Castle to rule in his place. On 23 May, a group of Protestants seized the men and—along with secretary Philip Fabricius—threw them out of the palace window, which was some 17 m above the ground! This event came to be known as the (Second) Defenestration of Prague. It marked the start of the Bohemian Revolt. The conflict spread quickly, and soon involved vast numbers of Protestants and Catholics across Europe.

▲ *The Bohemian Revolt ended with the Battle of Bila Hora (White Mountain). The rebel troops were put down by Ferdinand's army with support from the German Catholic League, led by Count Tilly. The Count's marauding armies were responsible for thousands of deaths during the first half of the Thirty Years' War, until he was crushed in 1631 by a cannonball while facing the Swedish armies of King Gustavus Adolphus*

Isn't It Amazing!

Surprisingly, the **defenestrated** men survived their long drop to the ground. The Catholics claimed that angels appeared and carried them to safety. The Protestants said that they landed in a pile of dung, which saved their lives!

▲ *A woodcut depicting the Second Defenestration of Prague*

French Wars of Religion

In the mid- to late- 16ᵗʰ century, millions of French people died in violent conflicts between Protestants (called Huguenots) and Catholics. The wars were also fuelled by the hunger of the French lords to wrest power away from their monarch.

▲ *In 1545, King Francis I of France ordered the Massacre of Merindol. Thousands of Protestants in Merindol and its surrounding villages were slaughtered or taken away as **galley slaves***

Catherine de' Medici

The greater part of the war took place during the reign of Catherine de' Medici, Queen of France. She became regent for her underage son Charles IX in 1560. Certain noble families—like the Catholic House of Guise—saw her rule as a chance to increase their power. This forced the Catholic queen to ally with the Huguenot House of Bourbon. Fighting broke out after the Guises attacked and slaughtered people at a Huguenot service. Eventually, the Duke of Guise was killed and a temporary truce was signed in 1563. Many were unhappy with the peace, and hostilities soon resumed, leading to two more attempts at peace in 1568 and 1570.

St Bartholomew's Day Massacre

On 18 August 1572, many notable Huguenots were gathered in Paris for the marriage of the king's sister to Henry of Navarre. By this time, Catherine was allied with the Catholics. She convinced her son, Charles IX, to grab this opportunity of getting rid of the Protestants' opposition. They set their plan in motion soon after the wedding. On the eve of St. Bartholomew's Day, thousands of Huguenots were slaughtered in Paris. Many more died in the provinces in the following days.

War of the Three Henrys

Charles IX died in 1574 and was succeeded by Henry III. In 1584, Henry's heir died. This made the Protestant Henry of Navarre the new heir. The Catholic head of the Guise family—another Henry—found this unacceptable. In 1588, Paris rose with the Guises against the king, who fled the city. In the ensuing negotiations, Henry of Guise was trapped and assassinated. In 1589, Henry III was also assassinated, leaving Henry of Navarre to claim the throne. The practical King Henry IV converted to Catholicism and ended the war by issuing the Edict of Nantes, which granted equal rights to Catholics and Huguenots.

▲ *Henry of Navarre needed to retake the staunchly Catholic Paris to unite his kingdom. With the famous phrase 'Paris vaut bien une messe' (Paris is worth a Mass), he announced his conversion to Catholicism and was crowned as Henry IV at Chartres in 1594*

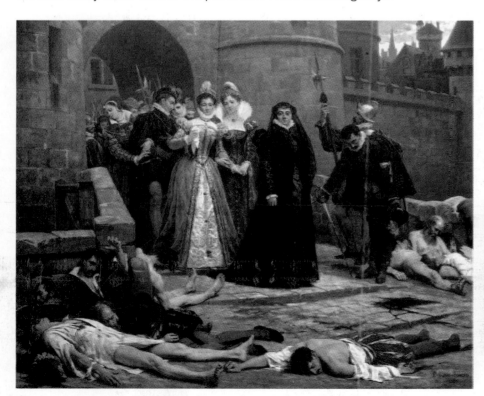

▲ *One Morning in Front of the Gate of Louvre shows Catherine de' Medici (in black) gazing upon the corpses of Protestants who died in the St. Bartholomew's Day Massacre*

The Napoleonic Wars

Napoleon Bonaparte (1769–1821) was a French soldier who rose to power during the French Revolution. In 1804, he took the title of emperor. Over the next decade, he waged many bloody wars across Europe, gaining an empire that included Spain, Portugal, Italy, and great swathes of modern-day Germany and Poland. He was ultimately defeated by an alliance of Great Britain, Prussia, Austria, Russia, Sweden, and others. These wars changed the way European armies fought, bringing in new technologies, tactics, and artillery. They were also enormously destructive for the **conscripted** men. The Napoleonic Wars ended with the restoration of the unpopular Bourbon dynasty of kings to France in 1815.

▲ On 18 May 1804, Napoleon Bonaparte was crowned emperor at Notre-Dame. He then placed a crown on the head of his wife Josephine, crowning her the Queen of France

▲ The Peninsular War (1808–14) refers to Napoleon's conquest and occupation of Spain and Portugal. Francisco Goya (1746–1828) created a masterpiece of war art by painting an incident from May 1808 in which Spanish rebels ferociously turned on French soldiers

 ## Battle of Austerlitz

In 1805, Napoleon crowned himself King of Italy. This enraged the Holy Roman Emperor, Francis II, who also owned territory in Italy. Allying with Russia, he sent a force of almost 90,000 soldiers against 68,000 French troops. They met on 2 December 1805, near a town called Austerlitz. Within two days, the allied armies had scattered in defeat. Austria was forced to sign a treaty with Napoleon in which it conceded so much money and land that the Holy Roman Empire came to an end.

▶ Napoleon meets Francis II after the Battle of Austerlitz

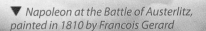

▼ Napoleon at the Battle of Austerlitz, painted in 1810 by Francois Gerard

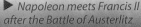

The Battle of Trafalgar

On 21 October 1805, the British navy—under Admiral Horatio Nelson—destroyed the French and Spanish fleets off Cape Trafalgar (in southwest Spain). Twenty-two ships were lost—none of them were British. Admiral Nelson, already famous from victories against the French at the 1798 Battle of Nile, died on his ship, pierced by a sniper's bullet. He became a national hero and the victory established Britain as the world's greatest naval power for a hundred years.

▲ The miserable retreat from Russia to Paris with many men dying by the wayside

▲ The Death of Nelson by Daniel Maclise. Nelson legendarily put his telescope to his 'blind' eye when he was told that there was a sign to retreat, giving us the phrase 'turning a blind eye'

▲ On 7 March 1815, Napoleon faced the French regiment that had come to arrest him. He shouted, 'Here I am. Kill your Emperor, if you wish.' The soldiers cried, 'Long live the Emperor!' They followed him back to Paris in whopping numbers. The unpopular Louis XVIII fled to Belgium

The Invasion of Russia

Napoleon's ambitions faced their first major check during his 1812 invasion of Russia. Rather than fight him in a face-off, the brilliant Russian General Kutuzov simply retreated with the troops and civilians into the vast Russian lands. They burnt all farms and towns behind them—even Moscow. Napoleon found an empty land with no food for his vast hordes of soldiers. With winter setting in, his army was forced to retreat to Paris empty-handed. Thousands died of starvation and cold in the long, freezing winter march. The event greatly reduced the strength of France, and made Napoleon vulnerable in later wars.

▲ British commander Wellington and his officers amidst the raging battlefield at Waterloo. Near the bottom left, the wounded Prince of Orange is being carried away. In the background the battle is raging

Abdication and Exile

In 1813, allied Europe defeated Napoleon at the Battle of Leipzig. Paris was captured and the brother of the old French king (who had been executed during the French Revolution) was crowned as Louis XVIII. In 1814, Napoleon was exiled to the island of Elba. On 26 February 1815, he escaped. He later returned to Paris and was joyously received by his soldiers. This marked the start of the Hundred Days. Once more, the allied powers of Europe joined against Napoleon. On 18 June 1815, the Duke of Wellington defeated him. The following month, Napoleon was exiled to the island of St. Helena, a remote island in the Mid-Atlantic which was 1,931 kilometres away from the African coast, where he died on 5 May 1821.

▼ Napoleon at St. Helena, where he was kept under strict watch, denied any newspapers, and subjected to a curfew as well.

Wars of Unification

'The empire, long divided, must unite; long united, must divide.' This quote from the ancient Chinese epic *The Romance of the Three Kingdoms* surmises the history of how long-divided territories in Europe united to form two nations—Italy and Germany. After the fall of Napoleon, the victorious powers met at the Congress of Vienna (1814–1815) and redrew the boundaries of European states. The areas that we now know as Germany and Italy were just a conglomeration of states till then.

Risorgimento

The political and social movements that led to the unification of Italy fall in the period of Risorgimento, meaning 'resurgence'. In the 19th century, different Italian states merged into the Kingdom of Italy. Soon after the 1815 Congress of Vienna, the Kingdom of Sardinia began its conquest of the Italian peninsula. The peninsular kingdom was ruled by the Savoy dynasty and had its capital in Turin. The conquest ended on 20 September 1870 with the acquisition of the Papal States. Rome became the capital of the new Italian Kingdom. Some of the most prominent men of this time were the influential philosopher and statesman Giuseppe Mazzini; the heroic fighter Giuseppe Garibaldi; the indefatigable officer and politician Camillo Benso, Count of Cavour; and the man who became the first king of united Italy, Victor Emmanuel II.

▲ *Victor Emmanuel II (1820–78) was King of Sardinia from 1849 until 17 March 1861. He then assumed the title of King of Italy until his death in 1878. The Italians called him Padre della Patria—Father of the Fatherland*

▲ *Garibaldi's unifying forces welcomed by the people of Naples, September 1860*

▲ *A political cartoon from 1861 shows Cavour and Garibaldi 'cobbling' Italy together; the boot represents the boot-shaped Italian peninsula*

The Carbonari

Before the Napoleonic wars, there was no thought of a united Italy. After that era, Italian leaders began to see a union as the only way to stand up to the rest of Europe. In the early 19th century, Italian rebels formed a secret political group called the Carbonari. In 1814, they began a revolution in Naples. In 1820, they led an army into Naples and forced the king to swear an oath to a new Italian constitution.

▶ *Citizens shot for reading Mazzini's journals, from the Life of Giuseppe Garibaldi, Italian hero and patriot (1888)*

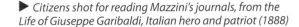

▲ Italian painter Carlo Bossoli (1815–84) captured the jubilant royal procession at the opening of the Parliament in the Kingdom of Italy

▲ On 20 September 1870, the breach of the Porta Pia gate, on the walls of Rome, soon led to the capture of the city from Pope Pius IX

The Unification of Germany

In the early 19th century, there were as many as 300 German-speaking states in Central Europe. Some of them were no larger than 8 kilometres across! After the Napoleonic Wars, they feared that the two powerful nations of Austria and Prussia would have an unfair advantage in a unified Germany. Nevertheless, the Prussian Chancellor Otto von Bismarck—through war and diplomacy—ensured that the nations came together under a single ruler. He engineered it so well that the Prussian ruler Wilhelm I became the first Kaiser (Caesar) of Germany.

▲ Wilhelm I is proclaimed German Emperor on 18 January 1871, in the Hall of Mirrors in the Palace of Versailles, France

▲ King Wilhelm on a black horse, with Bismarck, Moltke and others, watching the Battle of Königgrätz, 1866, between Prussia and Austria

The Franco-Prussian War

In the 1860s, Bismarck brought all the German states—except Austria—under Prussian control. Napoleon III of France felt that this shifted the power balance in Europe, and declared war. This resulted into the Franco-Prussian War that started on 19 July 1870. Under the military command of Field Marshal Helmuth von Moltke, the Prussians gained victory in January 1871. In the Hall of Mirrors at France's Palace of Versailles, the German princes declared a united German nation. Wilhelm I of Prussia was proclaimed the first German Kaiser. A formal treaty ending the war was signed on 10 May 1871.

▶ After the Battle of Sedan on 1 September 1870, Napoleon III of France surrendered by symbolically handing over his sword to Wilhelm I

⊙ Incredible Individuals

Prince Otto von Bismarck (1815–1898) was the leading statesman of 19th century Germany. He was the Prime Minister of Prussia between 1862–90. As the main architect of the German Empire, he became its first chancellor. Bismarck also waged wars against Denmark (1864) and Austria (1866) to acquire more land for Germany.

▶ The 'Iron Chancellor', inspired his people enough that his name was given to one of the most feared ships of WWII, the Bismarck

Conquest of the New World

Until the 15ᵗʰ century, most people thought that the world contained only Asia, Africa, and Europe. In 1492, the Genoese captain Christopher Columbus, while looking for a new passage to Asia, landed on western shores. He mistook the land for India. The Italian merchant-explorer Amerigo Vespucci (1454–1512) explained that this was, in fact, a New World. The unknown continent was called America in his honour. The Americas—North and South—soon developed a reputation for riches. European monarchs sent colonisers and **conquistadors** to explore and occupy the new territory. In the ensuing wars, Native Americans were forcibly subjugated, ousted, or slaughtered.

▲ *Vespucci Awakens America, an allegorical engraving by Belgian artist Jan Galle (1600–1676)*

1492

Sailing for the co-monarchs Isabella and Ferdinand of Spain, Columbus reaches the islands known to us as The Bahamas, Cuba, and Hispaniola. He establishes La Isabela, one of the first European settlements in the Americas.

1496

Columbus's brother Bartholomew Columbus establishes Santo Domingo, the first permanent European settlement in the Americas and the first base for Spanish colonial rule here.

1497

Commissioned by English King Henry VII, Venetian explorer John Cabot discovers (and claims) Canada—specifically landing in modern-day Cape Bonavista in Newfoundland.

▶ *In 1514, the Spanish founded a Cuban settlement in the area that would become Havana*

1511

The Spanish conquest of Cuba begins under conquistador Diego Velazquez de Cuellar. Chief Hautey of the local Tainos people leads guerrilla campaigns against the Spanish. Over 3 years, Hautey and other chiefs are captured and burnt.

1763

The French-Indian War ends with the Treaty of Paris on 10 February. France loses all its lands east of the Mississippi River. All of Canada, barring two small islands, is handed over to Britain. Britain also acquires the Spanish colony of Florida.

▶ *French forces surrendering at Montreal in 1760*

1754

The French-Indian War breaks out between what is now the US and Canada. The French fight the British. Both are supported by separate groups of Native American allies.

▶ *French and Native American forces ambush British soldiers near Monongahela River, 1755*

◀ The fall of
the Aztec city
Tenochtitlan in 1521

▲ The funeral of Atahualpa on 26 July 1533

1519-21

In the conquest of
Mexico, an expedition
of 508 men and 16
horses led by Hernan
Cortes discovers
and destroys the
mysterious Aztec
Civilisation. Coupled
with an epidemic that
killed 80 per cent of
the people, by 1680,
94% of the Aztec
population is dead.

1524

Pedro de Alvarado
(c. 1485–1541)
conquers most of
Central America,
including present-
day Guatemala,
Honduras, and
El Salvador.

1531–33

Conquistadors Francisco
Pizarro and Diego de
Almagro take 180 men
and 37 horses to Peru
and invade the Incas.
Through deception and
the power of gunpowder,
they plunder the Incan
empire and its rich capital
of Cuzco. Atahualpa
(c. 1502–33), the last
Incan emperor, is
captured, exploited,
and then executed.

1535

Explorer Jacques
Cartier (1491–1557)
reaches Quebec and
claims, what is now
Canada for France.
The French are,
however, unable to
establish permanent
colonies owing to
weather, disease,
and war.

1664

The English acquire
the Dutch colony of
New Netherland and
rename its capital
New York.

1620

Passengers (mostly English
Puritans) set sail for the
Americas on the *Mayflower*.

1607

The colony of Jamestown, Virginia
becomes the first permanent
English settlement in the Americas.

1579

Sir Francis Drake
claims New Albion
(a part of modern
California) for England.

◀ In autumn 1621, the
Mayflower settlers offered
thanksgiving for their first
harvest, sharing their bounty
with Native Americans

American Civil War

Over 1861–65, the USA was embroiled in a civil war over the issue of slavery. Eleven Southern states wanted slavery to be legal. They also aspired to be a separate country. They joined together to form the Confederate States of America. The states that declared slavery illegal and remained loyal to the US government were called the Union. Most of these states lay in the North. There were also five 'border states', that supported the Union but still engaged in legalised slavery. The war between the Union and the Confederates began on 12 April 1861, when the latter attacked Fort Sumter, which was held by a Union **garrison**. The war ended in victory for the Union.

▲ Jefferson Davis (1808–89) was the sole President of the Confederates, serving over the period of the Civil War

▲ The Union was governed by Abraham Lincoln (1809–65), 16th President of the USA, who proved to be an inspiring leader in this time of moral crisis and war

▲ Bombardment of Fort Sumter

 ## Fighting Begins

Fort Sumter was under Union control but lay in the Confederate State of South Carolina. Union soldiers were forced to surrender it after the Southerners attacked in April 1861. In response, President Lincoln called for volunteers from every Union state to join the Union Army. The United States Navy also **blockaded** the Confederate ships. This prevented them from selling their goods and acquiring weapons.

▶ Published in Harpers' Weekly: The Great Meeting in Union Square, New York, to Support the Government, 20 April 1861

▼ On 5 August 1864, the Battle of Mobile Bay resulted in the blockade of the last major Confederate port

The Battles of Bull Run

On 21 July 1861, the Confederates fought and won the first Battle of Bull Run in Virginia. In 1862, Lincoln's Army launched a series of battles, called the Peninsula Campaign, to capture Virginia's capital, Richmond. Southern general Robert E Lee (1807–70) defeated the Union army. In August, he won the second Battle of Bull Run. Lee pushed further to end the war by invading Maryland, but lost the Battle of Antietam and retreated to Virginia.

▲ *First Battle of Bull Run*

▲ *Second Battle of Bull Run*

Fighting in the West

A great deal of the war happened along the Mississippi River. Over 1682–83, Union general Ulysses S Grant (1822–85) forced back the Confederates from Kentucky and western Tennessee. Through his efforts, the North captured nearly all of the Mississippi. The Confederacy continued to hold the key city and fort of Vicksburg. In May 1863, Grant began the Siege of Vicksburg. On 4 July, the Confederates surrendered. This split the Confederacy into two and marked a turning point in the war.

▲ *The Union's ironclad gunboats running the Confederate blockade at Vicksburg on 16 April 1863*

The Battle of Gettysburg

Lee led his army into the North again in 1863, attacking Pennsylvania. He met the Union Army near Gettysburg on 1 July and battled for three days. Some 46,000–50,000 soldiers died, making this the most devastating of the Civil War battles. The Unionists won and Lee's troops retreated once again into the South. With not enough troops to continue the war, Lee eventually surrendered on 9 April 1865. Other Confederate Generals followed suit. On 23 June 1865, the last Southern leader, Brigadier General Stand Watie—the only Native American general in the Confederacy—laid down arms in Oklahoma.

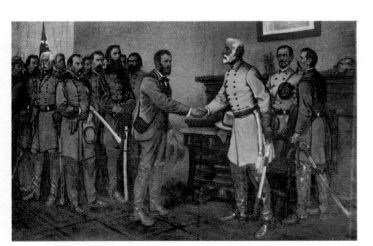
▲ *General Lee surrenders to General Grant at the Appomattox Court House, Virginia*

The Aftermath

The war devastated the South. The Reconstruction period, which lasted until 1877, saw the formal end of slavery, which further impoverished the Southerners. The US Constitution was amended to include equal rights for African Americans.

▶ *In a desire to avenge the South, stage actor John Wilkes Booth shot and killed Lincoln while he watched a play on 14 April 1865*

War of Spanish Succession

In 1700, Charles II, King of Spain, died childless. His older sister was married to Louis XIV, the Sun King of France, and their only son was the **dauphin**. Louis XIV agreed to let the dauphin's son Philip inherit Spain. Philip was proclaimed King of Spain on 16 November 1700. However, France had a long-standing law, which said that the right to rule could not be inherited through women. Therefore, Philip's rule was disputed by Charles II's cousins from the male line. This line belonged to the ruling family of Austria—the Habsburgs. Over 1701–14, Austria and France fought over the right to rule Spain.

▲ *Philip, Duke of Anjou, is recognised as Philip V, King of Spain, on 16 November 1700*

The Grand Alliance

The dispute between France and Austria led to war in 1701. A Grand Alliance of the English, Dutch and Holy Roman Empire's forces fought against France and Spain. This Alliance wanted the Spanish throne for Archduke Charles, who was the younger son of the Holy Roman Emperor. The battles overflowed into the New World colonies. In North America, it was called Queen Anne's War, after the then ruler of Great Britain.

▼ *At the battle of Almansa, 25 April 1707, the troops of Philip V of Spain defeated the troops of Archduke Charles of Austria*

Stalemate

By the end of 1706, the Alliance had gained Spanish lands in Italy and the Netherlands. They also controlled the seas. However, Archduke Charles was unpopular in Spain. So, the Allies could not hold on to the territories in the country. In 1711, the Archduke became Charles VI, Holy Roman Emperor, after his father and older brother passed away. This broke up the Allied partners, as European nations wanted neither France nor Austria to acquire Spain.

Peace in Spain

The war ended with the 1713 Treaty of Utrecht, which was followed by the 1714 Treaties of Rastatt and Baden. Britain and its allies accepted Philip as the King of Spain after he renounced his right to the French throne. Austria got most of Spanish Italy. Britain acquired Spanish Majorca and Gibraltar.

▶ *An 18th century print of the Treaty of Utrecht*

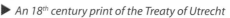

War of Austrian Succession

The daughter of Charles VI, Holy Roman Emperor, was also involved in a succession battle. Maria Theresa (1717–80) was an intelligent and able leader. Charles taught her all she needed to know to be a monarch. He even issued an edict—the Pragmatic Sanction of 1713—to ensure that his daughter would inherit his possessions. However, when Maria Theresa came to the throne, the kings and ministers of Europe declared her ineligible. This began the War of Austrian Succession, which lasted from 1740 to 1748.

▶ *Maria Theresa, with her three crowns of the Holy Roman Empire, Hungary and Bohemia*

The Silesian Campaign

The greatest thorn in Maria Theresa's side was Frederick II of Prussia. In 1740, his army swiftly invaded and took over Silesia— one of Austria's richest provinces. Silesian taxes made up 10% of the Imperial income. It had over one million people and was a major centre of the mining, weaving, and dyeing industries. In 1741, the Austrians raised an army and set off to free Silesia.

▲ *Frederick II receives the homage of Silesian representatives in 1741*

Europe Joins the War

Prussia's amazing victories in the Silesian campaign caused the rest of Europe to sit up and take notice. Here was a new military power upsetting the continent's balance! After 1741, most of Europe joined in the struggle, turning the Silesian Campaign into a larger War of Succession. Battles raged across southwest Germany, the Low Countries, and Italy. Prussia was supported by France, Spain, and Bavaria; Austria by the UK and Holland, and sometimes by Sardinia and Saxony.

▲ *Charge of the thoroughly organised Prussian infantry*

The War Ends

In 1748, the war ended with the Treaty of Aix-la-Chapelle. Maria Theresa kept all her lands except Silesia and minor territories in northern Italy. She went on to rule for 40 years! Prussia almost doubled the size of its economy, land and population. Frederick II would soon be called Frederick the Great. The war marked the start of a rivalry between two German states—Prussia and Austria—which would ultimately fuel German unification.

▶ *The Battle of Roucoux, 11 October 1746, between the French and the British, Dutch, and Austrians*

👤 In Real Life

The UK and France fought on opposite sides in the War of Austrian succession. Their battles spilled over to the colonies. In particular, it marked the start of French-British battles for supremacy in India. This series of 18th century conflicts, known as the Carnatic Wars, saw the fall of the Mughal Empire and the establishment of the British Raj.

The Great Northern War

Over 1700–21, the Great Northern War was fought between Sweden and the allied forces of Russia, Saxony, Poland, and Denmark-Norway. This was a fight between Russia and Sweden for supremacy over northern and central Europe. In 1715, the Germanic regions of Prussia and Hanover joined the war against Sweden. By this time, the ruler of Hanover had also become King George I of Great Britain.

▲ In 1701, Charles XII of Sweden crossed the Duna to fight the Battle of Riga, the first major battle in the invasion of Poland

▲ Peter the Great, the Russian monarch who modernised Russia and made it the pre-eminent power of Northeastern Europe

Swedish Victory and Retreat

Frederick IV of Denmark-Norway and Augustus II of Saxony, Poland and Lithuania were defeated by Charles XII of Sweden in 1700 and 1706 respectively. In 1709, Sweden invaded Russia. The Russian Army initially retreated, drawing the Swedes into the vast and hostile lands of wintry Russia. About half the Swedish troops died in the cold. Eventually, the two armies met in the Battle of Poltava. Russia won but Charles XII escaped and fled to the Ottoman Empire, where the Sultan captured him. Peter I of Russia then declared war on the Ottomans. This time, he lost and was forced to hand over the town of Azov to the Ottomans. The Ottomans released Charles XII in 1714. He went back to Sweden and was later shot and killed while invading Norway. Without their king, the Swedes retreated home.

▲ The 1709 Battle of Poltava

Russian Invasions

While Charles's army had been away, Russia had invaded Sweden. Peter the Great conquered Estonia, Livonia, and Ingria. By the time Swedish soldiers returned from Norway, Russia had captured Finland. Russia also used its new fleet of ships to raid the Swedish coast. Sweden surrendered in 1721. It had already made peace with Denmark in 1720. It now signed the Treaty of Nystad and other treaties that resulted in great loss of land and money. The treaty ensured the rights of German nobility living in the Baltic regions of Estonia and Livonia. They maintained their financial system, Lutheran religion and even their German language. This special position in the Russian Empire was reconfirmed by every Russian Tsar until Alexander II (ruled 1855–81). With this treaty, Russia became the dominant power of North-eastern Europe.

▲ The Skirmish at Bender, Moldove, took place on 1 February 1713 and resulted in the Turks capturing Charles XII

▶ Russian and Swedish ships engage in the Battle of Grengam, 27 July 1720, resulting in losses on both sides

The Russo-Turkish Wars

From the 16th–19th centuries, the Russians and the Ottoman Turks fought a series of wars over Crimea, the Balkans, and the Caucasus regions. This resulted in the gradual expansion of Russia and the weakening of the Ottoman Empire. The first war took place over 1676–81 and the last over 1877–78. The most complex of these engagements was the Crimean War of 1853–56.

▶ *Russians and Bulgarians defending the Shipka Pass against Ottoman troops in the war of 1877–78*

 ## The Crimean War

Also called the Eastern War, this was a fight between Russia and a coalition of France, the UK, the Kingdom of Sardinia, and the Ottoman Empire. It took place in the Crimean Peninsula. In western Turkey and around the Baltic Sea. The war saw the use of many new weapons and tactics. For the first time, an ongoing war was reported to the public over the telegraph and the newspaper. It revealed the many blunders and ruinous mismanagement of the leaders, as symbolised in Lord Tennyson's poem *The Charge of the Light Brigade*. The Russian Empire lost the war.

▶ *The Siege of Sevastopol, the capital of Crimea, lasted from October 1854 until September 1855 and led to the defeat of Russia in the Crimean War*

 ## The Charge of the Light Brigade

Tennyson's poem narrated a failed military action in the Crimean War. Owing to miscommunication in the chain of command, a British light **cavalry** was sent to face a full Russian assault of modern artillery. The Light Brigade withered under heavy, direct fire and endured heavy casualties. Back in the UK, this incident raised the alarm for the immediate need of better organisation and professionalism. The most heart-felt example of that was set by Florence Nightingale, who gained worldwide attention for pioneering modern nursing techniques while treating the wounded.

▲ *William Simpson's painting of the charge of the Light Brigade into the 'Valley of Death'*

 ### Incredible Individuals

The English nurse Florence Nightingale (1820–1910) helped create the modern techniques of nursing. The wounded soldiers of the Crimean War called her 'The Lady with the Lamp' as she made her nursing rounds at night by the light of a lamp. Nightingale wrote extensively in order to spread her medical knowledge. She was one of the early users of graphs, diagrams, and numerical data for understanding epidemics.

▶ *Florence Nightingale, the Lady with the Lamp*

A Subcontinent Divided

Aurangzeb, the last great Mughal Emperor, died in 1707, leaving behind a vast empire that stretched across the Indian subcontinent. But by the end of the century, the empire was almost completely gone. The Marathas—a warrior group of western India—took back the lands that Aurangzeb had wrested from them. (The Marathas themselves were defeated by the Shah of Afghanistan in the Third Battle of Panipat in 1761.) In 1739, the Shah of Persia sacked the Mughal capital of Delhi, taking away its greatest riches. Noble houses in southern India re-established their own territories. The Mughal monarchs increasingly became puppets in the hands of their viziers. After the 1764 Battle of Buxar, which cemented the British East India Company's hold over Bengal, the impoverished emperor became dependent on the British. With the help of the Marathas, he briefly returned to Delhi in 1772, but by 1803, the British once again got hold of the capital.

◄ In 1724, Mughal viceroy Asif Jah I proclaimed his own dynasty. He consolidated territory centred in Deccan India and became the first Nizam of Hyderabad

▲ Among the many treasures that Nadir Shah of Persia plundered from the Mughals, the amazing Kohinoor—one of the largest diamonds in the world—and the fabled Peacock Throne were significant

▶ In 1722, the Mughal vizier Saadat Khan took over territories around the Indian border with Nepal and established a flourishing province called Awadh. He became the first Nawab of Awadh, which remained a hereditary title until the land became a British protectorate in 1816

 ## The Nawab of Bengal

In 1717, Murshid Quli Khan was made the Mughal *diwan* (governor) of Bengal in eastern India. He proved to be an effective ruler. He is considered the first Nawab Nizam (prince) of Bengal. It was in Bengal that the British East India Company made clear that they didn't simply want to trade with India—they intended to rule the subcontinent. On 23 June 1757, under the leadership of Robert Clive, the British defeated Nawab Siraj ud-Daulah of Bengal and his French allies in the Battle of Plassey. Bengal became the base from which the Company expanded its control over most of India.

▶ Robert Clive bribed Mir Jafir, the commander-in-chief of the Bengal army, to betray the Nawab. This painting shows their meeting after the Battle of Plassey. In 1765, Robert Clive became the first British Governor of Bengal

The Sultan of Mysore

At the start of the 18th century, the Kingdom of Mysore in south-western India was ruled by the Wodeyar dynasty. In 1761, the army's commander-in-chief Hyder Ali seized power and became the de facto sultan of the kingdom. Inspired by the French army in the area, Hyder Ali invited them to train his own army. He created a modern arsenal and established a strong new navy. The British fought two battles against him but with little success. Hyder Ali died from cancer while still in camp during the Second Anglo-Mysore War in 1782.

▲ *French Admiral Suffren meets Hyder Ali*

▼ *Palace of the Maharajah of Mysore, India, as it appeared in the Illustrated London News, 1881*

The Kingdom of Travancore

In the 18th century, the southernmost part of India had a state called Travancore. In 1729, its King Marthanda Varma began to expand the borders through military conquest. His most famous battle took place in 1741 when he defeated the Dutch East India Company in Colachel. He captured the Dutch Admiral Eustachius De Lannoy and, interestingly, made him captain of the Travancore army. De Lannoy modernised the Travancore troops, by introducing firearms and artillery. Travancore became the most dominant state in the Kerala region and even defeated the Zamorin (king) of Kozhikode in the Battle of Purakkad in 1755. Travancore remained a princely state until it joined independent India in 1949.

▲ *Dutch Admiral Eustachius De Lannoy surrenders before King Marthanda Varma of Travancore*

Tipu Sultan

Hyder Ali's son Tipu Sultan held Mysore until 1799, remaining an implacable enemy of the British. He died in the Fourth Anglo-Mysore Battle while defending the Fort of Srirangapatnam against allied armies of the British, the Nizam of Hyderabad, and the Marathas. The British restored the Wodeyar dynasty to the throne but kept control over their kingdom.

War in Pre-Modern China

In the 1800s, China was ruled by the Qing dynasty. The country **exported** expensive goods like tea, silk, and porcelain. However, it didn't buy anything back from foreign traders. This changed when the British forced open China's ports in the Opium Wars. Historians mark this period as the start of modern China. After the Qing dynasty fell, the country faced a series of armed conflicts that ultimately made it a powerful nation.

▲ *European factories at the port-city of Canton in 1805–10*

First Opium War

The British East India Company began shipping opium into China. They hoped this addictive drug would force the Chinese into buying foreign goods. They completely ignored the effect opium would have on people's health and well-being. The Qing government responded by seizing thousands of incoming opium chests. This kicked off the First Opium War (1839–42). The British Navy easily defeated the outdated Chinese fleet and took control of important ports and coastal cities.

▶ *British and Qing troops fighting at close quarters*

▲ *At the end of the First Opium War, the Qing government was forced to sign the Treaty of Nanking, which opened up the country to further trade. China also had to pay $21 million and hand over Hong Kong to the British*

▼ *The British East India Company steamship Nemesis (in the background to the right) destroying Chinese war junks on 7 January 1841*

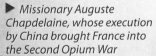 Second Opium War

Extreme British demands soon led to the outbreak of the Second Opium War (1856–60). The French allied with the British after a French missionary was executed by Chinese officials. In 1860, the Qing were defeated in Beijing. At the 1860 Convention of Peking, the Chinese were forced to legalise opium trade, permit freedom of religion, and pay **reparations**. This was the start of an era of unequal treaties that led to the end of the Qing and the rise of **republican** China.

▶ *Missionary Auguste Chapdelaine, whose execution by China brought France into the Second Opium War*

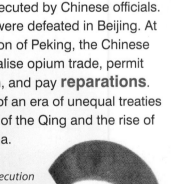

Sino-Japanese Wars

The First Sino-Japanese War took place in 1894–95 between the Qing dynasty and the Empire of Japan for dominance over Korea. The Japanese won a string of land and sea battles over the next few months. After the Qing lost the port of Weihaiwei, they surrendered and signed the Treaty of Shimonoseki. For the first time, Japan began to gain supremacy in this region of East Asia. The Second Sino-Japanese War (or the Chinese War of Resistance) began in 1931 and peaked over 1937–45. Initially, the Japanese subjugated China and set up a puppet state called Manchukuo. But by 1945, Japan had lost all its might in WWII and was expelled from China.

▲ Japanese troops landing near Shanghai, during the Second Sino-Japanese War

◀ Japanese soldiers beheading Chinese prisoners of war in the First Sino-Japanese War

Annexation of Tibet

The Tibet Autonomous Region (TAR) is an **autonomous** region of China. It was independent until the 1950s. China, however, had long considered it their **vassal** state. In 1949–50, communist China sent troops to 'liberate' Tibet. Over the next decades, thousands of Buddhist monasteries were destroyed, along with the traditional ways of life. In 1959, the Dalai Lama, the spiritual head of Tibet, escaped to India with his ministers. He has been in exile ever since.

▲ The People's Liberation Army of China marches into Lhasa, the capital of Tibet, towards the Dalai Lama's Potala Palace

Sino-Indian War

The McMahon Line is the border between Tibet and northeast India. Both countries had agreed to the border in 1914, while India was still under British rule. After China took over Tibet, it disputed this boundary. The Sino-Indian War took place in 1962 when China tried to invade this territory. The war was fought as a series of conflicts and military engagements under the harsh, high-altitude conditions of the Himalayas. China called a ceasefire in 1962 and the 3,225-km-long border remains a disputed line to this day.

▲ Armed Indian soldiers patrol the sweeping stretches of the Sino-Indian frontier

◀ Tibetan, Chinese, and British participants of the Simla Accord of 1914, which established the McMahon Line as the border between India and Tibet (later, China)

British Conquest of the Old World

Over the 17th–19th centuries, British merchant companies conquered and settled colonies and trading posts across Asia and Africa. These were eventually taken over by the crown and became part of the vast British Empire.

The English settle in Madras, in southern India. By 1644, they've finished constructing Fort St. George.

▲ Fort St. George, Madras, 18th century

The Levant Trading Company is established in London to trade with the Ottoman Empire.

The English defeat the Portuguese at Bombay in a battle over trading rights.

| 1578 | 1600 | 1615 | 1633 | 1639 | 1660 | 1661 | 1696 |

The British East India Company is established to set favourable trading colonies in India.

The English trading post in Bengal is established.

The Royal African Company is set up.

King Charles II receives Tangier and Bombay as dowry when he marries his Portuguese bride Catherine de Braganza.

The Company's Fort St. William is built on the Ganges delta. It develops into the city of Calcutta.

France and Britain draw up the boundaries for Senegal and Gambia in West Africa

Germany and Britain create the boundary between Tanzania and Kenya in East Africa.

Buganda and three other kingdoms are combined into the colonial Uganda Protectorate.

The First Boer War results in victory for the South African Republic.

| 1899–1902 | 1896 | 1890 | 1889 | 1886 | 1882-84 | 1880-81 | 1879 |

The Second Boer War breaks out over the Witwatersrand gold mines. It is won by the British. Thousands of Boer women and children die in concentration camps.

Businessman Cecil Rhodes sends people to settle the new colony of Rhodesia. Ruled by an Arab sultan, Zanzibar becomes a British protectorate.

The Zulu War leads to the British taking over the Zulu Kingdom.

▲ Boer troops firing from a trench

▶ The Mahdi's forces attack the Egyptian city of Khartoum and kill British General Gordon

Britain sends troops to quell anti-West riots in Alexandria, Egypt. Under the leadership of the **Mahdi**, Egypt and Sudan stun the world by overthrowing British rule.

Robert Clive defeats the Nawab of Bengal at the battle of Plassey and establishes British rule in Bengal. He later becomes the first British Governor of Bengal.

◀ *Mughal emperor Shah Alam gives Robert Clive, Governor of Bengal, the rights to collect revenue from Bengal, Bihar, and Orissa*

Encroaching British forces in the Punjab meet Sikh troops in the First Anglo-Sikh War. It ends the following year with the Treaty of Lahore, in which Jammu and Kashmir become British possessions.

1757 — 1798 — 1806 — 1819 — 1820 — 1821 — 1839 — 1845

1757 The British begin their conquest of the Persian Gulf by making Oman a protectorate.

1798 Cape of Good Hope is occupied by the British.

1806 Sir Stamford Raffles establishes the city of Singapore.

1819 Thousands of British settlers arrive in Cape Town, South Africa.

1820 Sierra Leone, Gambia and the Gold Coast combine to form British West Africa.

1821 The British seize the port of Aden (on the Red Sea), which links the East and West.

Egyptian government is placed under joint French and British control. Queen Victoria is given the title Empress of India.

The island of Cyprus is occupied.

Britain annexes Basutoland (modern-day Lesotho).

The British Crown takes direct control of India, putting an end to the Company's rule.

1878 — 1877 — 1876 — 1874 — 1868 — 1861 — 1858 — 1849

1877 Britain seizes the Boer republic in South Africa.

1874 The southern part of present-day Ghana becomes the British colony called Gold Coast.

1861 Britain seizes Lagos from its royal rulers.

1849 The Battle of Gujarat ends the Second Anglo-Sikh war—the British annex Punjab.

▶ *The Anglo-Ashanti Wars were a series of five conflicts between the Ashanti Empire, in the Akan interior of the Gold Coast (now Ghana), and the British Empire and British-allied African states*

World War I

A great global war broke out on 28 July 1914 and lasted until 11 November 1918. Some 135 countries fought in this war, which broke the great European empires, changed the boundaries of nations and took the lives of over 15 million people. Most of the actual fighting occurred on the Western and Eastern Fronts. Other important battlefields included the Middle Eastern Front, the Italian Front, Africa, and China. Battles raged on land, sea and—for the first time—in the air. WWI ended in many different peace treaties, of which the most significant was the Treaty of Versailles.

▲ The first warplanes were seen during WWI. They were initially used to photograph and spy on enemy camps. Later, they were equipped with guns for aerial warfare

 ## The Declaration of War

On 28 June 1914, the crown prince of the Austro-Hungarian Empire, Archduke Franz Ferdinand, was shot dead by a rebel student in the name of Serbian independence. The empire blamed Serbia and sought punishing reparations. Serbia refused to comply with all the demands. Austria then declared war on Serbia. Both countries' allies quickly became involved and Europe descended into an all-out war.

▲ The arrest of Serbian student Gavrilo Princip, who shot Archduke Franz Ferdinand and his wife while they were driving by. Tired of waiting, he had gotten a sandwich and was eating as the cars came on to that street because of a change of route.

 ## A Global War

Russia joined Serbia as they shared ethnic similarities. Germany suddenly found itself sandwiched between incoming Russian troops from the east and Russia's ally France in the west. Germany joined the war. It planned to defeat France first. Because the French had fortified their border with Germany, a direct invasion was impossible. Germany invaded neighbouring Belgium and moved through its border into France. The invasion of Belgium brought its ally Great Britain into the war. Britain's great navy put Germany at a disadvantage. The Kaiser of Germany signed a secret treaty with the Ottoman Empire, which brought the Turkish fleet into the war on his side. With the major powers of Europe all embroiled, their vast colonies—even those fighting for independence— were forced to contribute men and money towards the war efforts.

▲ German soldiers (wearing pickelhaube helmets) at the first Battle of Marne (5–12 September 1914), which cost the lives of more than 1,750,000 men and marked the end of the German advance into France; it also marked the beginning of trench warfare

◀ King George V of Great Britain inspects a munitions factory

Trench Warfare

WWI saw the widespread use of deadly new weapons such as machine guns, and long-range artillery. Soldiers could no longer charge against each other as rapid fire could instantly decimate troops. The armies now dug holes along the battlefront, so they wouldn't be killed. All along the Western Front, the holes joined up to form long trenches that protected the fighting soldiers. Some extended from Switzerland to the North Sea! Barbed wire and landmines were laid out in front of the trenches to deter enemies from infiltrating the line. Later on, poison gas was used to kill enemies in trenches.

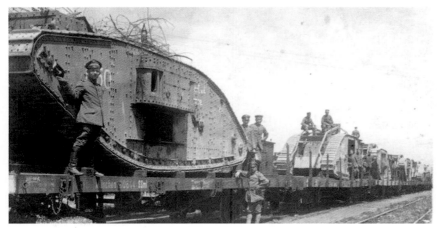

▲ *Tanks became popular in WWI, as they were the only means of getting over barbed wire and hostile trenches*

▲ *A German trench occupied by British soldiers during the Battle of the Somme, July 1916*

 ## USA Joins the War

Germany used submarines called U-boats in WWI. They attacked passenger ships in the Atlantic thinking that America was selling weapons to the British. American spies also picked up a secret telegram from Germany, inviting Mexico to attack the US. An angry America joined the Allies on 6 April 1917.

 ## The Aftermath

By 1918, the German side had lost the war. They were forced to sign a peace treaty while agreeing to pay approximately $31.5 billion in reparations. Many countries came together to form the League of Nations, which hoped to prevent another global war from ever taking place.

▼ *On 30 January 1915, the German submarine U–21 attacked and sank the Linda Blanche. Passengers can be seen disembarking in lifeboats*

World War II

The World War II took place over 1939–45. Nearly the whole globe was drawn into it. The war was fought between two opposing sides: the Allies and the Axis. The Axis Powers was a coalition of Nazi Germany, Italy, and Japan. At various points Finland, Slovakia, Romania, Bulgaria, Hungary, and Thailand joined or left this coalition. The Allied Powers consisted of the UK and its colonies, France, Poland, China, and others. In June 1941, the Soviet Union joined the Allies. In December 1941, the US also joined the Allies. By the end of the war, nearly 30–50 million lives had been lost. The majority who died were not soldiers but ordinary civilians.

▲ Soviet children take cover underground during a German air raid in the early days of WWII

▲ The Road of Bones is part of a highway in Russia. It was built by thousands of WWII prisoners who were forced into Soviet labour camps called gulags. The bones of the people who died building the road are buried beneath it

Rise of Hitler and Mussolini

After WWI, the Germans lost great sums of money—and their pride—to the Allies. The man who made them feel national pride once more was Adolf Hitler, leader of the Nazi Party. While Hitler conquered Germany with his rousing speeches, Italy had fallen under the spell of the dictator Benito Mussolini, who promised to make Italy a powerful empire.

▲ Hitler had millions of Jews put into concentration camps where they were killed in gas chambers. Others also whom the Nazis considered bad—non-whites, people, homosexuals, communists, people with disabilities, etc.—suffered a similar fate. This horrific period of mass killings is called the Holocaust

The War Begins

By 1939, Hitler had built a strong army to begin his plan of taking over the world. He signed an agreement with the Soviet Union to keep peace with each other for ten years—and to divide Eastern Europe between them! On 1 September 1939, Germany invaded Poland. France and Britain moved to help and declared war on Germany. But by 1941, a seemingly unstoppable Hitler had taken over most of Europe. Then, in June 1941, the Axis Powers invaded the Soviet Union. This caused irreparable damage to their cause.

⊛ Incredible Individuals

During WWII, the Nazis were terrified of a mysterious spy called the Limping Lady. Despite their best efforts to capture her, she slipped through their fingers like smoke. This extraordinary woman was the American spy Virginia Hall. She limped because she had a **prosthetic** leg—named Cuthbert! Even with her disability, Hall orchestrated jailbreaks for prisoners of war, ran resistance newspapers and sent vital information back to the Allies. Even Klaus Barbie, the Butcher of Lyon, considered her the most dangerous of Allied spies.

▲ Les Marguerites Fleuriront ce Soir (The Daisies Will Bloom At Night) by artist Jeffrey W. Bass is a painting of the brilliant and brave Virginia Hall

▲ WWII began on 1 September 1939, when Germany invaded Poland using a new strategy called Blitzkrieg, in which dense concentrations of tanks, supported by dive-bombing Luftwaffe (air force) planes, made short and speedy attacks resembling lightning strikes

▲ A member of the Observer Corps scans the skies for German bombers during the Battle for Britain. In the background is the dome of St. Paul's Cathedral, London

 ## Japan and the US

Some sources believe the war started even earlier, when Japanese troops invaded China on 7 July 1937. The US retaliated by placing an **embargo** on Japan. Tokyo and Washington were unable to resolve their differences through talks. On 7 December 1941, Japan bombed Pearl Harbour, along with many harbours in Southeast Asia. The US, which had stayed out of the war until then, joined the Allies. By May 1942, Japan had occupied many parts of Southeast Asia including Burma, Malaya, the Dutch East Indies, Singapore, and the Philippines. In August 1945, the US dropped two atomic bombs over Hiroshima and Nagasaki. Japan surrendered soon after.

The War Ends

With US aid, the Allies liberated France from Nazi control in 1944. To the east, the Germans were hemmed in by the Soviets. Germany surrendered in May 1945. Mussolini was captured while trying to flee the advancing Allied forces. On 28 April 1945, the Italians executed him and hung his body upside down at a gas station! Hitler ate poison and then shot himself on 30 April 1945, two days after Mussolini's death.

▼ The USS Arizona explodes in the Japanese bombing of Pearl Harbor

► The first nuclear bomb ever used in war was dropped over the Japanese city of Hiroshima. Hundreds and thousands of ordinary men, women, and children died in the explosion and only the mushroom clouds erupting thousands of feet above the city could be photographed

Cold War

After the end of WWII, the US and the Soviet Union—who had been allies—became rivals. The distrust arose because the two sides held differing political and economic beliefs. They didn't fight each other outright, but competed to become global superpowers. This long period of tension between the Western democracies, led by the US, and the communist countries of Eastern Europe, led by the Soviets, is called the Cold War. It lasted over 1945–1991 and came to an end with the collapse of the Soviet Union.

 ## Korean War (1950–53)

During the Cold War, both the US and the Soviet Union tried to establish dominance over Korea. The state split into two—the northern part became communist and was led by Kim Il-Sung; the southern part became capitalist under Syngham Rhee. The Korean War was fought by the armies of these two sides. When communist China, the Soviet Union and other 'eastern' nations entered the war to support the north, a coalition of the West, led by the US and the UK came to support the south. In the ensuing war, more than two million Koreans died, most of them in the north. Since then, the north and south have signed a peace treaty, but remain wary of each other.

In Real Life

The iconic TV show M*A*S*H (short for Mobile Army Surgical Hospital) was about American doctors serving in the Korean War. The show was based on a book and lasted longer than the war!

◀ *In 1959, the communist dictator Fidel Castro took power in Cuba. His policies made neighbouring America so upset that President John F Kennedy authorised the CIA to send trained Cuban exiles to invade the country and remove Castro from power. This Bay of Pigs Invasion (1961) ended in failure*

 ## Vietnam War (1964–1973)

In 1955, communist North Vietnam invaded non-communist South Vietnam in an attempt to unify the country. It was supported by other communist nations in this endeavour. US-led troops from various democratic countries sailed to aid South Vietnam in 1961, but withdrew in defeat after prolonged years of war. In 1975, the north seized full control of the south.

▲ *The fall of Saigon, the capital of South Vietnam, took place when the city was captured by the People's Army of Vietnam and the Viet Cong on 30 April 1975, marking the start of a unified communist Vietnam. Saigon was renamed Ho Chi Minh City, after the communist leader Ho Chi Minh*

◀ *The Viet Cong was a South Vietnamese communist force encouraged by the North. Its guerrilla warfare against anti-communist forces in the south was more effective than conventional war in routing the US-led coalition*

▲ US President Ronald Regan invaded the Caribbean nation of Grenada in the 1983 Operation Urgent Fury. The troops overthrew Grenada's government, which had close ties to Cuba, and remained to 'keep the peace' until 1985

▲ In 1965, US President Lyndon Johnson sent marines and troops to put down a civil uprising in the Dominican Republic, fearing the nation might become a second Cuba. This was called Operation Powerpack

The Cuban Missile Crisis, October, 1962

In response to the American deployment of missiles in Italy and Turkey, Soviet Russia agreed to adhere to Cuba's request of placing Nuclear missiles on their soil, which was just 90 miles away from the US shore. This act of aggression led to the major political and military tensions between the two nations. The 13 day complete stand-off compelled the world to believe, that it was on the brink of a Nuclear War. However, the tension eased when the Soviets decided to dismantle their arsenal of offensive weapons and retreated back in return of America's promise to not invade Cuba.

▲ Over 1989–90, the US invaded Panama in Operation Just Cause, to effect a regime change. A group of 60 Panama companies filed a lawsuit against the US claiming the action was 'done in a tortuous, careless, and negligent manner with disregard for the property of innocent Panamanian residents'

The Gulf War (1990–91)

Iraqi dictator Saddam Hussein invaded Kuwait, an ally of the US, in August 1990. This brought Iraq in conflict with a coalition of 34 countries, led by the US. On 17 January 1991, the coalition planes began to drop bombs on Baghdad (Iraq's capital city) in an attack called Operation Desert Storm. The Iraqi army blew up Kuwait's oil wells in response. They dumped millions of gallons of oil into the Persian Gulf. They even sent missiles towards Israel. Finally, in February, a ground force invaded and freed Kuwait. Saddam Hussein withdrew his troops and the war came to an end.

Isn't It Amazing!

The Gulf War was the first war to be heavily televised. For the first time, the front lines and bombing events were covered live by the media.

◀ Israeli civilians wear gas masks and take shelter from incoming missiles

▼ US aircraft fly over Kuwait oil fires set by the retreating Iraqi army

The War on Terror

Terrorism has been rampant since the late 20th century. However, the global war on terrorism became an international military campaign after the US was attacked by terrorists of the Al-Qaeda group on 11 September 2001.

▶ *The Nigerian terrorist group Boko Haram was once the world's deadliest terror group, having killed tens of thousands of people and displacing more than 2.3 million from their homes since 2009. It has been in decline since 2014*

The Taliban

A military group based in Afghanistan and western Pakistan, the Taliban was formed by students in 1994. They were led by a reclusive man called Mohammed Omar, who was helped by Pakistan and Saudi Arabia. In the late 1990s, the Taliban established a government called the Islamic Emirate of Afghanistan. Over 1996–2001, it imposed strict Islamic laws on the Afghan people. This was particularly hard on women, who had to cover themselves from head to toe, could not attend school or colleges. They were not even allowed to have any job or career of any sort, in short Taliban pushed their lives into a complete dismal state.

▶ *Taliban police patrol the streets in a pickup truck carrying weapons and missiles*

Taliban After 9/11

In 1997, Mohammad Omar forged ties with Al-Qaeda leader Osama bin Laden, who moved to Kandahar in Afghanistan. The Americans invaded Afghanistan soon after the 9/11 attacks in Operation Enduring Freedom, to prevent the Taliban from sheltering Al-Qaeda and to stop Al-Qaeda's use of Afghanistan as a base for the operation of their terror activities. By the end of 2001, the Taliban had lost all its strongholds and even the capital city of Kandahar. Despite peace talks, the Taliban is still fighting governments in Afghanistan and Pakistan. It is still causing the deaths of civilians, including women and children, through suicide attacks, bombing, and other methods.

▲ *US forces enter Afghanistan after the 9/11 attacks*

👤✓ In Real Life

On 2 May 2011, The US carried out a secret operation called Operation Neptune Spear, which was the culmination of an eight month plan enacted by the US President, Barack Obama and led by CIA Director Leon Panetta with the American special forces. Under the operation, special troops infiltrated bin Laden's private compound in Abbottabad, Pakistan, and shot and killed the world's most wanted terrorist.

The Rise and Fall of Al-Qaeda

In the late 1970s and 80s, the US and its allies supported Islamist guerrilla forces in Afghanistan as they were fighting against the Soviet Union. Among them was Osama bin Laden, who later founded the Al-Qaeda. The outfit later merged with the Egyptian Islamic Jihad and spread out as an armed Islamic group that took to terrorism. Members of the Al-Qaeda have been linked to many bombings and suicide attacks.

▲ *Pakistani journalist Hamid Mir (left) interviews Osama bin Laden (right) in Afghanistan two months after the 9/11 attacks*

Islamic State of Iraq and the Levant

In 2003, US invaded Iraq again to supposedly root out state-sponsored terrorism. Saddam Hussein's government was overthrown. The new Iraqi leadership soon faced rebellion from a branch of the Al-Qaeda. This Iraqi branch eventually split from its parent group and invaded Syria and the Levant, which were mired in civil war. The group quickly took over Iraq's western provinces under the name of the Islamic State of Iraq and the Levant (ISIL). ISIL enforced medieval Islamic law and carried out numerous public executions, crucifixions, and other horrendous acts. In 2015, it held some 3,500 people—mostly women and children—as slaves. The US sent troops to support Iraq in 2014 in bringing down ISIL. In late 2017, Iraq declared victory. ISIL lost its last stronghold in 2019 Battle of Baghuz Fawqani.

▲ *An ISIL terrorist captured by the Iraqi army*

Alt-Right Terrorism

Alt-Right is a way of describing the belief held by many white-skinned people that they are somehow superior to all other races and should therefore rule over society. Groups like the Ku Klux Klan and Neo-Nazis carry out these beliefs by terrorising members of other ethnicities. Violence by Alt-Right groups has been on the rise, as seen in the mass shootings of innocent non-white people in 2019, in places as far apart as New Zealand, Norway, and the USA.

▶ *Prime Minister Jacinda Arden of New Zealand visits the Muslim community in Christchurch after two mass shootings by a white supremacist at the city's mosque and Islamic centre*

SCIENTIFIC & INDUSTRIAL
REVOLUTION

INDUSTRIAL **REVOLUTION**

In Europe, the Agricultural Revolution began in the early 17th century and rapidly progressed in the 18th century. The quantity of crops increased with the use of crop rotation, selective breeding, enclosed fields, new tools, fertilisers, and manure. The new practices and inventions meant people no longer spent most of their time labouring in fields. Nor were so many people needed to farm. Many farmhands, therefore, moved to cities looking for jobs. This marked the start of the Industrial Revolution.

The Industrial Revolution marked the transition from handmade goods to machine-made goods as a result of technological inventions. This period is often referred to as the First Industrial Revolution and was confined to Britain, which by then had become a colonial superpower. Here, advances were made in science and technology, in the fields of iron, steam, textile, and transport. The Second Revolution took place in the late 1850s, when the new inventions of the First Revolution spread to America and Germany. This phase saw immense progress in the steel, electronics, and automobile industries.

This book will chronicle the discoveries and inventions, the inventors, and the progress made in every field, under both the First and the Second Industrial Revolution.

▼ *A Futuristic Vision is a coloured etching by William Heath that signifies the advancement of technology due to the Industrial Revolution. It led to mechanisation, progress in transport and lavish building projects*

An Overflow of Textiles

Textile production was the first to employ the factory system. Before industries began, people produced cotton cloth and woollen goods in their homes, or on a small scale, and it was referred to as a 'cottage industry'. Merchants or traders supplied the raw materials and equipment and returned to pick up the finished goods. But the demand for cotton grew when the upper class began to prefer it. Cotton was the first textile product to undergo mechanisation and mass production. The demand for inexpensive wool and yarn also increased within no time. By the late 18th century, Britain was the world's leading manufacturer of textiles.

▲ A flying shuttle showing metal capped ends, wheels and a **pirn** of weft thread

► The original fortified entrance to Richard Arkwright's mill in Derbyshire, Great Britain

1733

Mechanic John Kay developed the flying shuttle that led to a twofold increase in cloth production. It required four spinners to maintain one loom and ten people to develop yarn for one weaver.

1764

Englishman James Hargreaves invented the spinning jenny (or engine), after his daughter Jenny pushed the family's spinning wheel to the floor, by mistake. James noticed that the **spindle** had not stopped turning. This gave him the idea that one wheel could turn many spindles at the same time. The jenny drew threads from eight spindles.

► Model of the spinning jenny in the Museum of Early Industrialisation, Wuppertal, Germany

1769

Richard Arkwright patented the water frame—the first automatic spinning machine employing a water wheel. It produced stronger threads than the spinning jenny. The large water frame would not fit in the spinners' homes, so Arkwright built the first modern factory, a water-powered cotton mill next to a stream in Cromford, Derbyshire, England.

👤✓ In Real Life

The requirement for **manpower** started reducing in factories with the introduction of machines. Instead of one worker making a piece of fabric, a variety of machines worked simultaneously to produce it. And, instead of only one worker undertaking the entire process of converting the raw wool to dyed fabric, each worker was assigned only one task in the process, following the **assembly-line approach**. This increased the working speed, but performing the same task repeatedly became monotonous for the workers.

1856

William Perkin invented the first synthetic dye. He first called it aniline purple, but later renamed it mauve. Since the dye was cheaper than natural pigments, it was soon applied to cotton fabrics and used by everyone.

◄ Portrait of Sir William Perkin

▶ Boston Manufacturing Company, 1813–16, Waltham, Massachusetts

▲ The only surviving example of a spinning mule built by the inventor Samuel Crompton

1779

British inventor Samuel Crompton merged the features of the jenny and the water frame to create the Crompton's spinning mule. The mule could make both fine and coarse yarn, and one person could operate 1000 spindles at the same time! But Crompton didn't have the funds to **patent** his creation and was cheated by manufacturers. Soon, hundreds of Britain's textile factories were using spinning mules.

1780

English inventor Edmund Cartwright mechanised the process of weaving cloth with a power loom.

◀ Edmund Cartwright

▶ Portrait of Joseph Marie Jacquard (1752–1834), 1855

1804

Joseph Marie Jacquard's invention—the Jacquard loom—automatically controlled the **warp and weft** threads on a silk loom.

1830

The demand for cotton rose so high that the steam engine had to be introduced to speed up the textile industry.

1812

As Britain profited from the cotton production of its American colonies, the cost of producing cotton yarn reduced by nine-tenths. With the **industrialisation** of yarn production, workers who turned wool into yarn were also reduced by four-fifths.

1810

Massachusetts merchant Francis Cabot Lowell memorised the design of the textile machines when he was permitted to tour Britain's factories but not allowed to take notes. Back home, he recreated the designs and started the Boston Manufacturing Company—America's first cloth mill. Several large-scale mills came up in Massachusetts, so this time is considered to be the 'Cradle of the American Industrial Revolution'.

Coal & Iron

Before the Industrial Revolution, Britain, like the rest of Europe, produced coal in a limited quantity because of the small size of coal pits and the abundance of opencast mines (large, open pits dug into the earth). Only local businesses used them. With industrialisation, methods of production improved, and so did the methods of transportation. Fossil fuels like coal, natural gas, and oil became popular, though coal led the way.

⚛ The Demand for Coal and the Iron Industry

The iron industry became the major coal user. An English village, Coalbrookdale pioneered iron tramways that helped transport coal to buyers or even within the mines. Iron was used in the construction industry as well as to build coal-operated steam engines. Coal production increased by 50 per cent in 1700–1750, and by the year 1850, it went beyond 500 per cent. It was cheaper than wood and produced three times more energy. As the demand for coal increased, mines were dug deeper and mining became more dangerous. A series of steam-engine innovations helped pump water from the ground and dig deeper for coal. Richard Trevithick built the first moving steam engine in 1801. He believed that a steam engine on rails would be more effective than horse wagons to carry loads of coal and iron to and from the mines.

▲ *View of Coalbrookdale Ironworks, Shropshire, England (1758)*

⚛ Coal & Canals

Before 1750, Britain's roads were not smooth and well-connected, and ships were used to transport coal. In 1761, the Duke of Bridgewater inaugurated a **canal** from Worsley to Manchester for carrying coal. The demand for cheaper coal helped expand production and made him rich. Seeing his success, coal-mine owners built other canals.

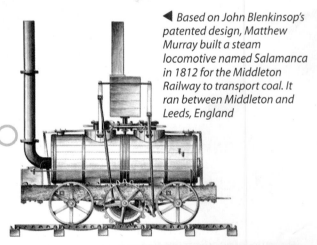

◀ *Based on John Blenkinsop's patented design, Matthew Murray built a steam locomotive named Salamanca in 1812 for the Middleton Railway to transport coal. It ran between Middleton and Leeds, England*

⚛ Coal & Brass

The West Midlands, England, was nicknamed the 'Black Country' because the entire area was covered with black smoke and soot from coal used in iron **foundries**, steel mills, and **furnaces** during the Industrial Revolution. In Birmingham, England, the metal industry boomed with the mass production of buttons, brass fittings, pins, guns, and nails.

⊙ Incredible Individuals

In 1700, the iron industry was on a decline and there was a shortage of charcoal. This was solved in 1709 by Abraham Darby, an ironmaster who, having worked with brass, moved to Coalbrookdale, Shropshire, England and purchased a semi-derelict blast furnace. He was the first to use coke—a form of processed coal—to smelt iron. This was a success story as it separated iron from ironstone. In 1715, he opened a second blast furnace. His son Abraham Darby II succeeded him and he learned to make better quality coke by burning coal in ovens and thereby improve the quality of iron. When Darby II died in 1763, his son Abraham Darby III continued the business, and he built a unique bridge above River Severn using iron from his late grandfather's furnace.

From Iron to Steel

With the rapid growth of industries and infrastructure, iron and steel became very important materials and were included in many building and construction processes. In time, steel began to be preferred over iron because it is stronger, though it is also more difficult to produce. Steel came to be used in weapons, transportation, telegraph lines, and buildings.

When Steel Mills Took Over the Landscape

In 1901, the United States Steel Corporation was formed and it was one of the world's largest steel-producing companies at the time. Throughout the 20th century, the scale of steel production increased dramatically for all stages of **infrastructure**. This included constructing large-scale blast furnaces to melt iron ore, open-hearth furnaces, oxygen furnaces, molten steel casting, and port-based mills from where ships transported raw materials and finished goods, as seen in countries like South Korea and Japan. Steel mills were being built close to locations that had huge deposits of coal and iron ore. For instance, such deposits around Birmingham, Alabama, Minnesota, and Michigan led to the construction of steel mills in the Great Lakes region of the United States.

The Rise of Buildings

The steel industry skyrocketed in the late 19th and 20th centuries during the Second Industrial Revolution and vastly transformed America. More and more buildings had to be constructed to accommodate the country's immigrant population. Steel was chosen for the inner skeleton inside stone constructions because it could withstand harsh conditions and was strong enough to support the skyscrapers it was used in.

▶ *The US Steel Tower in downtown Pittsburgh*

⊛ Incredible Individuals

In 1856, British engineer Henry Bessemer invented the first inexpensive process to produce steel on a large scale. The process could turn molten iron into steel within 20 minutes. Soon, Scottish-American industrialist Andrew Carnegie began building steel mills, following the Bessemer technique, to produce steel on a massive scale. Carnegie invested in and produced steel when he realised that the 2,858 kilometres transcontinental railroad from Nebraska to California would require a lot of steel. It was finally completed in 1869.

▲ *An illustration of Sir Henry Bessemer*

💡 Isn't It Amazing!

William Le Baron Jenney constructed the first skyscraper in 1885 called the Home Insurance Building. It was 138-feet tall and had 10 storeys.

▶ *The exterior of the Home Insurance Building in Chicago, USA*

Full Steam Ahead

Till the invention of steam engines, the industries had relied on energy harnessed from wind, water, animals such as horses, and manpower to operate small machines. Earlier, wood was burnt to produce fuel. This changed when Britain discovered that it had rich deposits of coal. The steam engine that was built to pump out the water from coal mines later helped run a variety of transport services such as ships, railway **locomotives**, and factories, which vastly improved transportation on land and water.

◄ *The 1698 Savery Engine*

◄ *The Newcomen Memorial Engine in Dartmouth*

1698

1712

1776

Thomas Savery patented a steam engine that he called the 'miner's friend'; it helped solve problems related to mine drainage and increased the public water supply. It was a pump with hand-operated valves. Steam from a boiler was condensed in a cylinder, creating a **vacuum** that sucked water from the mines into it. By controlling valves, the water was pumped upwards using the same steam. It generated about one **horsepower** (HP), but was ineffective given its short height and vulnerability to boiler explosions.

Englishman Thomas Newcomen's steam engine called Newcomen Atmospheric Machine caused a slight vacuum in the cylinder when cold jets of water condensed the steam. A **piston** was used in the process. The engine was large and used at the bottom of a mine, but it only produced five HP and used up a lot of coal. Still, when he passed away in 1933, 110 engines were found to be operational in France, Germany, Austria, Hungary, and Sweden.

Scottish inventor James Watt altered Newcomen's invention to produce steam. He added a separate condenser to his engine to prevent the heating and cooling of the cylinder. Watt's steam engine could rotate a shaft instead of the simple up-and-down motion of the pump. It generated 5–10 HP. By 1800, his company had built 496 engines that were used to power machinery, locomotives, ships, distilleries, canals, waterworks, paper, flour, cotton, and iron mills.

🔍 In Real Life

The first transoceanic voyage to employ steam power was completed in 1819 by *SS Savannah*—an American sailing ship with an auxiliary steam-powered paddle. Crossing the Atlantic at that time was dangerous and the sea captain Moses Rogers initially found it difficult to find a crew for the journey. There were hardly any passengers willing to risk their lives on the first steamship to voyage across the Atlantic Ocean.

The ship sailed from Savannah in Georgia, USA to Liverpool in England, in a little more than 27 days. Being a hybrid sail ship, the *SS Savannah* used a lot of steam power during the day, but also depended on traditional sail power for its journey. By the second half of the 19th century, larger and faster steamships were regularly carrying passengers, cargo, and mail across the North Atlantic, a service dubbed 'the Atlantic Ferry'.

▲ *A steam engine built as per James Watt's patent in 1848 at Freiberg, Germany*

British engineer Richard Trevithick built the first railway steam locomotive—the Penydarren locomotive—which undertook its first journey on 21 February 1804. Its 5 wagons carried 10 tons of iron and 70 men, and it travelled at a speed of 3.9 kmph (2.4 mph).

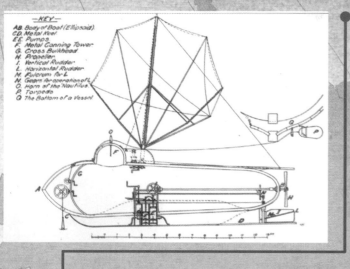

◄ *A 19th century drawing of Fulton's Nautilus submarine*

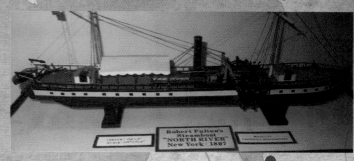

▼ *A model of the North River Steamboat designed by Robert Fulton at the Hudson River Maritime Museum*

1804   **1807**   **1807**

American engineer Robert Fulton built a paddle steamer—the *North River Steamboat* (later renamed *Clermont*)—and travelled up the Hudson River from New York City to Albany at five mph. It was more expensive to build than sailing vessels, but could handle tough storms.

▶ *This replica of Trevithick's 'Puffing Devil'— the first steam-powered passenger vehicle— was built by the Trevithick Society and is regularly demonstrated in Cornwall, England*

American Robert Fulton built the first steamboat to speed up the transport of raw materials and finished goods. Steam engines improved, becoming smaller and more efficient. By the mid 19th century, steamships transported cargo across the Atlantic.

◄ *Steam engines were used to run railway locomotives*

When Man Made Machines

Machine tools used in the production of manufacturing machines were important during the Industrial Revolution. They were originally developed in the 18th century as tools for clock, watch and for scientific-instrument makers to produce small, precise mechanisms in batches. These small mechanisms, when used in textile machines, were called 'clockwork' because of their metal gears and spindles. Birmingham, in 1830s England, is an example of how manufacturing changed because of machine tools. A new machine by William Joseph Gillott, William Mitchell, and James Stephen Perry helped mass-produce sturdy and cost-effective steel nibs (points) for dip-writing pens. The production of these items used to be taxing and costly.

▲ In 1827, English pen-maker Joseph Gillott started Joseph Gillott's, a company based in Birmingham, England to produce dip pens

 ## Growth of Bigger Machines

The early models of machines used very little metal because they were manually shaped with files, saws, hammers, chisels and scrapers. But after the Industrial Revolution, machine tools were used to make small metal parts and frames. Production of large machine parts was a problem till the cylinder **boring machine** was designed for steam engines. At the start of the 19th century, the **slotting machine** was developed and then the milling machine, which only gained prominence during the Second Industrial Revolution.

▲ Universal Milling Machine

▲ A slotting machine, built in 1863 in Netherlands, delivered to the Nagasaki Steel Mill

Incredible Individuals

Henry Maudslay, one of the famous toolmakers of the early 19th century, was responsible for training many engineers, toolmakers, and inventors of the next generation. During his stint at the Royal Arsenal, Woolwich, he saw large horse-driven wooden machines. He later worked for Joseph Bramah on the production of metal locks and machinery for ships' pulley blocks required by the Royal Navy at Portsmouth Block Mills, England. His workshops welcomed inventors like Sir Joseph Whitworth, Richard Roberts, James Nasmyth and Joseph Clement. Roberts made high-quality machine tools and encouraged the use of **jigs** and gauges for precision in workshop measurements.

▲ The bust of Henry Maudslay, a renowned tool maker of the 19th century

▲ Albert Edward, Prince of Wales, and Princess Alexandra at Gillott's Victoria Works in 1874

Transportation

The internal-combustion engine and the gasoline-powered automobile changed the face of transportation. Automobiles replaced the horse-and-carriage mode of transport and offered far greater mobility to the public.

 ## Building Infrastructure to Improve Transport

The increase in the trading of goods and services, a result of rapid industrialisation, instantly improved Britain's transport pathways. This created many jobs. Engineers were called in to construct more tunnels and bridges, and find more routes. The creation of railroads led to an increase in the demand for coal and fuel to construct locomotives, and iron was required to build railtracks. For instance, by 1815, Britain had around 2,000 miles of functional canals; and by 1840, the US had over 3,000 miles of railroad tracks.

 ## The Evolution of Automobiles

In 1859, Belgian inventor Étienne Lenoir constructed a working model of an internal combustion engine that mixed coal, gas, and air. In 1878, German engineer Nikolaus Otto tweaked the model into a four-stroke cycle comprising induction, compression, firing, and exhaust. Otto's models came to be used instead of steam engines. In the early 1890s, German engineer Rudolf Diesel used heavy oil, or diesel, in his engine as it was more efficient. His diesel engines were used in submarines, locomotives and heavy machinery. In 1885, the first motorcycle and motorcar by Daimler and Karl Benz used the gasoline-powered engine. Within two decades, American industrialist Henry Ford mass-produced automobiles, including his famous Model T, which was reliable and efficient. Mass production helped slash the prices of his automobiles and made them affordable to the average-income earning American.

▲ *Rudolf Diesel (1858–1913). His engines were so effective that it is speculated that he was killed by coal barons, who stood to lose a lot of money, when he went missing on a ship. His body was found on the shore a few days later*

▶ *Otto's 1876 four-cycle engine*

ⓘ In Real Life

It was found that cities situated near railroads prospered economically, compared to those away from the rail route. Factories began to thrive because a routine had been formed—finished goods were being transported from factory doorsteps to the markets, daily. Raw materials too were being transported from the markets to the factories, every day. Many companies only worked to build and operate railways. In time, large railway companies purchased the smaller ones and kept growing in the process.

◀ *The last home of Karl and Bertha Benz, now the location of the Gottlieb Daimler and Karl Benz Foundation in Ladenburg, in Baden-Württemberg*

Railways

The 1790s and 1800s were known for 'Canal Mania' as canal-building began and Britain invested a lot of money in building these waterways. By 1850, Britain had about 4,000 miles of canals. These helped transport coal, which was in high demand, from mines to factories. Horse-driven wagons were used to reach the waterways. The wagons were fitted with a steam engine to help push them over inclines, but this was rather a slow process. Then, in the 1840s, 'Railway Mania' began. Railroad construction in America boomed from the 1830s to the 1870s. European countries too followed Britain in building railroads (Belgium in 1834, France in 1842, Switzerland in 1847, and Germany in the 1850s). Perishable goods such as dairy products could now be transported across long distances without getting spoilt.

Landmark Moves in the Growth of Railways

In 1767, Richard Reynolds made a wooden set of rails for transporting coal from Coalbrookdale. The first act to create a 'railway' was passed by parliament in 1801. Till this point, horse-driven carts were used to pull coal. Then, in 1801, Richard Trevithick developed the first steam locomotive to be driven on roads. George Stephenson built the first steam-hauled public railway, the Stockton to Darlington railway, hoping to derail the monopoly of the canal owners, in the year 1821. The 40 kilometre long railroad connected coal mines at Shildon in North England to nearby towns, and to Stockton and Darlington.

▲ Trevithick's No. 14 engine was built around 1804 by an ironworks company, Hazledine and Company, in Bridgnorth. It can be viewed at the Science Museum (London) today

▲ Portrait of British engineer Richard Trevithick

In Real Life

White-collar workers moved out of cities and went to live in the suburbs because it was now possible to commute back and forth. Working-class districts were demolished for new rail buildings. In 1844, the British government passed a law stating that third-class accommodation would be allowed on at least one train a day travelling in each direction. The fare for each of these third-class passengers was not to exceed a penny for each mile travelled.

Stiff Competition From Canals

The Bridgewater Canal's owner initially opposed the building of a railway at Manchester, nonetheless the Liverpool and Manchester Railway opened in 1830. Seeing great potential for future passenger travel, the railways gradually created a permanent staff. In the same year, major railway lines were installed to connect big cities and towns. Canal companies rose to the challenge and reduced their prices, but industrialists sided with the railways, and from 1835–48 there was a massive boom in the creation of railways. In fact, a standardised time was introduced across the country so that trains could be timetabled, making Britain one of the first few countries to do so.

▲ The Bridgewater Canal, famous for its commercial success, crossing the Manchester Ship Canal, is one of the last canals to be built

◀ The development of railways not only brought about a monumental shift in trade and industry, but also helped connect people better

Roads

Before industrialisation, British roads were the decayed remains of what the Romans had built over a millennium and a half ago. Then, Mary I, also known as Queen Mary Tudor, passed a law stating parishes would be in-charge of improving their own roads using the assistance of workers six days a week, for free, and landowners had to provide the equipment. Unfortunately, the workers were not well-trained and didn't do much to restore the roads.

Legislation after 1750

Due to Britain's industrial expansion and population growth, the government passed laws to stop the road system from decaying any further, but it did not improve it in anyway. The Broad Wheel Act of 1753 widened the wheels on vehicles, and the General Highway Act of 1767 adjusted the sizes of the wheels and the number of horses per carriage. In 1776, a law was passed for parishes to employ men specifically to repair roads.

Improved Quality of Roads

By 1800, the quality of roads improved. Stagecoaches became so frequent that they had their own timetables. In 1784, the Royal Mail was introduced and its coaches delivered the post across Britain. While various industries used them, roads played only a small role in moving freight—a task that canals and railways did efficiently. Roads, however, played an important part in transporting goods (and people) once they came off the railways and canals.

▲ An oil painting of the Edinburgh and London Royal Mail, by Jacques-Laurent Agasse

Cemented Ties

Building lighthouses to prevent shoreline accidents involving warships and merchant ships became necessary for Britain, a naval superpower. For this, it needed a binding agent that could hold tall structures. In the 1700s, engineers experimenting with limestone discovered a powder that, when wet, would set and hold stone blocks together. This was cement.

⚛ Experiments in Cement

In the year 1757, engineer John Smeaton observed that good quality lime had a high amount of clay. Two years later, while building the third Eddystone Lighthouse at the Cornwall coast in Southwestern England, Smeaton found that mixing leftover clay, lime, and crushed **slag** from the iron-making process created a mortar that became hard when left to set under water. Smeaton's discovery motivated builders in England to come up with better quality cement.

British bricklayer-turned-builder Joseph Aspdin created a new type of cement in 1824 by firing clay and limestone till they calcined. He patented this cement and called it Portland cement because the concrete it produced looked very similar to the Portland stone that was often used to construct buildings in England. Portland cement became so popular that famous English engineer Marc Isambard Brunel used it to construct the Thames Tunnel in 1843. Two years later, Isaac Johnson improved the cement's quality by firing a mixture of chalk and clay at close to 1400° C–1500° C, which is what is used today.

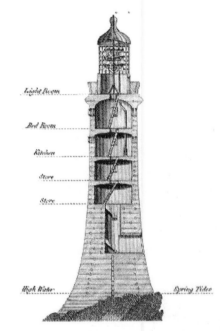

▲ A contemporary engraving of the lighthouse by engineer John Smeaton on the Eddystone Reef

◀ A blue plaque about Joseph Aspdin at Packhorse Yard in Leeds, England

JOSEPH ASPDIN
(1778 – 1855)

Portland Cement, one of mankind's most important manufactured materials, was patented by Joseph Aspdin, a Leeds Bricklayer, on 21 October 1824. Aspdin lived in this yard (then called Slip Inn Yard) and first sold his cement in Angel Inn Yard.

◀ One of the lighthouses built in the 18th century that played an important role in maritime safety was the Rear Lighthouse at Wicklow Head, Ireland

💡 Isn't It Amazing!

A ship carrying barrels of Aspdin's cement—named after the man who, some say, created a **prototype** of the first artificial cement—sank near the Isle of Sheppey in Kent, England. The barrels were found with cement set in them. After removing the wooden staves, these were given to a pub in Sheerness, England, where they can be admired even today.

An Explosion of Chemicals

The chemical industry saw the invention and large-scale production of chemicals right from the start of the Industrial Revolution. In 1635, John Winthrop Jr. became the first to open a chemical company in Boston to produce potassium nitrate. A century later, a series of inventions made chemical manufacturing a booming industry.

It Began with Sulphuric acid

Pharmacist Joshua Ward was the first to heat saltpetre and allow the sulphur to combine and oxidise with water to produce sulphuric acid in 1736. Englishman John Roebuck (James Watt's first partner) ensured large-scale production of the chemical in 1749 by establishing a big factory in Prestonpans. Sulphuric acid was used to bleach cloth and pickle (remove rust from) iron and steel. Roebuck increased his manufacturing by replacing costly glass vessels with bigger, cost-effective chambers made using riveted sheets of lead, later called leaden condensing chambers. Then, in 1791, Nicolas Leblanc patented the Leblanc process—the production of sodium carbonate (synthetic soda ash) from sea salt (sodium chloride)—which also created a lot of harmful wastes like hydrochloric acid and sodium sulphate. The chemical was used in the glass, textile, soap, and paper industries.

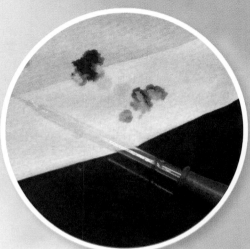

▲ Drops of 98 per cent sulphuric acid instantly char a piece of tissue paper. Carbon left as a residue from the dehydration reaction stains the paper black

Chemistry Takes Off

In 1800, Scottish chemist Charles Tennant created bleaching powder (calcium hypochlorite), based on French chemist Claude Louis Berthollet's discoveries that drastically reduced the process time from months to days. In 1855, Benjamin Silliman, from New Haven, Connecticut, obtained gasoline, naphthalene, tar, and other solvents by distilling petroleum. The first commercial oil well specifically drilled for oil was near Titusville, Pennsylvania, in 1859.

In 1888, chemical engineering was introduced as an undergraduate programme of four years, called Course X, and was taught at the Massachusetts Institute of Technology (MIT) in the United States. It was a combined course of mechanical engineering and industrial chemistry, training students to solve problems in engineering, especially those related to the use and manufacture of chemicals and their products.

In 1918, Fritz Haber received the Nobel Prize for the synthesis of ammonia, which German chemist Carl Bosh put to commercial use in 1930.

▲ An 1830 illustration of the cylinder furnace used in Leblanc's process of soda production

In Real Life

Before the Industrial Revolution, **greenhouse gases** like carbon dioxide (CO_2) and methane (CH_4) always remained at around 280 parts per million (ppm) and 790 parts per billion (ppb). Today, the concentrations are about 390 ppm and above 1,770 ppb respectively. Increasing levels of these gases are responsible for global warming and climate changes. Their increase is attributed to human activities that rely on fossil-fuel combustion, which causes an increase in emissions of these gases. The Industrial Revolution and subsequent industrialisation increased such emissions manifold.

▲ Fritz Haber (1868–1934)

▲ A plaque at the site where Charles Tennant's St. Rollox Chemical Works was originally located

Advancements in Medicine

Before the Industrial Revolution, bacterial (plague), viral (smallpox), and waterborne diseases (cholera, typhoid, and typhus) wiped out large chunks of the population. As **urbanisation** and industrialisation increased and the populations in cities grew, so did slums and poverty. The living and working conditions of the people worsened and there were further outbreaks of disease. However, the Industrial Revolution also brought many scientific breakthroughs in modern medicine. It improved the production of stethoscopes, scalpels, microscope lenses, test tubes, etc., and introduced **vaccines**, new cures, and treatments.

English doctor Edward Jenner discovered the cure for smallpox, which had been causing death and sickness since the 3ʳᵈ century BCE. He observed that milkmaids who contracted cowpox did not contract smallpox after **variolation**.

▲ *A stethoscope of the French physician René Theophile Laennec, who devised the first stethoscope in 1816. The brass and wood model consists of a single hollow tube*

1772	1776	1816

Joseph Priestly discovered nitrous oxide (NO_2). Later, Sir Humphrey Davy used it to numb the body parts on which surgery was to be conducted. From the 1930s onwards, it was also used to relieve the pain experienced during childbirth.

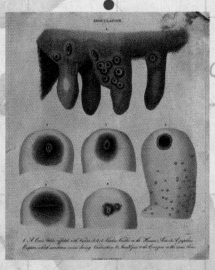

René Laennec invented the stethoscope. Before this invention, physicians had to put their ear on the patient's chest, used to be awkward for both the parties, and even produced inaccuracies in diagnosis as the internal sounds were muffled.

▶ *A coloured engraving done in 1811 by J. Pass, showing vaccinia pustules on a cow's udder as well as a smallpox and cowpox pustules on human arms*

1897	1895	1895

British doctor Ronald Ross won the Nobel Prize for his discovery of a parasite in the gastrointestinal tract of a mosquito, linking malaria to the insect.

Axel Cappelen performed the first open-heart surgery at Rikshospitalet (now Oslo) on a man who had been stabbed and was bleeding from his coronary artery.

Wilhelm Röntgen identified X-rays after he found a new ray that could pass through many substances and leave a 'shadow' for anything solid, like bones. Six months later, X-rays were used to locate and remove bullets from the bodies of wounded soldiers.

◀ *A record of 'pigmented bodies' in mosquitoes on a page from Ronald Ross's notebook. The bodies were later identified as malaria parasites*

▶ *Handmit Ringen (Hand with Rings) is a print of an X-ray taken by Wilhelm Röntgen. One of the first of its kind, it is an X-ray of his wife Anna Bertha Ludwig's left hand*

Isn't It Amazing!

Lady Mary Montagu was an English aristocrat, writer, and poet. She's often thought to have saved more lives than any other human. She brought smallpox inoculation practices from Turkey to Western medicine. Her actions led to the eradication of small pox. She is also credited for saving around 500 million lives in the 20th century alone.

▶ *Lady Mary Montagu*

▼ *James Blundell*

1818

British obstetrician James Blundell conducted the first successful human blood **transfusion** on a patient who had **haemorrhaged** during childbirth. Later, in 1901, Austrian physician Karl Landsteiner established blood groups.

1829

French chemist Charles Henri Leroux first isolated the 'miracle drug' salicylic acid (proto-aspirin). In 1853, Charles Frederic Gerhardt added an acetyl group to it and created acetylsalicylic acid (true aspirin). German chemist Felix Hoffmann developed it into the tablet form to mitigate fevers, headaches, common cold, and muscle aches. In 1899, the German company Bayer finally named it aspirin.

1845

English physician and pathologist John Hughes Bennet was the first to describe leukaemia as a blood disorder. Later, Franz Neumann linked the disease to bone marrow, and by 1900, experts connected it to a list of disorders.

1884

Jaume Ferrán y Clúa created a live vaccine that he had isolated from cholera patients in Marseilles. Later, Waldemar Haffkine developed a cholera vaccine with milder side effects.

▲ *Waldemar Haffkine*

1867

Joseph Lister, often referred to as the 'Father of Antiseptic Surgery', promoted cleanliness, antiseptic surgical methods, and carbolic acid to clean wounds and instruments as the vital elements in a patient's speedy recovery.

1847

Charles Babbage devised the ophthalmoscope that was popularised by Hermann von Helmholtz in 1851, and perfected by Greek ophthalmologist Andreas Anagnostakis soon after. This mechanism provided a magnified image of the patient's eye to the clinician.

◀ *The brain of Charles Babbage, called the 'Father of Modern Computing', displayed at the Science Museum, in London*

Blowing Glass into an Industry

The pace of glassmaking increased in 1635 when Sir Robert Maxwell began to use coal instead of wood, and glass industries no longer had to be based in forest areas. Several technological advancements from Germany and England brought glass production up to a level where it could be called an 'industry'.

Noteworthy Inventions in Glass

In 1851, one of the earliest uses of glass in structures was at the Crystal Palace for the Great Exhibition in London, where 3,00,000 glass panes were used as panels. Around 1900, American inventor Michael Owens created the automatic bottle-blowing machine that produced 2,500 bottles per hour. In 1923, the gob feeder was developed to supply consistently sized gobs in bottle production. Then, in 1925, the IS (Individual Section) machine was developed to work with gob feeders. The combination of an IS machine with the gob feeder that produces many bottles in one go is the crux of most automatic glass-container production today.

▲ A print of a photograph of the Owens Automatic Bottle Machine with ten arms. Each arm of the machine was fitted with bottle-making moulds. The fully automatic machine produced bottles faster and with different capacities

Float Glass

In the 1960s, Sir Alastair Pilkington's 'float' method of glassmaking was a revolution in the glass industry. He was looking for a more economical way of making high-quality glass that could be used for mirrors, shop windows, cars, and other applications where the requirement was distortion-free glass. The success of the Pilkington's method is based upon the careful balance of the volume of glass fed onto the bath, where it is flattened according to its height. Sir Alastair Pilkington's float glass method is used by 90 per cent of flat glass manufacturers even today.

▲ An engraved crystal vase by Gallé, circa 1900

Incredible Individuals

Over 1890-1920, **art nouveau** had a profound impact on glass art. Popular artists designing art nouveau glasses were Emile Gallé (France), Josef Hoffman (Austria), Louis Comfort Tiffany (USA), Joseph Maria Olbrich (Austria) and Karl Koepping (Germany). Early French glassmakers drew inspiration from Gallé for his '*pate de verre*' enamelling technique, which involved firing coloured glass to create translucent surfaces of different colours. Others worked with a thick, clear glass pressed into **moulds**, to trap bubbles in a '*verresouffle*' or 'bubble glass technique', or highlight relief surfaces (a type of sculpture).

▲ Emile Galle's self-portrait

Fossil Fuels: Unlocking New Energy Resources

Even before the potential of coal was discovered during the Industrial Revolution, oil and natural gas had long been in use, largely as a fuel for lamps and as grease for vehicles and equipment.

The Oil Industry

In 1853, one of the first oil wells was drilled in a forest near Bóbrka, Poland. In the same year, Ignacy Lukasiewicz, a Polish pharmacist and a rock-oil mine owner, was the first to distil kerosene from oil; he also invented the kerosene lamp.
It was found that although steam engines were efficient, they were slow starters, quite costly and could only be produced in small numbers. Petroleum-based fuel didn't have all these drawbacks. Moreover, the mass production of automobiles in the early 20th century increased the demand for petrol, and this fuelled the oil industry.

▲ The Lucas Oil Gusher at Spindletop Hill (an oil field), South of Beaumont, Texas, USA

▲ Bóbrka is an important landmark in the history of the oil industry

▼ A gas torch on an oil field

In Real Life

Carbon, apart from being released through evaporation, soil erosion, and volcanos, is stored below the ground in the form of fossil fuels and soil. It balances the Earth's 'carbon budget'. But that balance was disrupted during industrialisation, when fossil fuels were extracted on a large scale to produce energy and fuel. Their continued and increasing use has caused pollution of air, water, and climate.

Incredible Individuals

It was a merchant, John Austin, who introduced kerosene to the USA. He noticed a cost-effective oil lamp while travelling in Austria, and produced an upgraded version of it in the USA. This led to a boom in the country's rock-oil industry, as the prices of whale oil had already escalated because of the decrease in the number of these mammals. Suddenly, oil prices collapsed as production and refining increased. In 1859, an entrepreneur, Samuel Downer Jr. patented 'kerosene' as a trading name and put a licence on its use.

Electricity

The first reference to static electricity can be traced back to 600 BCE when ancient Greek philosopher Thales recorded that light materials were attracted to rubbed amber. He called materials like amber, glass, etc., 'electricks' after the Greek word for amber, 'elecktron'. Later, acclaimed 16th century physicist William Gilbert became the first to use the phrase 'electric force'.

The next notable landmark was German scientist Otto von Guericke's invention of the first electric generator in the mid 17th century. By the Second Industrial Revolution, electric power surpassed steam in its use. The pioneers of electricity were plenty and their inventions transformed the lives of generations to come.

Pioneers of Electricity

In 1752, the man who gave America its constitution, Benjamin Franklin, tried to collect electricity from lightning by flying a kite near thunderclouds. The kite was attached to a conductive wire; and to the wet kite string, a silk ribbon was tied along with a metal key that was connected to a Leyden jar. When Franklin moved his hand near the key, he got a shock. This led to the realisation that lightning could be diverted to the ground to prevent it from causing casualties.

▲ An artist's depiction of Benjamin Franklin flying a kite in an attempt to collect electricity from lightning

Discovery of Voltage

In 1799, Alessandro Volta gave the world the concept of Volt (symbol: V), the unit of measurement for electromotive force. He came up with it while inventing the electric battery. Belgian Zénobe Gramme conceived the dynamo, also called magneto, which was the first generator, in 1868. In the same year, the first hydroelectric power station became operational in Switzerland, and in 1891, the first high-voltage line was built between Lauffen and Frankfurt in Germany. Simultaneously, between the 19th and 20th centuries, Serbian-American engineer Nikola Tesla invented alternating-current (AC) motors, generators, and transformers as well as the Tesla coil used in radios, televisions, and other electronic equipment.

▲ Nikola Tesla (1856–1943) was one of the greatest scientific minds that the Earth has ever seen. An engineer, for whom money was not the primary goal, who would have changed the world if his Wardenclyffe project had come into being. Instead, he sadly died alone, penniless, and with only pigeons for friends

▲ Nikola Tesla's AC dynamo-electric machine (AC electric generator) in the 1888 US Patent 390,721

The Making of the Electrical Generator

In 1831, British scientist Michael Faraday successfully passed an electric current through a wire coil between two magnet poles, and by the next year, an electrical generator was built on this principle. This was a crucial step in our understanding of electromagnetism.

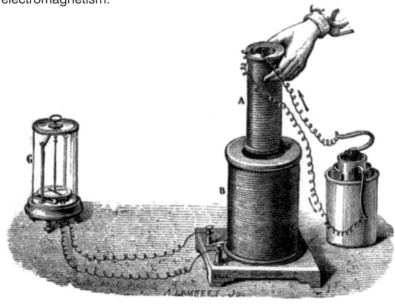

▲ One of Faraday's 1831 experiments demonstrating induction. The liquid battery (right) sends an electric current through the small coil (A). When it is moved in or out of the large coil (B), its magnetic field induces a momentary voltage in the coil, which is detected by the galvanometer

▲ Michael Faraday (1791-1867) came from a very poor family, but became one of the greatest scientists of history. It is even more impressive given that during his time science could only be pursued by those with enough wealth to support the education and resources that accompany scientific exploration

Another important discovery was the Ohm's Law, used to measure electrical current, in 1927 by Georg Simon Ohm. This eventually became the basis of the electric motor and the electric generator or dynamo.

▶ Georg Simon Ohm

▼ Nowadays, steel lattice transmission towers connect overhead power cables across electrical grids

👤 In Real Life

The Electricity Fairy is an enormous mural (10 x 60 m) painted by Raoul Dufy for the 1937 World's Fair in Paris. Now installed at the Paris Museum of Modern Art, it describes the history of electricity and its modern applications and has portraits of around 100 famous scientists and inventors who contributed to the development of electricity.

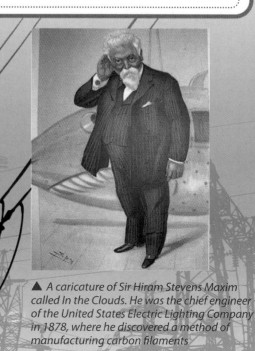

▲ A caricature of Sir Hiram Stevens Maxim called In the Clouds. He was the chief engineer of the United States Electric Lighting Company in 1878, where he discovered a method of manufacturing carbon filaments

Telegraph

The electric telegraph was the first electronic mode of communication that improved the delivery of letters. Prior to this, the Pony Express (a continuous relay of men on horseback delivering the mail) was the go-to mode of communication, and it would take 10 days to deliver a letter from Sacramento to Missouri.

Inventions before the Electric Telegraph

In 1809, Samuel Soemmering first invented a raw model of the electric telegraph, in Bavaria. He used 35 wires (for each encoded character) with a gold electrode placed in water. This way, messages could be read till 2,000 feet away, and interpreted depending on the amount of gas bubbles produced by electrolysis.

▶ *A sketch of Soemmering's electric telegraph*

Early Telegraphs

In 1828, Harrison Dyar invented the first telegraph in the USA, where the chemically treated paper tape would undergo electrical sparks to produce a coded message of dots and dashes. In 1837, British physicists William Fothergill Cooke and Charles Wheatstone patented the Cooke and Wheatstone 'needle' telegraph (the receiver had a number of needles that electromagnetic coils moved to point to letters on a board).

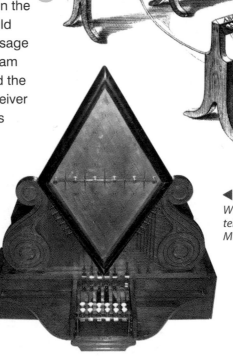

◀ *William Fothergill Cooke and Charles Wheatstone's electric telegraph (needle telegraph) from 1837, now in the Science Museum, London*

▲ *Charles Wheatstone and William Fothergill Cooke*

⊙ Incredible Individuals

Morse invented an electric telegraph system that was a great success. He built upon scientist Joseph Henry's discovery that electromagnets could be used to send a 'message' over a long distance. By 1835, he proved that signals could be **transmitted** by wire. His mechanism could move a marker to write codes on a paper strip, and soon emboss paper with dots and dashes. This is how the Morse code was born. On 1 May 1844, the first news transmitted over Morse's line was the nomination of Henry Clay from the Whig Party. It was carried by hand to the Annapolis Junction, between Washington and Baltimore, and wired to the capital by Morse's partner Alfred Vail. On 24 May 1944, Morse let Annie Ellsworth, the daughter of a friend, dispatch the famous message "What hath God wrought?" from a *Bible* verse, from the old US Supreme Court chamber, to his partner in Baltimore to officially declare that the line was completed.

▲ *Samuel Morse (1791-1872)*

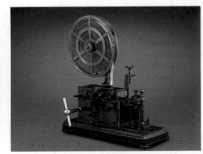

▲ *A Morse code receiver and recorder that dates back to the late 19th century*

Telephone

Till 1877, the telegraph was the only reliable source of long-distance communication. In the same year, several scientists were working on a new and effective way of communicating over long distances—the telephone. Alexander Graham Bell, who began his research in 1874, managed to win the first US patent for the telephone in 1876.

By 1879, the telephone had grown so popular that Western Union and the telephone system reached an agreement to operate as two separate services. Earlier in 1853, French professor Édouard-Léon Scott de Martinville, who was also a teacher of the deaf and mute, thought about 'electronic speech' and invented the phonautograph, which recognised the vibrations of speech.

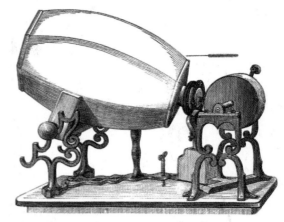

▲ *An illustration of French professor Édouard-Léon Scott de Martinville's phonautograph*

Father of the Telephone

The phonautograph and the telegraph both inspired the Scottish inventor Alexander Graham Bell to invent the telephone. On 2 June 1875, along with assistant electrician Thomas Watson, he observed that when the reed moved in a **magnetic** field, the frequencies and tone of spoken sound waves could be reproduced. On 10 March 1876, Bell spoke into the receiver of the instrument to Watson, who was in the other room with another telephone, saying the famous words, "Mr Watson—come here—I want to see you." This invention instantly lowered the demand for telegraphs as 'talking with electricity' was faster and more exciting. Bell went on to own the American Telephone and Telegraph Company (AT&T).

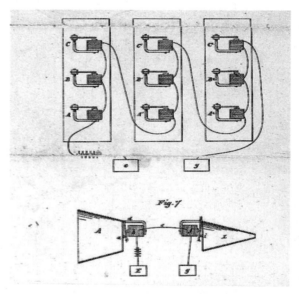

▲ *A patent drawing of Alexander Graham Bell's telephone. It was the first instrument that could transmit human speech through a machine*

Other Notable Inventions

While Bell patented the telephone first, American inventor Elisha Grey had also created prototypes of the same. The two inventors fought a long battle over taking credit, but Bell won. In 1849, Italian immigrant Antonio Meucci designed the telephone and, in 1871, even filed a caveat to announce his invention. Unfortunately, Meucci could not afford to renew the caveat and so his contribution to the discovery was not considered. But on 11 June 2002, the United States House of Representatives honoured Meucci's inventions.

▲ *Antonio Meucci, photographed by L Alman*

💡 Isn't It Amazing!

In 1888, Bell invented an advanced version of Thomas Edison's phonograph. Edison, in turn, invented the microphone that could be fitted into the telephone. People no longer had to scream into the receiver to be heard at the other end.

▲ *Alexander Graham Bell on the telephone, calling from New York to Chicago in 1892*

Lighting

Gas and kerosene lamps were the only source of artificial lighting till the early part of the Industrial Revolution, but their popularity declined in the next 50 years, after the invention of the electric light bulb during 1878–79.

⚛ A Tussle Between Gas Lighting & Electricity

Gaslight technology evolved in England in the 1790s, and by 1879 people had grown used to the idea of lighting with gas. Gaslight manufacturers started to provide better quality gas and brighter lights. Besides, they had existing infrastructure, while electric lighting required power-generating plants to be built with connecting wires across the entire distance. Edison decided to design his electric lighting system based on the model of the gaslight technology. But, unlike the manually operated gas lamps, Edison's electric lighting system was automatic. Then in 1880 came Sir Hiram Maxim's lamp which contained a high-resistance **filament**. It was produced quicker than usual because Maxim hired Edison's expert glassblower, Ludwig Boehm. The United States Electric Lighting Company used the Maxim lamp in their installed electric lighting systems for many years.

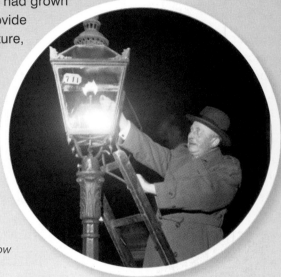

▶ *A gas lamp being manually lit on a street in Stockholm. Can you imagine how difficult it must have been to light up an entire city using such lamps?*

⊛ Incredible Individuals

The electric bulb underwent many inventions. Between 1878–79, an English inventor, Joseph Wilson Swan, and an American, Thomas Alva Edison, both invented an incandescent lamp. They were engaged in a long tiff till they agreed to form a joint company called Edison & Swan United Company in 1883. Swan got patents for many features of the lamp before Edison, but since the latter conceived power lines and other lighting equipment, he is given more credit. In 1886, inventors Elihu Thomson and Edwin Houston jointly began manufacturing incandescent lamps under Sawyer-Man patents. In 1892, J. Pierpont Morgan orchestrated a merger between Edison and Thomson-Houston, and together they formed General Electric.

▲ *Thomas Edison's first successful light bulb model, used in a public demonstration at Menlo Park, December 1879*

▲ *Thomas Alva Edison's portrait*

▲ *Inside Thomas Edison's Menlo Park Laboratory*

Banking and Financial Institutions

The three banking tiers in existence at that point in England comprised the Central Bank of England established in 1694, 30 private banks preferred by traders and industrialists, and 12 county banks. Prior to 1750, copper was used for daily transactions, and gold and silver for major ones. Commercial bills and paper money too were in existence. By 1750, private banks kept growing, in terms of both status and business.

⚛ Development of the Banking system

Increasing business opportunities and the resultant wealth brought with them the need to deposit the earnings in one place, and also acquire loans for building equipment and infrastructure for factories, railways and canals. This gave rise to specialist banks that catered to certain industries. The merchants supplied some of the circulated capital. Some of it came from the **aristocrats**, who had acquired money from land and estates and were now keen on increasing their wealth by investing it and assisting others. They were able to supply land, capital and infrastructure.

By 1800, England had 70 private banks and 24 county banks. But the Napoleonic Wars scared the public and led to a mass withdrawal of money, till the government passed a rule stating that only paper notes, not gold, could be withdrawn. The Country Bankers Act of 1826 put a limit on the issuance of notes, and many banks had to make their own notes. This resulted in the formation of joint-stock companies. The end of the 19th century saw the merger of many localised banks.

▲ An illustration of the interior of the Central Bank during working hours in the 1800s

⊛ Incredible Individuals

The finance sector produced a group of individuals from the Midlands called 'shock troops' who inadvertently helped spread the revolution by buying land with their profits. These were managers, capitalists, merchants, financiers, and salespersons, who ranged from key figures to small-scale players in the finance industry.

▼ The Bank of England gained a monopoly over the issue of banknotes with the Bank Charter Act of 1844

How Industrialisation Was Smuggled Out of Britain

Britain tried hard to keep the benefits of industrialisation to its home shores so it could dominate the global economy and trade. But visiting Europeans and Americans who had learnt the secrets and techniques of creating machines went back to their countries and reproduced factories and railroads. At times, the machines were even smuggled out of Britain in rowboats to other countries. The first few countries to follow Britain's lead were France, Belgium, Germany, and Switzerland.

⚛ Outside Europe

The American Civil War (1861–65) was an 'industrial war' where the urban, industrially advanced people of the Northern states fought the agriculturally inclined people in the Southern states that used slave labour. As a result, both sides reacted differently to the Industrial Revolution. Industrialisation continued despite the war, and by 1900, USA was producing 24 per cent of the world's output in manufacturing, overtaking Britain. In 1870, the **monarchy** in Japan adapted quickly to early industrialisation. But in Russia, the czar and the nobility struggled with the harmonious implementation of industrialisation. Industrialised nations, with the help of their armies and naval forces, were able to colonise countries that were not at par with them, and exploited these colonies for raw materials which they used in their own factories.

▲ Crew members of the ship USS Wissahickson standing beside a Dahlgren XI-inch pivot gun during the 1863 American Civil War

⊙ Incredible Individuals

In 1789, Samuel Slater took industrialisation to American soil when he **migrated** from Britain to Rhode Island, USA. He built the first textile factory there, purely from memory, as British authorities would have seized any written notes. Between 1810–12, Francis Cabot Lowell returned to Massachusetts after a trip to England and set up the first power loom that merged mechanical spinning and weaving in the USA.

▲ Located on the banks of the Blackstone River in the United States, the historic Slater Mill used water-powered machines to spin cotton

▲ Samuel Slater (1768–1835) is popularly called 'The Father of the American Industrial Revolution'

Prose During the Industrial Revolution

Many authors were influenced by the Industrial Revolution and wrote stories based on the lives of working class people and the oppression and injustices they experienced in industrial England. A new genre of writing known as the 'industrial novel' emerged, it dealt with the lives of the workers. Authors used their works to portray how, although on the surface society looked like it was progressing, the poor and working classes experienced severe hardships. Child labour was common in factories and mines, moreover the working conditions were in such a dismal state that it often put their lives at high risk. Authors contributed to bring about change by highlighting the plight of this particular strata, eventually the society and government took notice and worked towards their upliftment; laws were passed and changes were made to improve the lives of the working class as well as of women and children.

▲ *An illustration from the novel North and South by Elizabeth Gaskell*

 ## Charles Dickens

In his famous classic *Oliver Twist*, English author Charles Dickens depicted the harsh living conditions during this time in history. *The Pickwick Papers, Hard Times, A Christmas Carol*, and *David Copperfield* are some of his works that reflect his own experiences while working at a blacking factory. His works justly portrays the horrid conditions of the working class in the light of his own experiences. He openly wrote about the treatment of children across England. His stories focus on social injustices and upon people whose lives were ravaged by poverty during the Industrial Revolution.

Elizabeth Gaskell

She was a famous female author from the mid 1800s. Belonging to England's Manchester—a city that was an industrial powerhouse known for its cotton—she wrote *North and South*. In the novel, she covered the plight of the working class, poverty, and other social issues during the Industrial Revolution. Her novel *Mary Barton* is about the struggles of a working-class family. She received a lot of criticism because she openly sympathised with the working class.

👤 In Real Life

Robert Owen was a businessman and social reformer from New Lanark, Scotland. In the early 19th century, he managed a cotton mill which became a model community. He worked hard for the rights and upliftment of the working class. His famous work, *A New View of Society* focused on his principles of educational philanthropy.

▲ *Robert Owen (1771-1858)*

The Industrial Revolution and Poetry

Child labour, the plight of the working class, the destruction of nature, etc., were some of the consequences of the Industrial Revolution that led many poets like William Blake, Percy Shelley, John Keats, and William Wordsworth to criticise the revolution. Some of them felt that it had caused more harm than good, and they called upon the people of Great Britain to remember the times when industrialisation and urbanisation had not spread across the country.

▲ *An extract from the poem, The Chimney Sweeper by William Blake*

 ## William Blake

Labour laws prevalent at the time of the Industrial Revolution allowed children to work. They were discriminated against and paid much lower wages than those received by adults. They had to work for long hours and some of them even began working as early as age four. William Blake's poem, *The Chimney Sweeper*, from his collection *Songs of Innocence and Experience*, is about the injustice suffered by child chimney sweeps. Blake explains the sad lives of innocent children who, on the pretext of their small size, were forced to climb up the chimney's and clean them.

 ## William Wordsworth

Industrialisation lead to an increase in the number of factories, and the need for more labour. Many people moved to the cities for jobs. But the workers were underpaid and lived in small houses with poor living conditions. They no longer lived near nature but in polluted cities. William Wordsworth was a poet famous for his love for nature. Although the Industrial Revolution did solve some problems, he felt that it violated the relationship between humans and the environment in many ways. In response to the effect of the Industrial Revolution on nature, William Wordsworth, in his poem *Lines Composed a Few Miles Above Tintern Abbey*, recalls happier times spent in nature as compared to the lonely rooms and din of towns and cities.

▲ *A portrait of the English poet William Wordsworth*

In Real Life

Caroline Norton (1808–1877) was a poet who wrote about the issue of child labour, and through her poems such as *A Voice from the Factories* spoke about the harsh conditions and suffering of the children working in factories at the time of the Industrial Revolution.

▲ *Caroline Norton*

The Effect of the Industrial Revolution on Society

Industrialisation and urbanisation led to increased demands for greater social welfare, labour rights, education, equality, and political rights. In 1807, the African slave trade was abolished in America. In 1832, the British Great Reform Act was passed, which saw the representation of the manufacturing cities of Birmingham and Manchester for the first time, causing a change in the organisation of the parliament and governance.

 ## Industrialisation Changed all Sectors

Industrialisation had increased the production of coal by twentyfold, 'pig' (crude) iron by thirtyfold and textiles by fifteenfold. There was development in the iron, textile, transportation, banking, and communication industries. The number and variety of manufactured goods increased, they became more affordable and were easily available to the masses. The standard of living for middle and upper classes improved. The **oligarchical** ownership that initially controlled the means of production encouraged a bigger distribution of ownership through common stocks. Britain's working class' conditions improved by the end of the 19th century as the government passed various labour reforms, including the workers' right to form trade unions.

▲ *Iron and Coal by William Bell Scott illustrates the rise of coal and ironworkers in the Industrial Revolution and the complex engineering projects they made possible*

 ## More Spending Power

The costs of clothes, tools, and household items reduced due to mass production. Employment opportunities rose as new factories were constructed and the need for manpower required to operate the machines increased. Factory employees earned more than farmers. People were no longer dependent on their farms for income. The growing middle class now had access to economic power that, till now, was held by aristocrats.

💡 Isn't It Amazing!

The Great Exhibition in London, 1851, was testimony to the progress Britain had made with industrialisation. On display were revolvers, telegraphs, reaping machines, sewing machines, and steam hammers to showcase how the British were the world's best manufacturers of machinery.

 ## The Rise of Specialist Professions

Industrialisation led to a change in the nature of work as well as manufacturing, and encouraged specialisation. Teachers and trainers were hired to impart specialised skills. Workers were divided into groups. Some had to transport raw materials such as coal, iron and steel. Some handled the functions of different machines, others repaired them, and still others upgraded or improved their efficiency. Work was divided in this manner and each department gained expertise in particular areas. Specialised departments handled **sanitation**, traffic, and taxation. The significance of specialised professionals such as lawyers, builders, physicians, and others increased as well.

Pitfalls of the Industrial Revolution

While the Industrial Revolution was known to have heralded rapid growth and change while improving the quality of life in Britain, America, and several other countries, it also had its drawbacks. While it brought large profits to the upper classes, it also led to subhuman living and working conditions for the working class that often lacked even basic **amenities**.

 ## Decreased Quality of Life

Young children were employed for long hours in dangerous environs at very low salaries by textile mills and factories. In the early 1860s, one-fifth of Britain's textile industry had workers younger than 15 years of age. Factory workers had to toil 14–16 hours per day, 6 times a week. Men earned twice the amount women did, and children earned even lower. The working conditions, especially in the mines, were dangerous. Unskilled workers had no job security. Machines replaced craftspeople. Most machines were dirty, produced soot and smoke, and their use caused many ailments and accidents resulting in death and injuries.

 ## Poor Work and Housing Infrastructure

Alongside modern buildings, inferior low-cost housing options such as shanties and shacks also cropped up. Better wages attracted migrants to industrial cities and towns, but these places were unable to tide the flow and number of new workers from the countryside. Local sewerage and sanitation systems took a toll. This—along with overcrowded homes, pollution, and unsanitary living conditions—caused a number of disease outbreaks such as smallpox, cholera, typhus, and tuberculosis.

 ## Rise in Obesity

Use of tractors, trains and automobiles certainly made life easy. With the rise of automation, various professions became **sedentary** and the invention of the TV and the radio gave rise to 'couch potato' culture. This way of life has led to an array of lifestyle diseases including obesity, diabetes, and hypertension.

▲ *Michael Sadler was a British historian and educationist. He led the factory reform movement in England and worked to regulate and improve factory conditions and working hours, especially for children*

▲ *A 19ᵗʰ century representation of the cholera epidemic. Cholera, an unknown disease in the Western Hemisphere before 1830, turned out to be one of the most feared diseases of the 19ᵗʰ century*

 ## Root Cause of Environmental Threats

Most of the world's current environmental problems began or were exacerbated during the Industrial Revolution. Depletion of Earth's natural resources such as water, trees, soil, rocks, and minerals, fossil fuels, etc., began with the Industrial Revolution. While coal was responsible for kick-starting the Industrial Revolution and changing the way people utilised energy, it eventually had an ill-effect on the environment and, in turn, the health of all living beings. Air and water pollution, loss of flora and fauna, and global warming are considered to be the ghastly after-effects of industrialisation. Before 1750, atmospheric carbon dioxide existed in concentrations of 275 to 290 parts per million by volume (ppmv). It had crossed 400 ppmv by 2017.

Word Check

Ancient World

Aqueduct: It is an artificial channel for conveying water, typically in the form of a bridge across a valley or other gap.

Bronze Age: In the history of human civilisation, this is the period when people shifted from using stone tools to metals. The time period varies from region to region. In Greece and China, for instance, it started in 3,000 BCE but it Britain, it only began during 1900 BCE.

Citadel: It is a fortress, typically one on high ground above a city.

City state: This is when a city and its immediate surroundings are considered an independent nation.

Confucianism: This system of thought focuses on being rational and true to social and familial hierarchies. It was developed by Chinese philosopher Confucius (551–479 BCE).

Cult: This is a group of people who share beliefs or customs that are markedly different from those of the majority.

Doab: It is the basin of two rivers.

Dynastic: It is a term used to describe a line of rulers belonging to the same family.

Egyptologist: An expert on ancient Egypt—especially its customs, culture, history, language, and often on Egyptian archaeology as well

Ethnicity: It is the fact or state of belonging to a social group that has a common national or cultural tradition.

Feng Shui: It is a system of rules that is used while deciding the plans or position of furniture in buildings to guide positive energy.

Glazed: It is a technique of fitting glass panes into a structure like glass or door frame.

Mesoamerica: It refers to the cultural civilisations that belonged to ancient Mexico, Guatemala, Honduras, Belize, El Salvador, Nicaragua, and Costa Rica.

Metallurgists: They are experts in the branch of science and technology concerned with the properties of metals and their production as well as purification.

Mummify: This refers to the use of specific physical and chemical processes to embalm a dead body and prevent it from rotting away.

Neolithic: It marks the New Stone Age, which is characterized by the development of settled agriculture and the usage of polished weapons and tools.

Nomadic: It is an adjective used to describe travelling or wandering people.

Oracle: It refers to a priest or priestess acting as a medium, sharing a prophecy from the gods.

Pagoda: A temple with tiered towers, typically seen in Hindu or Buddhist architecture of East and Southeast Asia

Pictography: It is a method of writing that uses pictures or drawings to represent words or letters.

Relief: This a type of sculpture that is raised above (but remains attached to) its background surface.

Ridge: It is a long, narrow hilltop, mountain range or watershed.

Sarcophagus: This is a decorated stone coffin of the ancient civilisations of Egypt, Rome, and Greece.

Siege warfare: It is a military strategy from the ancient and medieval times where an army surrounded a fortress or castle and weakened it by cutting off essential supplies in order to capture it.

Surplus: It means to have extra or excess of something.

Taoism: This system of philosophy highlights humility and religious piety. It is based on the writings of philosopher Lao-Tzu who is believed to have been lived in 4th or 6th century BCE.

Yin and Yang: The Yin-Yang philosophy states that the universe is governed by duality—opposite yet complementing energies, such as darkness and light, young and old, etc.

Middle Ages

Abbess: This was the senior, the leader, of all nuns in a convent.

Abbot: This was the senior, the leader, of all monks in a monastery.

An Lushan Rebellion: General An Lushan went against the Tang emperor and made himself the emperor of northern China in 755 CE. His Yan Dynasty fell in 763 CE, but the fight greatly weakened his Tang rivals.

Caliph: It refers to the Islamic rulers who succeeded the Prophet Muhammad. The word comes from Arabic kalifa, meaning deputy of God.

Celtic: A collection of cultures/peoples, including Picts and Scots, who settled in the British Isles and parts of Spain. They are known today by their culture and languages (e.g. Irish, Scottish Gaelic, and Welsh).

Cloisonné: A decorative work in which enamel, glass, or gemstones are separated by strips of flattened wire on a metal backing.

Gaul: The ancient name for France.

Guilds: Professional groups formed by people of a trade.

Hundred Years' War: This was a series of European conflicts, divided by short periods of truce. It was spread over a century; hence the name.

Iberian Peninsula: The south-westernmost peninsula of Europe, comprising Spain and Portugal.

Nativity: The occasion of a person's birth, most often used to refer to the birth of Jesus Christ.

Niall of the Nine Hostages: A part-historical, part-legendary king of the northern half of Ireland. He lived sometime during the 4th–5th centuries CE.

Nika riots: Many people, unhappy with Emperor Justinian I's reforms, tried to overthrow him. They shouted 'Nika!' (Conquer!) and assaulted the palace. Half the city burned and thousands died before the riots were quelled.

Patriarchal: Relating to a system or government that is controlled by men.

Polymath: A person of wide and varied learning.

Purgatory: In Catholicism, this means a temporary place of suffering for dead souls of sinners before they go to heaven.

Sa cking: This is the capturing and plundering of cities by invading armies.

Schism: This is a word for discord that leads to a formal division/splitting of a group.

Serf: In feudal times, workers were often compelled to serve their landowners without pay, as if they were their property, much like slaves. Such bonded labourers were called serfs.

Siege: This is when an army blockades an enemy's city or fort, cutting off communication and supplies to force it to surrender.

Renaissance

Baptistery: This is the part of a church that is used for performing baptisms, a rite of passage for being accepted as a Christian.

Boyar: This is the term for Russian nobility.

Catholics: Christianity is divided into many groups that hold slightly differing beliefs. Catholics form the largest of these groups. They are guided by the Pope, the Bishop of Rome.

Chanson: This is a song with French words or a song whose words have been set to music by a French composer.

Chiaroscuro: This refers to the effect of contrasting light and shadow in an artwork.

City state: A small territory, centred on a powerful city, that acts as an independent nation

Classical: In the context of scholarship and art, this refers to the knowledge and learning of Ancient Greece and Rome.

Colosseum: This refers to a large open theatre or stadium built by Ancient Romans.

Condottieri: In medieval and Renaissance Italy, this referred to leaders of troops that fought for money (rather than out of loyalty for a country or cause).

Conquistador: The men who led the Spanish and Portuguese conquests of South America.

Constantinople: Modern-day Istanbul in Turkey was the centre of the Eastern Roman Empire—or the Byzantine Empire—during the Middle Ages. The city was then called Constantinople, after the Roman Emperor Constantine the Great (c. 272–337 CE), who made it his capital city.

Diet: An imperial council; the Diet of Worms was held in the city of Worms.

El Greco: This is the nickname of Doménikos Theotokópoulos (1541–1614). His dramatic, twisted artworks were way ahead of his time and puzzled many of his contemporaries.

Epidemic: An epidemic is the widespread occurrence of infectious diseases at any given time.

Execution: This is the act of carrying out the death sentence on a person judged to be a criminal.

Fresco: This is the art of painting on a wall while its coating of plaster is still fresh and moist.

Marranos: Jews who converted to Christianity officially but still practised Judaism secretly.

Motet: This refers to church music sung by a choir without using any instruments. The words are usually in Latin. If the words are in English, it is called an anthem.

New World: This refers to the Americas and many Pacific islands, which became prominent from the 16th century onwards, after Western explorers began to conquer them.

Old World: This refers to Africa, Asia, and Europe, lands that have been known to humankind since ancient times.

Page: A young attendant, usually a boy.

Perspective: This refers to the way in which three-dimensional objects are painted or sculpted so as to give a viewer different ideas/perceptions of height, width, depth, and relative position.

Polymath: This refers to a person of great and varied learning.

Protestants: This refers to Christians who broke away from the Catholic Church in the 16th century. They believed Catholicism had become corrupt and sought a way back to the original teachings of Christianity.

Retable: This is a frame that holds carved or decorated panels. It is placed just behind the altar.

Sack of Rome: Sacking is the brutal pillaging of a town or city by an invading army. In the course of history, Rome has been sacked seven times!

Sfumato: This is an art technique that creates soft forms using gradually changing tones, shades, and colours, rather than sharp, clear outlines.

Spanish Inquisition: This was a Roman Catholic court set up by Spain to root out any religious beliefs that were contrary to Catholicism.

Stucco: This is a fine plaster used inside buildings for decoration or ornamentation.

Tintoretto: This Italian painter lived over 1518–94. A master of the Venice school of art, he was hailed for both the speed of his painting and his powerful brushwork.

Treatise: A formal, written work that is a scholarly exploration of a subject.

Triptych: This is an artwork that is spread over three panels.

Triumvirate: This refers to a group of three people holding power over a territory (instead of a single monarch). Ancient Rome of the 1st century BCE was sometimes ruled by a triumvirate of men.

Revolution & Independence

Autonomy: This refers to conditional self-government under a greater authority.

Besiege: This is the military act of blockading a city or fortress, with the purpose of forcing it to surrender by cutting off its food and other supplies and assaulting its defences.

Capital: In finance, this refers to resources that business people must have to buy what they need to operate a successful enterprise.

Communism: This is a system in which all property is owned by the community; each person contributes and receives according to their ability and needs.

Coup: This is a sudden, usually violent, seizure of power.

Economic sanctions: These are financial and other types of penalties (punishments) levied on misbehaving states or institutions.

Equality: In civilisation, this term means that all humans have the same rights and are equal in the eyes of the law. It is not to be confused with the math term 'equal', which is only a comparison of quantities.

Fraternity: In civilisation, this is the idea that all humans are linked in kinship and should support each other.

Guerrilla: This refers to small groups of combatants who fight larger armed forces using hit-and-run tactics, sabotage and harassment.

Guillotine: The instrument of choice for beheading people during the French Revolution. It comprised two long poles with a sharp blade in between, at the top. A condemned person would kneel under the blade, which, falling from such height, would slice cleanly through the neck.

Inquisition: In European history, this refers to a tribunal set up to find and remove religious heresy.

Insurrection: This is a rebellion or uprising against ruling powers.

Junta: This refers to a military group that seizes political power—usually in Spain, Portugal or South America.

Literary salons: A gathering of like-minded people under a roof to discuss important subjects of the day.

Minutemen: This refers to the militiamen of the American Revolution who volunteered to be ready for service at a minute's notice.

Mutiny: A refusal, especially by soldiers, to follow orders and rebelling against authorities.

Pamphlet: A booklet or leaflet that is given out to people to spread a message or give information on a subject.

Polymath: This is a person of wide knowledge and understanding.

Republic: A form of government in which the affairs of a nation are considered a public matter, and not the private concern of the people in power.

Stadtholder: Over the 15th–18th centuries, this term referred to the chief magistrate of the Netherlands.

Vodou: This is the religion of certain African and Creole people.

Scientific & Industrial revolution

Amenities: Desirable or useful features or facilities of a building or place.

Aristocrats: A social class of the highest order in society, it often consists of the nobility and people who hold ranks and titles.

Art nouveau: A new style of art that began around the year 1890 and spread through Europe and the USA. It was often used in architecture, design, etc., and was based on the idea of art being a part of daily life and applying art to everyday objects.

Assembly-line approach: It refers to a process where a line of workers or machines complete a specific job on a product as it is being produced or built. The production process is divided into steps, and no single worker or machine completes the entire task.

Boring machine: A machine with a

cutting tool that is used to either make a smooth and accurate hole, or to enlarge a hole that has already been drilled in a material.

Canal: Artificial waterway or man-made channel of water to allow transport of goods and services.

Factory: A space that produces goods and services using machines operated by trained staff.

Filament: A thread or conducting wire with a high melting point at the centre of an electric bulb or thermionic valve that gets heated by an electric current.

Foundries: Workshops or factories for casting metal.

Furnace: Closed area where materials can be heated at very high temperatures to harden objects.

Greenhouse gases: Gases that trap the Sun's energy and cause warming of Earth's surface, also known as the greenhouse effect.

Haemorrhage: When blood escapes from a damaged blood vessel.

Horsepower: A unit of power that measures the rate at which a device performs mechanical work.

Industrialisation: The development of industries in a country or region on a wide scale.

Infrastructure: Man-made structures (e.g. buildings, roads, power supplies) that assist in the functioning of a society.

Jig: A special device that holds a work piece and guides the machine tool as the operation is carried out

Locomotive: A powered (usually electric or diesel) railway vehicle used for pulling trains

Machine tools: These are power-driven tools used to cut, drill or fashion metals or other hard materials into useful parts

Magnetism: A physical phenomenon produced by the motion of electric charge, which results in attractive and repulsive forces between objects

Manpower: The total number of people working on a project or for an employer

Manufacturing machines: These are machines used to create or assemble items (like cars), with little or no help from humans

Migration: Relocating or moving to a new place, usually for job opportunities

Monarchy: A form of governance where the monarch (ruler/king/queen) rules the land till death; power is then transferred to the monarch's heirs

Moulding: A piece of wood or other material fitted as a decorative architectural feature

Oligarchical: A small group controlling the affairs of a country or organisation

Oxidiser: A chemical with which a fuel burns

Patent: An exclusive right to a product or process given to the inventor (an individual or a firm), which permits the manufacture, use or sale of the invention and excludes others from doing so, usually for a limited period of time

Pirn: A rod-like device similar to a reel or spool on which weavers wind thread for weaving

Piston: A disc or a piece of solid metal that is part of an engine and moves back and forth inside a cylinder to press a liquid or a gas into a small space to impart or derive motion

Prototype: The original version of a product from which the final version is developed. It is mostly created during the testing and evaluation phase and is found to lack a few features that the final product has.

Revolution: A drastic change in the way a system/organisation/country works; the change can be for the better or worse, and can be sudden, temporary or ranging over a long period.

Sanitation: Public health conditions, including provisions for clean drinking water and disposal of human excreta and sewage

Sedentary: Sitting most of the time, somewhat inactive

Slag: Stony waste matter that is separated from metals during the process of smelting or refining ore

Slotting machine: A machine with a tool that moves up and down and is used to cut slots and grooves of different sizes in materials

Spindle: A straight wooden spike used for spinning and twisting fibres of wool, flax, hemp, and cotton into yarn

Static electricity: An electric charge caused by friction

Transfusion: The process of transferring blood from one human being into the circulatory system of another human of the same blood type

Transmission: The process of broadcasting or transferring something from one person or medium to another

Urbanisation: The process by which large numbers of people shift from living in the countryside to towns and cities.

Vaccination: Administration of a vaccine to the body to build immunity or strength to fight off a particular disease

Vacuum: A space entirely devoid of matter

Variolation: A method of immunising patients against smallpox by infecting them with a mild form of the disease (using a substance taken from the pustules of patients). It is no longer in use.

Warp: It is a term used to describe the direction of threads in a fabric. These threads run vertically, parallel to the selvedge (fabric's edge).

Weft: It is a term used to describe the direction of threads in a fabric. These are the threads that run perpendicular to the selvedge.

Wars

Arquebusiers: This is the word for soldiers who were armed with an arquebus, an early form of the rifle.

Autonomous: This is the right of an organisation to govern its internal affairs.

Battalions: This refers to a large body of troops.

Blockade: This is the act of sealing off or barricading something—a port, a street or a town—so that nothing and no one can enter or leave.

Cavalry: This refers to soldiers who fight on horseback.

Conquistadors: This refers to a Spanish or Portuguese conqueror of South America in the 15th–16th centuries.

Conscripted: This is the act of forcing someone to join the armed services.

Dauphin: This was the title of the crown prince of France.

Defenestration: This literally means throwing someone out of a window. In modern times, it is used to refer to removing someone from a position of authority.

Embargo: This is an official ban on trading or doing business with another country.

Exported: This refers to goods being sold to another country.

Galley slave: This is a person who is condemned to rowing in a galley, which is a large ship often used for naval battles.

Garrison: This is a group of soldiers stationed in a town or fort, usually to defend it.

Guerrilla: This refers to a small independent group of fighters, who take part in irregular fighting, typically against larger regular forces.

Mahdi: This refers to a Muslim leader in certain parts of the world. The Mahdi who captured Khartoum was Muhammad Ahmad (1843-85) of Dongola, Sudan.

Prosthetic: This denotes an artificial body part, like an artificial leg.

Puritans: A group of English Protestants in the 16th–17th centuries who held particularly strict and overcritical moral rules.

Reparations: This is the action of making amends for a wrong done to someone or to some group. It usually involves payment and other forms of assistance to set things right.

Republican: This is a person who believes that the governance of a country is the business of all its citizens.

Vassal: This refers to a person or state that owes allegiance to another person or state.

a: above, b: below/ bottom, c: centre, f: far, l: left, r: right, t: top, bg: background

Cover

Shutterstock: Francesco Scatena; Everett Collection; Sean Pavon; Simon Mayer; posztos; Veniamin Kraskov; jejim; Jaroslav Moravcik;

Wikimedia Commons: Front: File:Dschingis Khan 01.jpg / https://commons.wikimedia.org/wiki/File:Dschingis_Khan_01.jpg; File:Moctezuma I, the Fifth Aztec King.png / https://commons.wikimedia.org/wiki/File:Moctezuma_I,_the_Fifth_Aztec_King.png; File:Chaussure chinoise Saverne 02 05 2012 1.jpg / https://commons.wikimedia.org/wiki/File:Chaussure_chinoise_Saverne_02_05_2012_1.jpg; https://commons.wikimedia.org/wiki/File:Weltliche_Schatzkammer_Wien_(190)2.JPG / https://commons.wikimedia.org/wiki/File:Weltliche_Schatzkammer_Wien_(190)2.JPG; File:CHINE, 1 Yuan à l'effigie du Président Yuan Shikai.jpg / https://commons.wikimedia.org/wiki/File:CHINE,_1_Yuan_à_l' effigie_du_Président_Yuan_Shikai.jpg; File:Birmingham Quran manuscript.jpg / https://commons.wikimedia.org/wiki/File:Birmingham_Quran_manuscript.jpg; File:Washington Crossing the Delaware by Emanuel Leutze, MMA-NYC, 1851.jpg / https://commons.wikimedia.org/wiki/File:Washington_Crossing_the_Delaware_by_Emanuel_Leutze,_MMA-NYC,_1851.jpg;

Back: File:Timur reconstruction03.jpg / https://commons.wikimedia.org/wiki/File:Timur_reconstruction03.jpg; File:Ming-Schale1.jpg / https://commons.wikimedia.org/wiki/File:Ming-Schale1.jpg; File:Neolithic pottery, Museum of Western Bohemia, 187697.jpg / https://commons.wikimedia.org/wiki/File:Neolithic_pottery,_Museum_of_Western_Bohemia,_187697.jpg; File:Xian 2006 6-5.jpg / https://commons.wikimedia.org/wiki/File:Xian_2006_6-5.jpg; File:MilosObrenovic 1848.jpg / https://commons.wikimedia.org/wiki/File:MilosObrenovic_1848.jpg

Ancient World

Shutterstock: 4&5t/Everett Collection; 5tr/Juan Aunion; 5bl/Naaman Abreu; 6t/invisiblepower; 6bl/Mountains Hunter; 7tl/pryzmat; 7cr/Vladimir Korostyshevskiy; 7br/De Viacheslav Lopatin; 8tr/Fedor Selivanov; 8b/Homo Cosmicos; 9t/Jukka Palm; 9bl/Dima Moroz; 9br/Luti; 10tr/Jose Ignacio Soto; 10&11b/Gordana Adzieva; 11tr/Kamira; 11cr/Nomad_Soul; 12 & 13 background/; 12tl/Ashwin; 12br/EleniMac; 13br/Jakub Kyncl; 12& 13/matrioshka; 14tr/Murat Hajdarhodzic; 14cr/rysp_z; 14b/Daily Travel Photos; 15bl/Supavadee butradee; 15tr/Delbars; 15cl/Leon Rafael; 16tr/posztos; 16 & 17b/zhao jiankang; 17tr/fotohunter; 17cr/yienkeat; 18tc/Romolo Tavani; 18cl/cc; 18b/cc; 18tr/ StockAppeal; 19tr/HelloRF Zcool; 19cr/GuoZhongHua; 19bl/Mark Brandon; 19br/cl2004lhy; 19br/jianbing Lee; 20b/Jawwad Ali; 21br/steve estvanik; 22t/Thotsaporn.S; 22tr/arun sambhu mishra; 22br/Gumpanat; 23tr/GCapture; 23cr/Natalya Erofeeva; 23bl/javarman; 23br/Lukiyanova Natalia frenta; 24tr/Vladimir Korostyshevskiy; 24bl/ Hurst Photo; 24b/IR Stone; 25br/jejim; 26tr/Sean Pavone; 26cl/Simon Mayer; 26b/Anton_Ivanov; 27t/AlexandrinaZ; 27bl/Pung; 28tr/Blue Planet Studio; 28cl/Kamira; 28bl/Francesco Scatena; 28bl/TTstudio; 28b/javarman; 29t/anyaivanova; 29cr/matrioshka; 29c/Slava Gerj; 29bl/Tatiana Popova; 30&31bg/SS pixels; 30&31border/luma_art; 30tl/markara; 30tc/Svetlana Mahovskaya; 30tr/Anastasios71; 30bl/aquatarkus; 30br/itechno; 31tl/markara; 31tl2/markara; 31tc/MidoSemsem; 31bl/Fernando Cortes; 31br/ Zvonimir Atletic

Wikimedia Commons: 3b/Egyptian_harvest/Anonymous Egyptian tomb artist(s) / Public domain/wikimedia commons ; 4tr/Neolithic_pottery,_Museum_of_Western_Bohemia,_187697/Zde / CC BY-SA (https://creativecommons.org/licenses/by-sa/4.0)/wikimedia commons; 4b/; Orkney Skara Brae.jpg/John Burka / CC BY-SA (http://creativecommons.org/licenses/by-sa/3.0/)/wikimedia commons; 5cr/ Figurine feminine Harappa Guimet 2.jpg/Zunkir / CC BY-SA (https://creativecommons.org/licenses/by-sa/4.0)/wikimedia commons; 6tr/ Cacao Aztec Sculpture.jpg//wikimedia commons; 7tl/Lamassu. From Khorsabad, Iraq. Gypseous alabaster. Isolated with clipping path./By Dima Moroz/wikimedia commons; 8bl/ Sumerian account of silver for the govenor (background removed).png/Gavin.collins / Public domain/wikimedia commons; 9cr/King_Hammurabi_raises_his_right_arm_in_worship._Detail_of_a_votive_monument._Limestone._Circa_1792-1750_BCE._From_Sippar,_Iraq._The_British_Museum,_London/Osama Shukir Muhammed Amin FRCP(Glasg) / CC BY-SA (https://creativecommons.org/licenses/by-sa/4.0)/wikimedia commons; 12tr/Geb_and_Nut03/E. A. Wallis Budge (1857-1937) / Public domain/wikimedia commons; 12bl/; Standing Osiris edit1.svg/Jeff Dahl / CC BY-SA (https://creativecommons.org/licenses/by-sa/4.0)/wikimedia commons; 12bc/ Amun the state god of Thebes.JPG/Suraj at ml.wikipedia / CC BY-SA (https://creativecommons.org/licenses/by-sa/3.0)/wikimedia commons; 13tl/ Goddess Ma'at or Maat of Ancient Egypt - reconstructed.png/TYalaA / CC BY-SA (https://creativecommons.org/licenses/by-sa/4.0)/wikimedia commons; 13tr/ Thoth.svg/Jeff Dahl / CC BY-SA (https://creativecommons.org/licenses/by-sa/4.0)/wikimedia commons; 13cl/ Set.svg/Jeff Dahl (talk · contribs) / CC BY-SA (https://creativecommons.org/licenses/by-sa/4.0)/wikimedia commons; 13bl/ Re-Horakhty.svg/Jeff Dahl / CC BY-SA (https://creativecommons.org/licenses/by-sa/4.0)/wikimedia commons; 15br/ Achaemenid king killing a Greek hoplite.jpg/Marco Prins / CC0/wikimedia commons; 16bl/ ChangXingongdeng.jpg/User Refrain on zh.wikipedia / CC BY (https://creativecommons.org/licenses/by/1.0)/wikimedia commons; 17tr/ Cai-lun.jpg/Unknown author / Public domain/wikimedia commons; 17bl/ Fu Haocrop.jpg/https://commons.wikimedia.org/wiki/; Fu_Hao.jpg / CC BY (https://creativecommons.org/licenses/by/2.5)/wikimedia commons; 18tl/ King Yu of Xia.jpg/Ma Lin / Public domain/wikimedia commons; 19tc/Jar,_Han_dynasty,_stoneware_with_glaze,_Honolulu_Museum_of_Arts/Hiart / CC0/wikimedia commons; 19cl/; Laozi a.jpg/Laozi_002.jpg: Thanatoderivative work: Fewskulchor / CC BY-SA (https://creativecommons.org/licenses/by-sa/3.0)/ wikimedia commons; 20tr/Cut_brick,_Indus_Valley_Tradition,_Harappan_Phase,_Chanhu_Daro,_Pakistan,_c._2500-1900_BC_-_Royal_Ontario_Museum_-_DSC09716/Daderot / CC0/wikimedia commons; 20cr/Soban / CC BY-SA (https://creativecommons.org/licenses/by-sa/3.0); 21tl/Great_bath_view_Mohenjodaro//wikimedia commons; 21cr1/Mohenjo-daro_museum_relics13/Saqib Qayyum / CC BY-SA (https://creativecommons.org/licenses/by-sa/3.0)/wikimedia commons; 21cr/Pottery_artifacts_Harappa_Krishnapuram_Palace/Akhilan / CC BY-SA (https://creativecommons.org/licenses/by-sa/3.0)/wikimedia commons; 21cl/Unicorn._Mold_of_Seal,_Indus_valley_civilization/Ismoon (talk) 17:48, 21 February 2012 (UTC) / CC0/wikimedia commons ; 21c/ Mohenjodaro_toy_002/Gryffindor / Public domain/wikimedia commons; 22cl/WimaKadphises/No machine-readable author provided. World Imaging assumed (based on copyright claims). / Public domain/wikimedia commons; 22bl/Charles_le_Brun_-_Alexandre_and_Porus_(Louvre,_INV_2897)_details/Charles Le Brun / Public domain/wikimedia commons; 25cl/20041229-Coatlicue (Museo Nacional de Antropologia) MQ.jpg/Luidger / CC BY-SA (http://creativecommons.org/licenses/by-sa/3.0/)/wikimedia commons; 25cr/Moctezuma_I,_the_Fifth_Aztec_King/Juan de Tovar / Public domain/wikimedia commons; 27cr/ Attack on Pearl Harbor Japanese planes view.jpg/Imperial Japanese Navy / Public domain/wikimedia commons

Middle Ages

Inside

Shutterstock: 6c/Hans Coppens; 10t/Oleksandr Shestakov; 15br/Udompeter; 16tl/David Benton; 16cr/jorisvo; 17tc/chrisdorney; 20tl/creativica; 21b/Shaineast; 23tl/Anton Kudelin; 26tl/beibaoke; 27cr/Michael Rosskothen; 28&29b/NG Shutterbug; 29tr/ Leonid Andronov; 29cr/Nataliia Sokolovska; 30b/cowardlion

Wikimedia Commons: 3b/BLW The Battle of Roncevaux, 1475-1500.jpg/Valerie McGlinchey / CC BY-SA 2.0 UK (https://creativecommons.org/licenses/by-sa/2.0/uk/deed.en)/wikimedia commons; 4tr/Sack_of_Rome_by_the_Visigoths_on_24_August_410_by_JN_Sylvestre_1890/JN Sylvestre 1847-1926 / Public domain/wikimedia commons; 4b/Genseric sacking rome 456 /Karl Bryullov / Public domain/wikimedia commons; 5tl/Invasions_of_the_Roman_Empire_1/MapMaster / CC BY-SA (https://creativecommons.org/licenses/by-sa/2.5)/wikimedia commons; 5tr/MorThanFeastofAttila/Mór Than / Public domain/wikimedia commons; 5bl/Bracteate from Funen, Denmark (DR BR42)/Bloodofox / CC BY-SA (https://creativecommons.org/licenses/by-sa/3.0)/wikimedia commons; 5br/Romulus_Augustulus_and_Odoacer//wikimedia commons; 6br/Codex Manesse 052r Walther von Klingen (detail)/Master of the Codex Manesse (Foundation Painter) / Public domain/wikimedia commons; 7tr/Mathilde_von_Tuszien_(Rom_16Jh)/possibly by Giuseppe Rivelli (fl. mid-16th century) / Public domain/wikimedia commons; 7cl/Blackdeath, tourmai/Unknown author / Public domain/wikimedia commons; 7br/Great_famine/English: Scanned (by me) from the cover of The Great Famine (1996) by William Chester Jordan. Original cover art from a photograph courtesy of Stiftung Weimarer Klassik, Herzogin Anna Amalia Bibliothek. / Public domain/wikimedia commons; 8tl/Hagia Sophia Southwestern entrance mosaics 2/Photograph: Myrabelladerivative work: Myrabella / Public domain/wikimedia commons; 8b/Mosaic_of_Theodora_-_Basilica_San_Vitale_(Ravenna)/Basilica of San Vitale / CC BY-SA (https://creativecommons.org/licenses/by-sa/4.0)/wikimedia commons; 9tl/Weltliche_Schatzkammer_Wien_(190)2/MyName (Gryffindor) CSvBibra(Gryffindor) CSvBibra / Public domain/wikimedia commons; 9bl/Friedrich Kaulbach - Krönung Karls des Großen/Friedrich Kaulbach / Public domain/wikimedia commons; 9r/Otto,_Otto,_Otto,_Conrad/Leslie Philipp from Wetaskiwin, AB, Canada / CC BY (https://creativecommons.org/licenses/by/2.0)/wikimedia commons; 10cl/Gregorythegreat.jpg/Jusepe de Ribera / Public domain/wikimedia commons; 10bl1/Jensky_kodex_selma_z_apokalypsy_a_prelati/Janíček Zmilelý z Písku (?) / Public domain/wikimedia commons; 10bl2/Jensky_kodex_satan_prodava_odpustky/Janíček Zmilelý z Písku (?) / Public domain/wikimedia commons; 11br/Assisi - Basilica di San Francesco 04.jpg/ Luca Aless / CC BY-SA (https://creativecommons.org/licenses/by-sa/4.0)/wikimedia commons; 11tl/Dante exile/Galleria d'arte moderna di Firenze / Public domain/wikimedia commons; 11tr/Pedro_Berruguete_Saint_Dominic_Presiding_over_an_Auto-da-fe_1495/Pedro Berruguete / Public domain/wikimedia commons; 12tl/Birmingham Quran manuscript/AnonymousUnknown author / Public domain/wikimedia commons; 12b/Dome of the Rock, Jerusalem (16197850416)/yeowatzup / CC BY (https://creativecommons.org/licenses/by/2.0)/wikimedia commons; 13tl/Age of Caliphs.png/United States of America federal government / Public domain/wikimedia commons; 13tr/Persian_painting_of_Hülegü's_army_attacking_city_with_siege_engine/Unknown author / Public domain/wikimedia commons; 13bc/Harun-Charlemagne/Julius Köckert / Public domain/wikimedia commons; 13br/ManuscriptAbbasid/See page for author / CC BY-SA (http://creativecommons.org/licenses/by-sa/3.0/)/wikimedia commons; 14tl/ChirurgicalOperation15thCentury/Unknown author / Public domain/wikimedia commons; 14cr/Biruni-russian/The original uploader was Romanm at Slovenian Wikipedia. / Public domain/wikimedia commons; 14bl/Lunar_eclipse_al-Biruni/Al-Biruni / Public domain/wikimedia commons; 15tr/_Captured_Indian_Raja.jpeg/Metropolitan Museum of Art / CC0/wikimedia commons; 15cr/Seljuk Empire (greatest extent).svg / Ali Zifan /(https://commons.wikimedia.org/wiki/File:Seljuk_Empire_(greatest_extent).svg); 16b/West_Stow_Anglo-Saxon_village/User:Midnightblueowl / CC BY (https://creativecommons.org/licenses/by/3.0)/wikimedia commons; 17tl/Normand_-_King_John_Signing_Magna_Charta/Ernest Normand / Public domain/wikimedia commons; 17tr/ Robert_the_Bruce_Statue,_Stirling.jpeg/Ally Crockford / CC BY-SA (https://creativecommons.org/licenses/by-sa/3.0)/wikimedia commons; 17bl/James_Doyle_s_Battle_of_Bosworth/James William Edmund Doyle / Public domain/wikimedia commons; 18tl/ Prise_caen_1346/Jean Froissart / Public domain/wikimedia commons; 18br/Ingres_coronation_charles_vii/Jean Auguste Dominique Ingres / Public domain/wikimedia commons; 18tr/King Edward III/See description / Public domain/wikimedia commons; 19tr/Three_Mamelukes_with_lances_on_horseback/Daniel Hopfer / Public domain/wikimedia commons; 19bl/Empire mansa musa.jpeg/HistoryNmoor / CC BY-SA (https://creativecommons.org/licenses/by-sa/4.0)/wikimedia commons; 19br/Harîrî Schefer - BNF Ar5847 f.51/Yahya ibn Mahmud al-Wasiti / Public domain/wikimedia commons; 20tr///wikimedia commons; 20bl/Counquest of Jeusalem (1099)/Émile Signol / Public domain/wikimedia commons; 20br/Konrad_III_Miniatur_13_Jahrhundert/Unknown author / Public domain/wikimedia commons; 21tl/Saladin_and_Guy//wikimedia commons; 21tr/ConquestOfConstantinopleByTheCrusadersIn1204/David Aubert (1449-79) / Public domain/wikimedia commons; 21cr/Cathars expelled/Workshop of Master of Boucicaut / Public domain/wikimedia commons; 22c/Funeral of ruthenian noble by Siemiradzki/Henryk Siemiradzki / Public domain/wikimedia commons; 22br/Vlad_Tepes_002/AnonymousUnknown author / Public domain/wikimedia commons; 23cr/ Vasnetsov_Ioann_4/Viktor Mikhailovich Vasnetsov / Public domain/wikimedia commons; 23b/Eggink VelKnVladimir/Эггинк Иван / Public domain/wikimedia commons; 24tl/YuanEmperorAlbumGenghisPortrait/National Palace Museum / Public domain/ wikimedia commons; 24bl/Dschingis Khan 01/Sayf al-Vâhidî. Hérât. Afghanistan / Public domain/wikimedia commons; 24bc/Gold coin of Genghis Khan, struck at the Ghazna (Ghazni) mint/Classical Numismatic Group, Inc. http://www.cngcoins.com / CC BY-SA (https://creativecommons.org/licenses/by-sa/2.5)/wikimedia commons; 24&25b/Liu-Kuan-Tao-Jagd/Liu Guandao / Public domain/wikimedia commons; 26&27t/Eighty-seven Celestials/Unknown Chinese artist from c. 8th century / Public domain/ wikimedia commons; 26bl/Luoyang_2006_7-27/G41rn8 / CC BY-SA (https://creativecommons.org/licenses/by-sa/4.0)/wikimedia commons; 26br/Xian_2006_6-5/G41rn8 / CC BY-SA (https://creativecommons.org/licenses/by-sa/4.0)/wikimedia commons; 27b/Ming_soldiers_wielding_pikes_and_guandaos/Yprpyqp / CC BY-SA (https://creativecommons.org/licenses/by-sa/4.0)/wikimedia commons; 28tr/Indian Kanauj triangle map.svg/w:user:Planemad / CC BY-SA (https://creativecommons.org/licenses/by-sa/3.0)/wikimedia commons; 28cl/Belur si1059/G41rn8 / CC BY-SA (https://creativecommons.org/licenses/by-sa/4.0)/wikimedia commons; 29tl/Razia_Jital/Overlord12 / Public domain/wikimedia commons; 30tl/Prince Shotoku (574-622 AD) at Age Two, Japan, Kamakura period, c. 1292 AD, cypress, polychromy, rock-crystal inlaid eyes - Arthur M. Sackler Museum, Harvard University - DSC01169/Daderot / Public domain/wikimedia commons; 30tr/Wadokaichin_coin_8th_century_Japan/PHGCOM / CC BY-SA (https://creativecommons.org/licenses/by-sa/3.0)/wikimedia commons; 30cr/Daibutsuden at the Todaiji Temple - Nara (41441116434)/Ajay Suresh from New York, NY, USA / CC BY (https://creativecommons.org/licenses/by/2.0)/wikimedia commons; 31tr/ Minamoto_no_Yoritomo/Fujiwara no Takanobu / Public domain/wikimedia commons; 31cl/Kongorikishi_(Ni-o)/Thiago Santos / CC BY-SA (https://creativecommons.org/licenses/by-sa/2.0)/wikimedia commons; 31cr/Moko_Shurai_Ekotoba/English: Author unknown. Illustration rolls were ordered by Takezaki Suenaga himself / Public domain/wikimedia commons; 31b/MuromachiShip1538/Unknown author / Public domain/wikimedia commons

Renaissance

Inside

Shutterstock: 4&5bg/Lukasz Szwaj; 6&7bg/maodoltee; 7tl/Lukasz Janyst; 7tr/Viacheslav Lopatin; 9cr/Yury Dmitrienko; 15tr/ArTono; 16tl/Desmochicco; 16tr/Vladimir Korostyshevskiy; 16cl/SeregaYu; 17r/Veniamin Kraskov; 18c/Babich Alexander; 18br/ FrimuFilms; 19tr/kavalenkau; 19cr/silky; 19br/Anna Pakutina; 19b/Phant; 22&23bg/Andrey_Kuzmin; 26b/YURY TARANIK; 28bl/Sean Pavone

Wikimedia Commons: 33b/Gozzoli_magi/Benozzo Gozzoli / Public domain/wikimedia commons; 4tr/Florenca146/Ricardo André Frantz (User:Tetraktys) / CC BY-SA (https://creativecommons.org/licenses/by-sa/3.0)/wikimedia commons; 4cr/ Lorenzo_de_Medici/Agnolo Bronzino and workshop / Public domain/wikimedia commons; 4bl/Hanging_and_burning_of_Girolamo_Savonarola_in_Florence/Museum of San Marco / Public domain/wikimedia commons; 4br/Behaim_Globus/Pirkheimer / CC BY-SA (https://creativecommons.org/licenses/by-sa/3.0)/wikimedia commons; 5tr/The_Last_Supper_Leonardo_Da_Vinci_High_Resolution_size_32x16/Leonardo da Vinci / Public domain/wikimedia commons; 5c/Gutenberg_Bible,_Lenox_Copy,_New_York_Public_Library,_2009._Pic_01/NYC Wanderer (Kevin Eng) / CC BY-SA (https://creativecommons.org/licenses/by-sa/2.0)/wikimedia commons; 5br/La_Rendicien_de_Granada_-_Pradilla/Francisco Pradilla y Ortiz / Public domain/wikimedia commons; 6tl/ ShahAbbasPortraitFromItalianPainter/Unnamed Italian painter / Public domain/wikimedia commons; 6cl/Mona_Lisa,_by_Leonardo_da_Vinci,_from_C2RMF_retouched/Leonardo da Vinci / Public domain/wikimedia commons; 6br/San_Gregorio_VA_(6)/ Queninosta / CC BY-SA (https://creativecommons.org/licenses/by-sa/3.0)/wikimedia commons; 7cl/Italy-3208_(5387284501)/Dennis Jarvis from Halifax, Canada / CC BY-SA (https://creativecommons.org/licenses/by-sa/2.0)/wikimedia commons; 7c/Babur_crossing_the_Indus_in_the_heat_of_battle/a painting commissioned by Akbar / Public domain/wikimedia commons; 7br/863px-Carlos_V_en_Mühlberg,_by_Titian,_from_Prado_in_Google_Earth/Titian / Public domain/wikimedia commons; 8bl/Simone_Martini_-_Frontispice_du_Virgile/Simone Martini / Public domain/wikimedia commons; 8br/FirenzeOrsanmichele03/Nanni di Banco (Italian, 1375–1421) / CC BY-SA (http://creativecommons.org/licenses/by-sa/3.0/)/wikimedia commons; 9tr/Sandro_Botticelli_-_Madonna_del_Magnificat_-_Google_Art_Project/Sandro Botticelli / Public domain/wikimedia commons; 9cl/Urbino,_bottega_di_guido_durantino,_grande_piatto_con_sacco_di_roma_del_1527,_1540_ca./Sailko / CC BY-SA (https:// creativecommons.org/licenses/by-sa/3.0)/wikimedia commons; 9c/Girolamo_Savonarola/Fra Bartolomeo / Public domain/wikimedia commons; 9bl/KatharinavonMedici/Unidentified painter / Public domain/wikimedia commons; 9bc/Peter_Paul_Rubens_043/ Peter Paul Rubens / Public domain/wikimedia commons; /omap 8 (3) [Converted].ai//wikimedia commons; 10tr/Charles_VIII_Ecole_Francaise_16th_century_Musee_de_Conde_Chantilly/After Jean Perréal / Public domain/wikimedia commons; 10cl/Bayard_sur_le_pont_du_Garigliano/Henri Félix Emmanuel Philippoteaux / Public domain/wikimedia commons; 10cr/Louis-xii-roi-de-france/Workshop of Jean Perréal / Public domain/wikimedia commons; 10br/Ferdinand_of_Aragon,_Isabella_of_Castile/Jebulon / Public domain/wikimedia commons; 11tr/Peter_Paul_Rubens_120b/Peter Paul Rubens / Public domain/wikimedia commons; 11cl/Battle_of_Pavia,_oil_on_panel/Birmingham Museum of Art / Public domain/wikimedia commons; 11cr/Sack_of_Rome_of_1527_by_Johannes_Lingelbach_17th_century/Johannes Lingelbach / Public domain/wikimedia commons; 11b1/Elderly_Karl_V/After Titian / Public domain/wikimedia commons; 11br/Philip_II_portrait_by_Titian/Workshop of Titian / Public domain/ wikimedia commons; 12tl/La_nascita_di_Venere_(Botticelli)/Sandro Botticelli / Public domain/wikimedia commons; 12tr/Caravaggio_Judith_Beheading_Holofernes/Caravaggio / Public domain/wikimedia commons; 12bl/_The_School_of_Athens__by_Raffaello_Sanzio_da_Urbino/Raphael / Public domain/wikimedia commons; 12br/Mona_Lisa,_by_Leonardo_da_Vinci,_from_C2RMF_retouched/Leonardo da Vinci / Public domain/wikimedia commons; 13tr/Michelangelo_-_Creation_of_Adam_(cropped)/ Michelangelo / Public domain/wikimedia commons; 13c/Pieter_Bruegel_The_Peasant_Dance/Pieter_Bruegel_d._Ä._014.jpg: File Upload Bot (Eloquence)derivative work: Wikielwikingo / Public domain/wikimedia commons; 13cr/Hieronymus_Bosch_-_The_Garden_of_Earthly_Delights_-_Hell/Hieronymus Bosch / Public domain/wikimedia commons; 13bl/Tizian_041/Titian / Public domain/wikimedia commons; 13bc/Madonna_dell'Orto_(Venice)_-_Presentation_at_the_temple_of_the_Virgin_(1552-1553)_by_Tintoretto/Jacopo Tintoretto / Public domain/wikimedia commons; 13br/El_Greco_-_The_Burial_of_the_Count_of_Orgaz/El Greco / Public domain/wikimedia commons; 14tl/Henry_Fuseli_rendering_of_Hamlet_and_his_father's_Ghost/Henry Fuseli / Public domain/wikimedia commons; 14tr/Foxe's_Book_of_Martyrs_-_Tyndale/John Foxe / Public domain/wikimedia commons; 14cr/Shakespeare's_Globe_(8162111781)/Steve Collis from Melbourne, Australia / CC BY (https://creativecommons.org/licenses/by/2.0)/wikimedia commons; 14br/Calle_Martin_de_los_Heros_59bis_(Madrid)_05b/Luis García / CC BY-SA 3.0 ES (https://creativecommons.org/licenses/by-sa/3.0/es/deed.en)/wikimedia commons; 15tl/Portrait_de_Dante/Sandro Botticelli / Public domain/ wikimedia commons; 15tc/File:Francesco Petrarca00.jpg/Unknown author / Public domain/wikimedia commons; 15tc///wikimedia commons; 15cr/Giovanni_Palestrina_and_Pope_Julius_III/Sémhur / Public domain/wikimedia commons; 15bl/Claudio_Monteverdi/After Bernardo Strozzi / Public domain/wikimedia commons; 15br/Pietro_Bembo_-_Titian/Titian / Public domain/wikimedia commons; 16br/Florence_-_David_by_Donatello/Donatello / CC BY-SA (https://creativecommons.org/licenses/by-sa/2.0)/

Revolutions & independence

Inside

Scientific & Industrial Revolutions

Inside